Dear Dan
40 is the beginning!
Happy Birthday

Love
Joe & Judi

MEMOIRS *of a* FORTUNATE JEW

MEMOIRS
of a
FORTUNATE JEW
An Italian Story

DAN VITTORIO SEGRE

Translated from the Italian
by the author

ADLER&ADLER

First English language edition published in 1987 by
Adler & Adler, Publishers, Inc.
4550 Montgomery Avenue
Bethesda, Maryland 20814

Library of Congress Cataloging-in-Publication Data

Segre, Vittorio.
  Memoirs of a fortunate Jew.

  Translation of: Storia di un ebreo fortunato.
  1. Segre, Vittorio. 2. Jews—Italy—Biography.
3. Jews, Italian—Israel—Biography. I. Title.
DS135.I9S45713 1987   945.091′04924024 [B]   86-17495
ISBN 0-917561-32-5

Printed in the United States of America

In the same manner in which the just are rewarded in the world to come even for their smallest merits, so are the evildoers in this world.

Babylonian Talmud, Tractate *Ta'anit*

Dispersed in diaries written daily or intermittently since 1940, the memories contained in these pages would not have been turned into a book without the encouragement of many friends.

The Rockefeller Foundation, to which I owe the generous invitation to stay at its Villa Serbelloni during the winter of 1983, will probably never know to what extent the enchanted silence of Bellagio contributed toward persuading the phantoms of my past to allow themselves to be imprisoned by the typewriter on which my wife patiently produced the many drafts of the original Italian manuscript.

As for the English translation, it would certainly not be intelligible without the compassionate help of Devorah Bar-Zemer, who worked with me on every page of the English version. I am deeply indebted to Martine Halban and Amy Pastan, who read through the manuscript with great care and suggested many improvements. If I have been able to convey to the English reader some of the original Italian flavor, I owe this to Susan Rose, who unstintingly gave me the benefit of her sense of both languages and sensitively edited many pages of the manuscript.

I.

The Pistol

I WAS probably less than five years old when my father fired a shot at my head. He was cleaning his pistol, a Smith & Wesson 7.65, when it went off —nobody knew how.

My father was sitting at the same desk at which I am writing these lines, a massive oak table, well fitted for the huge ledgers in which he carefully entered, in his clear handwriting slightly slanted to the right, the daily expenses, purchases of animals and seeds, income from the sales of wine and grain, the taxes he paid, as well as the small sums he put in the neck pouch of Bizir, his massive Saint Bernard dog trained to fetch his cigars from the tobacconist. In the village everyone knew the hairy, good-tempered dog of the village mayor. If the tobacconist was not prompt enough in giving Bizir the correct packet, it was only to make him growl for the admiration of the villagers. On the oak table, now mine and still unburdened —as before—by modern gadgets such as a telephone, transistor radio, typewriter, or calculating machine, I keep my father's photograph. Bizir is standing on his hind legs, his forepaws on my father's shoulders. The picture is fading and still smells of tobacco like the desk drawers full of aging possessions: pipes, spring tape-measures, erasers, rusty compasses, penholders, a dry inkwell—things I no longer use but carefully preserve as remnants of the vanished world of my family.

On the day I was shot, in the sixth year of the Fascist revolution, I would certainly have been killed had my father held his pistol at a slightly lower angle. I had crawled into his study, placed myself in front of the huge desk without his noticing me, and suddenly stood up at the very moment when the pistol went off. The bullet grazed my head, burned—so I was told time and again—a lock of my then-blond hair, and penetrated an Empire-style armoire behind me.

This was one of those pieces of furniture with a front panel opening into a desk, which was known incorrectly in the family as a *serre-papier*. I still occasionally see this type of desk-cum-drawers in the windows of antique shops, converted into bars with places for bottles and glasses. My wife, who is convinced that furniture, like flowers, has a dignity of its own, is furious whenever she sees one of these aberrations. She regards them as a perversion of nature. I do not share this belief with her, yet I am convinced that this particular *serre-papier* possessed a personality of its own. I wonder how it would have perceived my funeral after having witnessed my death.

There would be a small, white coffin at the center of my father's library, transformed for the occasion into a funeral parlor. The rabbi would arrive from Turin with a hexagonal black ceremonial hat on his head, standing just in front of the Sisters of Saint Vincent—who nursed in the village hospital —with their wide, starched caps, rosaries in their hands, praying for the salvation of my soul. I would be carried to the cemetery in a hearse drawn by two, or perhaps even four, horses with white plumes on their heads and embroidered caparisons as in Paolo Ucello's pictures. A lot of people would be weeping around my bier. Our faithful maid, Annetta, would be there in her black uniform and white cap; Cecilia, the cook, with the special chocolates she made for my mother's Thursday tea parties; Vigiu, the coachman, with a top hat adorned by a pheasant's feather; the two collies, the huge cat, my tin soldiers, and, naturally, the entire family crying around me.

Their sorrow did not affect me. Even apart from dreams of this kind, I have always asked myself what it really means to share someone else's sorrow. The cases in which people genuinely empathize with other people's feelings are few. After all, an ingrown toenail hurts one more than the death of a thousand Chinese, and we live in a world where we share our "deep grief" or our "great joy" with distant people through cabled messages, which cost less if transmitted by a coded number. Nobody ever seems to learn from the suffering of others; rarely from his own. Only in the look of confidence and love of a dog, or of fear in a wounded animal is it possible to catch a fleeting instant of the pain of the world.

For years I have empathized with that piece of furniture wounded in my place. I do not claim that it felt pain instead of me, but I have often thought that the shot established a peculiar link between us; that that piece of oak, old and polished, possessed a strange vitality, as if it were holding a particle of my destiny. The little hole, round and clean-cut, discreet and unexpected in the folding panel, has winked at me for years. Long before I was told so by a gypsy, it convinced me that I had been born under a lucky star. Not one supposed to grant glory, wealth, and social success, but a minor star, full of a sparkling life that still gives me courage in the ever more frequent hours of doubt and sadness.

Late in the 1950s I once accompanied an Algerian sultan to Nazareth. According to his calling card he was a direct descendant of the caliph Abu Bakr, and he wanted to visit the lodge of the Clarisses convent. Here the viscount of Foucauld, touched by grace, had prepared himself for his mission of conversion of the Arabs in the Sahara, where my sultan's grandfather had murdered him. The nuns of the Order of the Père de Foucauld, who had transformed the lodge into their small convent, received my companion with the enthusiasm due to those who are clearly part of a divine design.

We sat on low, rush-seated stools, chatting quietly in the big room, clean and tidy, smelling of new whitewash, opening on two sides onto a secret, shady garden. Gusts of wind carried in the perfume of orange blossom while we kept measuring out, like the beads of a rosary, polite phrases and conspiratorial smiles, full of spent hatreds and aging vanity. We had left outside the thick convent walls the diversities of our religions, politics, and cultures. All that reached us from the outer world was the muffled sound of traffic, waves of flower scent, and the smell of burning charcoal spattered by mutton fat.

History had lost its dimension. The conversation veered almost naturally toward the idea of death. The sultan was saying that life is made up of bursts of energy constantly struggling with death. To exist was, for him, to be like a flicker of light shining for shorter or longer periods on the black inertia of matter. This descendant of Abu Bakr, to whom the French had for a moment thought of handing over control of the French Sahara, spoke, in this place of peace and faith, so remote from my village in Piedmont, in the same manner that my father spoke to me for the first and last time about his soul, two weeks before he died.

We were looking down from the top of our terraced garden into the valley, soft and green, which sloped gently down to the Tanaro River. To our left, like a caravan of brown roofs and whitish walls, the houses of San Defendente undulated above vineyards already dressed in autumnal red. The farmhouses and the courtyards stood aligned in their ancient order, still unaffected by the new, undisciplined way of life with which the farmers now had to cope. From the tops of the hills the houses overlooked the plants still growing in their appointed seasons. Here and there, however, one could already see the first signs of change. Men who only yesterday had been at the mercy of drought and hail, now crushed the land with tracked vehicles, dusted crops with small planes, and tricked the climate with plantations of imported pines and aspens. Here too, as in the Levant, one was able to perceive the deep wounds that modernity was opening in the old system of cultures. Yet at the end of the fifties, the valley still showed the face that, like that of my father, I had known since my childhood.

Scattered over the fields were bushes of cobnuts and a few lines of poplars, slim and wavering up to the sky; there were orchards that by that time had already given their crops of peaches, figs, and apricots. The land, tired by the summer toil, was lying exhausted, like a woman's body resting after the élan of love. Punctuating the deep silence, crickets chirped, thirsty birds darted from tree to tree. The hay was drying, fragrant, in the meadows. Unpicked clusters of grapes rotted on the vines amid the buzzing of wasps and in the shade of vine leaves spotted by copper spray.

From every side it seemed as though a message of farewell was rising to us. It was still hot, but my father sensed a chill overcoming his body. He calmly explained to me how the feeling of death was spreading, surprised at not feeling any fear. He had the impression, he told me, that his bones, sinews, and muscles, which still held him upright in spite of his years, were no longer his own; that his life was leaving his body like a flickering flame, deserting the cinders of his earthly life. Sooner or later, he said, these cinders would disperse into nothingness, and the flame of his soul mount, with travail, to the place from which it had come.

He was speaking slowly, to himself, about himself, head slightly bent to one side as if he wanted to catch a consensus from the rustling of the leaves in the vineyards he had planted in his youth. His eyes wandered along the rows of vines, from the houses to the dusty paths, from sky to valley, caressing the brooks, stopping at every milestone on the provincial road, following the tracks along which he had ridden, the meadows over which he had hunted hares, the poplars under which he had dismounted to drink wine with his peasants and eat slices of bread, tasting of olives and garlic.

I looked at his purplish hands, clutching the railing of the steps leading down from the garden to the bowling green. From here he had called on the youths of the village to go and fight and get killed in the war that was to have given back to Italy the towns of Trento and Trieste and brought perpetual peace to the world. His patriotism had not been the reason for his becoming the youngest mayor in Italy. The villagers had consistently voted for him because he was the largest landlord and a Jew, two things that made him more credible than others in matters of money. Villagers who had emigrated used to send him money to have mass said for their dead, trusting him more than the local priest. He had sold many tracts of land to his peasants with deferred payments and without interest. To those who suggested guarantors, he used to answer that the mouths to be fed in the buyer's family were as good as any security. At that time he was loved, admired, and respected.

It was only natural, therefore, that when he decided to volunteer in the Great War, many of the villagers followed his example, believing that it would be, as he had promised, a glorious and short war. Instead it had been just the opposite, long and painful, with few of the soldiers coming back from the front. Although there were fewer than half a dozen socialists in the village and nobody really held him personally responsible for the slaughter, the dead had been too many not to reproach him for the military interventionism he had defended with such fervor. Insulting graffiti appeared on street walls, his poplars were slashed, subversive slogans were shouted at him as he drove through the village in military uniform. They did not appreciate the garden he had planted on the castle grounds in memory of the fallen soldiers. My father felt deeply wounded; he became convinced, like many other landowners of the time, that nothing would stop the "Bolshevik hydra" except a new, strong, patriotic regime, capable of forcing draft dodgers to recognize the contribution of blood and suffering that the veterans had given the country. He could not accept emotionally the social changes that war had brought, even though intellectually he understood them. More out of anger than ideology, he enrolled himself in the Fascist party, which was gathering strength and credibility with the help of enraged war veterans like himself and with the covert support of the police and the army.

After the March on Rome, which he understood as the triumph of order over anarchy and of which he totally missed the political consequences, he threw himself with enthusiasm into the burgeoning electrical industry. He invested the income from the sale of his magnificent estate in the building of dams. In this way he ruined himself twice over: first in politics and then in the financial chaos created by the Great Depression. However, these were things of the past, memories faded by time. The more recent ones, of anti-Jewish persecution, had been mellowed by the help extended to him by those very farmers who had forced him to run away from the village at the end of the Great War. During World War II they had risked their lives to save him and his family from the Germans. In these more recent memories I had no share. Our lives had evolved in different directions. We had parted too early and for too long to share common adult experiences. If my father now allowed himself to speak to me of his innermost feelings, something he would never have done before, it was because he knew he was on the point of leaving this world forever.

Listening to him talking about his image of his soul, I had the impression of quite literally seeing a flicker of life emerging from his shabby, gray, peaked cap. It was a flickering, bluish flame of delusion and failure. I was his only triumph in life, but for the wrong reasons. The long war, from which we had both emerged unharmed, was a conflict in which a third of world Jewry had disappeared; in it he had lost his motherland, Italy, and I had found a new one, Israel. I had returned home victorious but dressed in a foreign uniform; he had survived six years of civil ignominy, two of flight into the mountains, and had witnessed the defeat of his country. Humiliated by the king, whom he had personally served, persecuted by the Fascist regime that he had helped to create, he had no other reason for pride except my contribution to that Zionist cause against which he had so tenaciously fought as an Italian nationalist.

I perceived his embarrassment toward me as soon as I saw him after five years of separation. In May 1945 I discovered that, after years of being in hiding, he was still alive and living in our old village home. I rushed in my command car to look for him, on roads still torn up by Allied bombing and Partisan operations. I felt an arrogant satisfaction in making peasant carts move out of my way, in the stupefied and frightened looks of local people seeing a British uniform for the first time.

When I got to the village I stopped under the outer archway of my home, uncertain how to behave. I was sensitive to the silent feeling of awe and curiosity in the villagers gathering in the street behind me, brought together by an event that was breaking the monotony of life in the small, rural center, forgotten by history and overlooked by war. I did not dare enter the courtyard, afraid that a sudden meeting with my father might be too much for him. At the same time I was trying hard to remember his face. I was terrified at the thought that he might recognize me first, while my expression might give away that I did not know who he was. We had not written to each other for years. The last Red Cross card I received from my family was dated 1941, before I joined the British army. I was wondering how he would react to seeing me dressed in a foreign uniform (he who had dreamt of a military career for me in Italy), discovering that without his permission I had abandoned the agricultural studies on which he had spent so much money. Behind my back people surrounded my Italian driver, bombarding him with questions and telling each other who I was. I could feel, without turning around, that they were pointing me out, could hear them mentioning my name and that of my father, exchanging comments without daring to approach me. To them I was the representative of the new authority, of those Allied forces who had won the war and whom they had not yet had a chance to meet.

From the inner courtyard of my home one of our tenants emerged. Pinin was his name. I recognized him by his thick, drooping moustache and the black scarf tied around his neck, looking exactly as he did when he used to help me mount my horse. I told him who I was. I asked him about my father. When I heard that he was in his study, in good health, and that my mother was alive and living with my sister in a nearby convent, I asked him to inform my father that I had returned. I was nervous. I had assumed a brisk tone of command that, in those circumstances, made me feel I was acting a part. With all those people clustered behind me, I stood facing the big gates that opened onto the inner courtyard. I lacked the courage to go through them, wondering if somebody would pull the iron chain of the entry bell in my honor, feeling like part of a cheap theatrical piece, of one of those serialized novels that I remembered from my father's library. Shamefacedness prevented me from crossing the threshold of a world of affections and hopes that I felt was no longer mine but that my father probably still associated with me. I had a confused premonition that a breach, deeper than that opened by time, had developed between us: between his Italian world, which had been destroyed, and my new Jewish one in which, as Joachim Murat, who Napoleon made King of Naples, once said proudly, I was my own ancestor.

My father suddenly appeared under the archway. He was panting; he must have run all the way from the library. He stopped abruptly in front of me, wondering if someone was perhaps playing a trick on him. We scrutinized each other for a moment, suspiciously, because we were both greatly changed. The man with his military beret at an angle over one ear, a blond moustache, the silk scarf of the Special Units around his neck, a pistol dangling in its canvas holster at his side, must certainly have looked to him very different from the boy, dressed in navy blue jacket and linen collar, whom he had accompanied to embark at Trieste in 1939. He, with a long white beard that had grown during his life underground, his hair thinner but still black, his leaner body barely filling a crude corduroy suit, had a patriarchal look quite new to me. Only his button-up boots were familiar.

He did not stretch out his hand or make any gesture of affection. We both stood silent and still, unable to disentangle ourselves from the images of each other that we had preserved during the long years of separation. Changed in our outward appearances, we felt both the same and different inside: linked by blood ties but separated by experiences so divergent. All this, of course, lasted only an instant, but the shock was great for us both. He spoke first, asking me which regiment I belonged to. I answered him: the Palestine Regiment. Probably he did not understand what I meant, but it was only after that answer that he stretched out his right hand and then hugged me with his left arm. By this time people behind us were talking at the tops of their voices. Someone even started clapping. We paid no attention. With our backs to them so that no one could see our emotion, side by side, we slowly crossed into the inner court and moved toward the garden, now full of weeds. My father had his arm around my shoulders. In silence we stopped at the top of the steps leading to the bowling green, untended and overgrown, to look at the valley that had been his domain and that of his parents.

The valley was unchanged except for the airfield that the German army had built near the river Tanaro. It held part of our common memories and had witnessed the sadness of our parting five years earlier. Here, we felt, we could again converse in silence, overcoming that void of disappointed experience that neither of us had been able to fulfill. For this reason, when my father suddenly chose this spot to speak to me about his soul, I knew that he was nearing his end. Convinced as he was of having failed in his task of guiding me in my life, his halting words had no other aim but to teach me how to face death, with dignity and detachment.

I, too, as I grow older, find myself thinking about death while standing at the top of the steps that lead to the bowling green, looking at the shadows drawn by the sun on the banks of the Tanaro. But I am unable to imagine my soul as a small flame flickering out of the cinders of my life. My soul looks more to me like a light reflected by an insignificant star, one of those that Saint Exupéry would have given his Little Prince to ride on: a happy and sociable star, which at least twice helped me to escape my mortal destiny, once as a child and again on a rainy evening in still-occupied Bari.

I had gone to look for a cardigan in the kit bag that the king of England had lent me, together with two sets of underwear, two winter shirts and three summer ones, two pairs of trousers, and a leather jerkin, all to make me fight better in the war. I had also been issued a jackknife, one pair of boots, a pouch with needles and thread, two gaiters, and that combination of webbing, pouches, and packs that, with the help of a flat steel helmet, made us look like ancient warriors in a modern world.

At the bottom of the kit bag I kept a big revolver taken from a captured Italian arms depot. It was heavy, cumbersome, and I had forgotten that it was loaded. I took it out of the kit bag and laid it on the corner of my bed, which I then inadvertently hit with my knee. The weapon fell onto the cement floor, butt downward. It was a fall of less than half a meter, but it was enough for the hammer to jerk and the bullet to explode.

At that moment I was crouched over the weapon. The flash blinded me for a second, and I still carry with me, intact after all these years, the memory of a deafening bang. I am surprised today at not having felt any fear, though I am not by nature particularly brave. But I cannot rid myself of the image that flashed through my mind, of myself bent forward as if I were stretching my neck on the block, looking like an illustration from the *History of Illustrious Men,* which my father kept, bound in three volumes, on the second shelf of his library.

As a child I used to spend long hours leafing through these books that, more than any others, I think, infected me with a romantic taste for the heroic. Each volume contained a collection of primitive watercolors protected by tissue paper, torn at the corners and spotted with rust. I recalled them, looking at the rust spots on the barrel of the revolver, now lying warm and vulgar, on the floor near my bed.

I do not remember how long it took before I found the strength to pick it up and unload it—three seconds, two minutes, three hours? But I know that when I looked at myself in the mirror hanging askew from two hooks on the wall over the dirt-encrusted washbasin, I saw the reflection of a pallid face, not belonging to me, with a lock of burned hair standing up over a pair of eyes that had stared, without seeing, at the void of my death.

There was deep silence in the room. On the floor below nobody in the mess seemed to have heard the noise of the explosion. If I had died they would certainly have attributed it to suicide. In a way it was true: I had that day thought of killing myself, and I felt now as though I had wriggled out of my human destiny.

I went on believing in my special lot until the day my wife, without my knowledge, decided to repair the *serre-papier* and plug up the hole made by my father's pistol. The spell is now broken. Yet from time to time I find myself believing that hidden in the shining oak there still slumbers a shred of my peculiar destiny.

2.

Faith and Boredom

My mother, born Jewish, is buried in a Christian cemetery. In her case destiny really seems to have played tricks with our family. True, she loved to travel, yet nobody could have imagined that after having provoked such dismay by her conversion to Christianity in reaction to my departure for Palestine, she would become the first member of our family in two thousand years to go and die—as is the custom among pious Jews—in the Holy Land.

My mother rests in the small cemetery of the nuns at Ein Kerem, the meeting place of Mary and Elizabeth. She is buried in the shadow of tall cypresses in a square of ground surrounded by high walls, which naturally invite one to raise one's eyes to the sky. Wild geraniums and lazy lizards follow the sun's rays around the stone that covers her body and that is slowly sinking into the earth. The smell of rosemary always reminds me of the black square beneath which Camus lies in a little Provençal cemetery. "The Motherland," he wrote, "is the land which covers the bones of one's ancestors." If this is true, I have, thanks to my Christian mother, planted roots in

my Jewish ancestral land, though fifty years of active life have
not succeeded in making me feel it is mine.

Be that as it may, nobody would have imagined such an
ending for my mother who, at the beginning of the century,
was not only one of the most beautiful Jewish girls in Piedmont but also one of the most sought after *partis* in Turin. In
the miniature painted on the occasion of her marriage she looks
like a fairy: the mass of brown hair combed up in the fashion
of the time crowning the perfect oval of her face; the long
neck, adorned with three rows of pearls falling over the laced
bodice; the long, white, manicured hand catching them with
the gentle gesture of a palm already destined to play with a
rosary. There is another picture showing her in all her beauty
dressed in a Japanese kimono. It was taken on the eve of World
War I, in the small trellised pavilion of the garden, with Mrs.
Petrella, an artist who for a fleeting moment had some fame
in provincial theaters, sitting admiringly next to her. This poor
woman ended her days in the village old-age home which,
before being restored and modernized in the 1960s, was a hovel
where inmates had to eat out of tin bowls, using their beds as
tables.

In the 1950s Mrs. Petrella shared the misery and dirt of her
room with two other skinny old women. When I visited her
from time to time, she liked to talk about the parties that my
mother gave in our country home. Today, no one could
imagine the past splendor of these rooms, emptied as they have
been of their furniture, smelling of mold and invaded by
woodworm, which has eaten the gilded reliefs of the door
frames and the wood of the old window sashes. Yet many years
before I was born, the bishops of Cuneo and Alba used to
converse in the hospitable atmosphere offered by the Jewish
mayor of the village, with the count of Mirafiore, offspring
of the morganatic marriage of Victor Emmanuel II. On other,
less official occasions, when the notables of the area gathered
in these salons to talk about wine, cattle, and the fight against

Phylloxera (the American pest that was ruining their vine-yards), it was my mother who set the tone of the meetings, playing the spinet and inviting some guest to exhibit his singing talents. Mrs. Petrella loved to linger over the description of this village society, which for her had been the unsuccessful springboard into the Italian fin-de-siècle society. She was easily moved when recalling for me the luxury of the white silk-lined landau in which my mother drove with her to the nearby towns of Alba or Asti. Mrs. Petrella, an expert in city fashions, advised her what clothes to buy for the forthcoming theater season, or for one of those special "family evenings," when the ladies played rummy and the gentlemen "three-seven" until they all gathered together to admire the performance of the newly acquired magic lantern.

Mrs. Petrella apparently never realized how much my mother hated the country life she was forced to live after her marriage. She did not share my father's passion for riding and hunting; she found no interest in the conversation of the local gentry, even less in political discussions. She was not even excited by such extraordinary events as the arrival in Asti of the Buffalo Bill Circus or by Colonel Cody's invitation to my father to race his horses against ours. She was bored to death in the gilded cage in which my father had imprisoned her. Childless for over ten years, she envied her more fortunate friends who could enjoy the amusements of Turin's society life, still gravitating, as it did at the time, around many members of the royal family.

The Jews of Piedmont recently had emerged from the ghetto: my great-grandfather on my father's side had grown up in that of Ivrea, on my mother's side, in that of Turin. They did not belong to the families that had distinguished themselves in the wars of the Italian Risorgimento—the nineteenth-century movement for Italian political unity—but they had fought for their emancipation and were fiercely faithful to the House of Savoy which, in 1848, had granted them civic equality. In the thirty years that followed they had forgotten most of the rites and values of their ancestral faith. My grandfathers were already unable to read Hebrew, still a language of current knowledge in the preceding generation. My maternal grandmother used to recite her daily prayers in a shortened form without understanding their meaning; for over seventy years she apparently recited in Hebrew the morning blessing in which a Jew thanks the Lord for "having made me a man."

Italian Jewry at the time suffered from the effects of emancipation for reasons common to other European Jews but also quite particular to Italy. First of all there was the question of numbers. The Italian Jewish population at the end of the last century was slightly over thirty thousand, one-tenth of the Jewish population of France and less than a fraction of the Jewry of the Austro-Hungarian Empire. Italy did not have—and to a certain extent still does not have—a capital city like Paris, London, or Vienna polarizing the intellectual, political, and economic establishment. In these metropolises, Jews had become numerous and rich enough to carry out the responsibilities of modern, communal religious institutions. In Italy, Jews had remained for centuries scattered all over the peninsula in small communities that at times were no more than a dozen families strong. From these Italian villages or country towns they had taken their new names when the state authorities required them to drop their old Jewish patronymics: Moses, son of Jacob or of David, became Alatri, Orvieto, Sermoneta, Padua, or Pavia. The "universities," as the Jewish communities were called, had developed, in the separateness of the ghettos and notwithstanding the outwardly miserable appearance of their members, strong cultural traditions in the fields of music and art unparalleled by any other European Jewish community. With the emancipation, however, they rapidly lost their members to the urban centers, former capitals of the states that the united Kingdom of Italy had meanwhile turned into provinces. In the course of these rapid social and topographical changes, the centuries-old tissue of Italian Judaism, still strong in the eighteenth century, had frayed, while the falling of the ghetto walls put an end to an isolation that discriminated against, but at the same time protected, the integrity of these communities.

The Italian Jews at the beginning of the twentieth century had not lost their pride in their origins. They understood that the events that allowed them to become financially richer, and politically equal with the rest of the population, also made them religiously poorer. They compensated for the loss of content in their separate collective identity by constructing grandiose synagogues, in which liturgy and decorum tended to imitate church pomp, while increasingly moving away from the atmosphere of sacred life and study that had permeated the small, beautiful synagogues of the Italian ghettos. In Turin this process reached a significant peak—fewer than three thousand Jews, already forgetful of their ancestral traditions, decided to build a synagogue competing in height and architectural originality with the Eiffel Tower. Lack of funds finally prevented the Mole Antoneliana from becoming the Jewish house of prayer, and this enormous and useless building eventually became the symbol of the capital of Piedmont.

The need to compensate for long centuries of misery and oppression, however, pushed the Italian Jews to use the new riches acquired through the emancipation to purchase—whenever and wherever they could—lands and castles, less as an investment than as a natural reaction to the state of inferiority in which they had lived for so long. To buy, as my great-grandfather did, a castle that had belonged to a branch of the royal family, the dukes of Genoa, was a doubtful investment but a social consecration. This desire to climb socially, shared at that time by all the Jews of Western Europe, was probably less resented in Italy than elsewhere. Yet it helped to link the traditional currents of church hostility to the Jews to the new, secular forms of anti-Semitism on both Right and Left, the strength of which Jews seemed unable to measure and in most cases refused even to perceive. In Italy, as elsewhere, the nationalist Right regarded them as intruders, and the Left as marginal people who preferred to join the bourgeoisie than to identify with the proletariat. However, the success of the House of Savoy in uniting the peninsula, and the unlimited support that the Jews gave to this nationalist, unitarian Italian policy, allowed them to integrate into the Gentile society more quickly and more deeply than in any other country, including the United States, and to believe in the existence of unique historical conditions.

Indeed, it was not by chance that Italian Jewry was able to provide a minister of war, the first in modern Jewish history, and two prime ministers as well as contribute to the Italian wars of independence and to Garibaldi's militias thirty times more, proportionally, than the rest of the population. In the thirty most crucial years of the Risorgimento, from 1840 to 1870, the Jews in fact felt more Italian than the Italians, because, unlike most of the inhabitants of the peninsula, they had no links of loyalty to the aristocratic and Catholic regimes of the Italian states, which had traditionally kept the Jews apart from the rest of the population. By supporting the cause of the Risorgimento, guided by men like Mazzini, Cavour, Garibaldi, and Victor Emmanuel II, the Jews stood squarely behind a political movement that justified its territorial conquests and the reunion of the various Italian regions into one kingdom with an aggressive nationalist, liberal, and anticlerical ideology.

The Jews thus found themselves also defending ideas befitting not only their particular communal interests but also those of a rising political and military power—the Piedmontese, who could not rely on the unequivocal support of the Italian masses. Indeed, the Piedmontese government, especially after the military defeat suffered in the years 1848–1849 at the hands of the Hapsburgs, could not rely on wide popular sympathy.

Neapolitans, Romans, Florentines, Modenese, Venetians, tied to ancient local regional loyalties, hesitated to throw in their lot with the ambitious but—to many—foreign Savoy dynasty. The Jews, however, as a "landless tribe," were ready to serve it unconditionally and work for the creation of a new "fatherland" in which they could feel equal to others. They therefore brought to the Risorgimento an unlimited enthusiasm and faithfulness, supported by a relatively high cultural and economic level and reinforced by valuable international relations. The marriage between the dynastic Piedmontese interests and the communal ones of the Jews opened for the latter all the doors of political, cultural, and economic influence as nowhere else in Europe. Thus, for some decades, Jews like my great-grandfathers and grandfathers felt themselves to be not only the citizens but also the founding fathers of a new nation. This transitory but exhilarating situation also gave the majority of the Piedmontese Jews a psychological compensation and moral justification for the abandonment of their ancestral traditions, making them believe that they were both "true Italians" and "true Jews"—a hybrid situation and the source of that "fascination" that would later on so greatly surprise a Zionist leader like Chiam Weizmann, the future first president of the State of Israel. In the thirties he could not fathom how Jews who were so assimilated could be so free of what he called in his memoirs, the "fatuous presumptions of the so-called Frenchmen or Germans of the Mosaic persuasion."

My grandparents on my father's side had become bankers. On my mother's side they traded successfully in land and cattle. In both cases they had become affluent and—to judge by their portraits—fat bourgeois, with all the prejudices, aspirations, social conformism, moral values, and weaknesses common to a generation of "new" Italians interested in the greatness of their fatherland as much as in the success of their own affairs.

To preserve Judaism in these conditions was an unrewarding

and difficult task for them. In 1848, when a group of Jewish students in Turin on the fiftieth anniversary of Jewish emancipation in Piedmont asked Max Nordau, the then-popular French writer and ardent Zionist, to contribute an article to their paper, he answered with a message that analyzed correctly the new situation of Italian Jews:

> Up to 1848, oh Italian Jews, you were Jews in Italy; since then you have become Italians of Jewish extraction. What will you be in the future? Pure and simple Italians, without even the adjective "Jew" which reminds you of your past? People assure me that this is what will happen. They tell me that the majority of the Jews in Italy—excuse me—of the Italian Jews, have forgotten their origins, have no longer any Jewish interest, do not know or want to know the history of their race, are indifferent to the sufferings of their brothers in other countries, do not even admit the existence of a brotherhood of faith and do not desire to preserve any link with those of their blood who live under less blue and sunny skies. Is this true?

For my family, at least, this was perfectly true. I do not claim that my grandfathers were ashamed of their Jewishness—quite the opposite. But their Judaism had become something purely formal, devoid of its ancient values. Mixed marriages were considered shameful, but Jewish girls of good families, like my mother and her sister, were sent to study (little and badly) in convent schools where they would acquire a "better education." No self-respecting Jewish family of the time would have dared to eat bread during the eight days of Passover (during which Jews are required to eat only unleavened bread in memory of their liberation from slavery in ancient Egypt). Both my maternal and paternal grandmothers were proud of their beautiful Pesach (Passover) porcelain dinner services, used only for that one particular week of the year. But the thought of not having bread in the kitchen for the use of the servants, or of not consuming forbidden foods or wines would never cross their minds. When, out of respect for some elderly and "bigoted" member of the family, they observed some "unusual" details of the Mosaic tradition, they did it convinced that such rituals had no further reason to exist in modern society, although most of the assimilated families continued to exalt the value of Jewish tradition.

Nobody, for instance, had taught my mother Hebrew, or explained to her the rudiments of Jewish traditions, with the exception of some vague notions in preparation for her bat mitzvah, celebrated in the style of a Christian girl's confirmation. My father used to recite by heart, morning and evening, a small section of the Shema, the Biblical passage that forms the center of the daily liturgy. He also carried in his wallet the text of a Kaddish, a sanctification of God also recited by mourners, printed in Latin characters on a card. On the back of this card there were lines on which to record the names and dates of the "dear departed" according to both Jewish and Gregorian calendars. On these anniversaries even the least observant Jews felt it their duty to visit the synagogue. On the Sabbath preceding the Jahrzeit, that is, the anniversary of the burial, my father made sure to be called up to the podium in the synagogue, next to the rabbi, to attend the reading of the weekly portion of the Bible. At the end of the reading, of which he did not understand a word, he had the name of the departed relative announced together with the sum of money he was offering in his memory. For the rest, and in spite of his pride in being Jewish, my father was totally ignorant of Jewish culture. One could not accuse him of consciously breaking the Mosaic law, since nobody had ever taught it to him. He knew that pork and hare, which he enjoyed immensely, were forbidden foods according to some outdated Jewish ideas. He would have been sincerely surprised to learn that it was also forbidden to light a fire on the Sabbath.

Thus, almost as a reaction to this ignorance, his generation and that of my mother had invented, faute de mieux, a series of their own private "rites" to mark the Jewish holidays. God forbid that at the end of the Yom Kippur fast, which in my family only my father kept, we should not eat the *bruscadela*, a traditional Piedmontese dish consisting of slices of toasted bread soaked in strong wine. Yet the idea of stopping work or giving up a business deal or trip because of a Jewish festival would never have crossed their minds.

We children had all made our entry into *da-minyan*, a corrupted Jewish expression indicating our coming of age. Jews of thirteen years of age enter into a minyan, or group of at least ten men, without which it is not possible to recite most of the prayers in the synagogue. To prepare for this they used to send us to Talmud Torah, courses of Judaism, on Thursday afternoons, a day chosen to avoid the study of religion clashing with a tennis party or a skiing outing, which usually took place on Saturdays and Sundays. Between the solemn engagement to uphold Judaism, which the young Jew undertook on the day of his religious initiation in front of happy, proud, and usually tearful families, and the subsequent observance of Jewish precepts there was, of course, no theoretical or practical connection. It was obvious to us that "Jewish life" and "normal life" belonged already to two separate spheres. They usually overlapped in the request of Jewish parents to exempt their children from the study of Christian religion at school, a request automatically granted by the school authorities (and regarded as a privilege by one's non-Jewish schoolfellows).

My mother, therefore, like my father, grew up in a climate of obsolete Judaism and of vigorous Italian nationalism, and, as a result, she shared all the virtues and prejudices typical of a generation of Jewish bourgeois sure of themselves, affluent, and respected, and totally unconscious of the dangers that lay waiting for them in the future.

As was proper for young ladies from good and wealthy families, my mother had not followed a regular course of study. She could play the piano, embroider, had tried painting with little success, knew French and German, read fashion magazines, and took a passionate interest in books that dealt with religious questions. Her interest in such subjects was part of her inner nature. It had been developed by the nuns in the school in which my grandmother had enrolled her, convinced as the old lady was that the proximity of the *munie* (nuns) and a better knowledge of their system of life would immunize her from any "religious phobias." This turned out to be a correct forecast. My mother never turned into a bigot. Yet once she was installed on my father's estate it became natural for her to fill the long hours of boredom, while she waited for her husband to return from hunting parties or tours of inspection in the fields, by reading stories of the saints and martyrs of Christendom supplied by the local church, together with the picaresque novels about royal courts that my father had brought into his library during his bachelor days.

The emotional relationship between my parents ran on different levels throughout their lives. From the day he met her, by chance, at a university students' party, my father's love for my mother became his principal reason for living, and so it remained in spite of all the unexpected trials it underwent. "Neither of you," he used to say to my sister and me, half serious and half laughing, "is worth your mother's little finger-nail." She, on the contrary, had an entirely different idea of married life—she looked on it as a duty of faithfulness, without burning love. The kindest and most thoughtful of people in her behavior, there was in my mother a core of coolness that married life was never able to warm, a coolness that inclined her to search for violent spiritual adventures, leaving the physical ones to remain part of a cluster of social and material interests that people of her class and generation believed could best serve the contractual engagements of respectful marriages.

Strangely enough, my father's and mother's families had not

previously been acquainted in spite of the fact that they had lived for a long time in the same city. One originated in Spain and had lived for generations in the ghetto of Ivrea. The other came from France and had settled in a small village near Turin. My father had to work hard to obtain permission to marry my mother. Her parents did not regard favorably the union of their daughter, "beautiful, delicate and innocent" (this was written in a song composed by a poet on the occasion of their betrothal), with a dowry of three hundred thousand golden lire, with a "good-for-nothing." This is how my father was regarded because of his inexplicable retirement at the age of twenty-four into the country after having tried in vain to persuade his mother to allow him to follow a military career instead of banking. As a compromise he had agreed to study law and for a time was even apprenticed to a famous lawyer. But the heavy sentences that a couple of his clients, petty thieves, had received at the conclusion of his impassioned defenses, had convinced him that he should withdraw from the bar and follow his un-Jewish passion for agriculture.

My maternal grandfather, who was a shrewd dealer in grain and land, suspected that this flight into the province concealed something shady. Before giving his consent to the marriage, he dressed himself in the shabby clothes proper for a cattle dealer and went to the village where my father was the mayor and the largest landowner. He took a room in the local inn and, between a glass of wine and a query about the price of cows, began to make some sly insinuations about Jews who had become heads of local administrations. He barely escaped being beaten up. Ashamed but happy, he returned to Turin convinced that my father, although indeed a queer fellow, was an honest one, capable of taking good care of public property as well as of his own, which consisted of four hundred hectares of excellent land, a rich hunting reserve, broad meadows along the Tanaro River, and a kiln for making bricks. My mother accepted her suitor without enthusiasm but also without reservations, happy to get married and in this way put an end to her parents' fears that she might elope with a non-Jew.

My father's love for her, especially after the late birth of my sister and myself, grew with the passing years. However, when the marriage was celebrated in June 1908 with great pomp in the Turin synagogue, the feelings between the two spouses differed profoundly from the type of sentiment engraved on the gold medallion struck for the occasion. Among the numerous sources of friction between the two were also my mother's refusal to be separated during her honeymoon from a little fox terrier, which my father hated, and his refusal to drop his habit of smoking smelly Tuscan cigars, which she loathed.

On a warm July day, my parents arrived at their village home, tired from their long and uneventful honeymoon trip. Vigiu drove the landau, lined with white silk and shining with black varnish outside, drawn by two lively black trotters. He wore a top hat with yellow and green pheasant feathers, a long gray coat decorated with golden frogs, and with his gloved hands barely controlled the horses, excited at the clapping of the villagers and the firecrackers. The municipal council had lit up the main street of the village with Chinese paper lanterns and with torches in the windows of the castle that my grandmother had sold to the municipality soon after her husband's death. A deputation of notables offered the newly married couple a message of good wishes embroidered on silk, in a wide oak frame decorated with their two portraits, the work of the orphanage nuns. In this message my mother was described as "a woman of sublime beauty and virtue." The village priest accompanied by the clerics, one of them a future cardinal, had organized a torch parade for the evening from the Chiabo quarter to the gate of the castle park. The carabinieri in full uniform maintained order; the municipal band played lively tunes; my father's peasants who, at that time, made up the majority of the village population, were lined up in the outer court of our home. Dressed in festive attire, their black kerchiefs around their perspiring necks, their Sunday jackets creased, they stood next to their wives and children, clapping and shouting at the tops of their voices, "Long live the mayor," "Long live Madamin," and anxiously waiting for the golden half sovereign that had been promised to every head of a family. They certainly did not think that a few years later my father would ask them to go and get themselves killed in battle. That night nobody thought of war or of the possibility that in the course of yet another bloody conflict my father and mother would be chased out of their home because they were Jewish.

My parents' total assimilation did not prevent them from being conscious of their difference from other people. Annetta, the maid who had entered my father's service before he married, also knew that there was something wrong with "the master." A minute person, deeply religious without being a bigot, she became my mother's confidant almost from the day she was promoted to the rank of personal maid. She carried out her daily work as though it were a mission, never tired, never sad. I could not understand why she had not married. In the course of the fifty-five years she remained in our service, with the exception of the brief period during which the Fascist laws against the Jews forbade her to work for us (though she continued to come secretly to help my mother), I do not remember ever having seen her in tears. On the contrary, she was always ready to laugh, even when things went wrong for her. When she was nearing her end, she kept telling my sister and me how fortunate she was to be dying in the apartment we had arranged for her in the attic of our village home. The only thing she could never understand or admit was how decent people like us could not be Christians. She consoled herself, in the course of the years, with the idea that there must exist some strange links between us and God since on certain days of the year my parents used to go to pray in Turin and on other occasions they ate food that appeared sacred to her, although quite different from the consecrated host she took every morning at communion. For this reason, and although nobody ever asked her to do so, she had taken upon herself the task of cooking the family's "religious dishes." She did not know a thing about Jewish dietary laws but it was she who, more than anybody else, took care that we should follow, at least as far as the kitchen was concerned, our strange religious obligations.

Naturally it was at Passover that Annetta felt in her element. The great spring cleaning suited her Christian principles. Although she never understood why, at Easter time, we suddenly stopped eating pasta, bread, and cakes, she took over from the cook for an entire week and sent up to the table the *quaietta d'Pitu*—salted turkey meat, and unleavened bread soaked in meat gravy with peas, instead of the usual meat, ham rolls, and roast rabbit.

On Yom Kippur it was she who, at the end of the fast— which she thought inhuman because of my mother's migraines —carried to the table the famous *bruscadela,* with which my father liked to break his twenty-five hours of total abstinence. At Purim, the Jewish carnival, which usually coincided with Lent, Annetta prepared small crisp squares for us. They bore little resemblance to the "Haman's ears" with which Jews celebrate the victory of Esther and Mordecai over the Chaldean prime minister who, in the Bible, symbolizes the prototype of the political anti-Semite; but they were equally tasty and agreeable to our Christian friends.

Annetta certainly would have liked to see us become Christians, but she would not have dared to interfere in such a delicate matter. Without knowing what it was all about, she never forgot to ask me when she tucked me into bed whether I had recited the Shema. I believe she imagined this prayer to be a pagan version of the Pater Noster and Ave Maria. I always answered "yes," and then she sat next to my bed, falling asleep before me. In the twilight I liked to listen to her breathing, looking at her miniature features drowsing in the deep arm-chair. Only once did I have a conversation with her that I could define as religious, and the initiative was certainly not hers.

I must have been six or seven years old, and we lived then in a villa in the center of the estate near Turin bought with my mother's dowry. Running away from the clutches of a French governess whom I detested, I sneaked up one quiet afternoon to the servants' quarters—absolutely forbidden to the children—and entered the room where Annetta was resting. It was a large, clean, tidy room, with a big window from which one could see the Castle of Rivoli on top of the hill and get a new view of the gardens and fields of the estate. Annetta got up from her big, iron-framed bed and offered me small pieces of licorice, which she kept in a candy dish on her bedside table. I noticed a bunch of dried leaves tied up with a blue ribbon at the head of her bed and asked what they were. She explained to me that these were olive leaves blessed by the priest at Easter. She also showed me the small picture of a saint she kept next to the bowl of licorice and told me that it possessed great power. She had tested it each time she asked for help in looking for something she could not find, for instance the gloves that my mother regularly lost in the house. It was enough to hold the image in one's hand and murmur in Piedmontese, "Saint Anthony, full of virtue, help me to find what I have lost," for the sought-after object to jump out of its hiding place.

I asked her whether this picture understood only Piedmontese. She laughed and explained to me that saints like Saint Anthony of Padua understood all languages even if they had never studied them, as Jesus did. This last name was familiar to me since I had heard it pronounced on occasion in the family, though in muffled tones, as if it were a relative who had gone bankrupt. I thought the time had come to elucidate the matter. Annetta looked highly embarrassed. She explained to me that Jesus was the son of God; that many years ago he had been crucified by the Romans after having been denounced by a disciple called Judas; that he had died on the cross but been resurrected; and that upon him depended the salvation of every human being. "Also of those who don't know about his existence?" I asked her. She answered, "Of course." It was at that point that, blushing and sweating slightly, she took the black and silver crucifix down from the wall and gave it to me to kiss. I found this strange but not repulsive because the crucifix had a strong, sweet taste of licorice.

It was not Annetta who influenced my mother to convert. Her conversion was the result of a dramatic affair during World War I and my departure for Palestine during World War II.

My mother's sister, educated like her in a convent school, had converted to Christianity—I believe in 1908 or 1909—after a long struggle with her family. Unlike my mother, who had a docile and mystic temperament, my aunt possessed an anxious and aggressive character. She was still very young when she fell madly in love with a lawyer in Turin, a fervent Catholic and the son of a noble family. Concerning this gentleman's birth, various versions were current in the family, all of them false, due partly to envy, and to the fact that he was physically and psychologically different from his two brothers. One, a well-known doctor, lived in an odor of sanctity; the other was to reach the top of the Italian naval hierarchy. When the lawyer met my aunt, none of his family had yet become famous. This, of course, made it even more difficult for my maternal grandparents to agree to the romance of their daughter. Their opposition only made her passion fiercer. In the bourgeois romantic atmosphere prevailing at the time, it was only natural that she threatened to commit suicide or run away from home with her lover. This second alternative would have been even more dishonorable than self-inflicted death, so after my grandfather died, consent was grudgingly given. My aunt converted and married, and the entry of this Christian uncle into the family made relationships within the "clan" even more complicated than before.

This uncle whom I acquired by marriage was a tall man, thin as a rake, a frequent sufferer from rheumatic pains, austere and authoritarian as befitted his profession, and with little sympathy for Jews. He was certainly not an anti-Semite. He had broken openly with the Fascist party—which he had supported in the beginning—after Matteotti's assassination, a gesture that showed his political farsightedness and his moral stamina. But to him, the utilitarian and bourgeois conformism that my family had developed toward the Fascist regime made "certain types of Jews," as he used to say, unbearable to him. I knew him too little and I was too unaware of our family intrigues to discuss the judgment I often heard people passing on him. His long, drawn face, the offensive tone he often used to underline his ideas, his fits of temper, about which I often heard but never witnessed, made him unlikable.

In fact he scared me. An unpleasant remark he made about the Jews the day I went to say good-bye to him before leaving for Palestine gave me, quite unjustly, an excuse to break with him. After the war he let me know that he wanted to see me and clear up the misunderstandings that were keeping us apart. I refused to meet him. I was certainly wrong; as one of the first Piedmontese intellectuals to join the Fascist party and one of the first to give back his party card—something that for a man in his position was neither easy nor convenient—he could have enlightened me on many political and family matters for which I cannot find answers in the family archives. But another fact, which I learned only after my return from Palestine, had in the meantime helped to raise a barrier between us: that uncle had played an important role in the life of my mother.

At the outbreak of World War I my father found himself exempt from military service because he was a mayor as well as the firstborn son of a widowed mother. His filial duties had prevented him from entering the military academy as he had wanted. In 1916, a year after Italy's entry into the war, it became impossible for a fervent nationalist like him, who had preached participation in the war, to stay at home. He felt ashamed each time he had to take news of deaths to the houses of his villagers, transmitted to him ever more frequently by the military authorities. The event that finally drove him to join up as a volunteer, however, was the death of his favorite horse.

The army had requisitioned three of his horses at the outbreak of the war. He had seen them leave the stable for the front line, one after the other, docile, clean, full of energy: the gray, his hunting mare, and Bayard and Harlequin, who were the matched pair for his landau. Only Blackie, a wonderful six-year-old gelding, born and reared in his stables, was left behind. My father succeeded in having him classified as a workhorse, although he had never pulled a cart or a plow in his life. I never understood why the army, which was already stuck in the trenches, needed so many riding horses. In any event, my father's first three horses were sent immediately to the front line, and soon came the military postcards announcing their deaths. Each time the unknown hand of some possibly romantic or melancholy officer had written to my father expressions of condolence more suited to the death of a man than that of an animal. But in that first year of war the peasants who filled the trenches counted little. Italy, as much as other European countries fattened by forty years of peace, seemed to need—as Churchill said—a good bloodletting.

At the beginning of 1916 they came to take Blackie. Before he left my father photographed him. This picture, enlarged to life size, was framed and hung in Blackie's stall in the now empty stables. Later the photograph was moved to the attic. Yellowed by time, it still shows, under the glass, a military postcard signed by a certain Colonel Depaoli of a cavalry regiment and dated April 12. It reads: "Most illustrious lawyer:

I am sorry to have to announce to you that Blackie has died a hero's death. He was hit by a grenade which also killed seven men and a sergeant-major. He was a courageous and faithful animal. He gave the best of himself to the Fatherland. Please accept the expression of my most sincere sympathy." Three weeks later my father enlisted, unrequested, at the nearest recruiting depot.

He was short in stature and for this reason he was registered in the infantry. After a few weeks as a private, they discovered that he had a university degree and sent him on an officers' training course and from there straight to the front. For him, as for so many other members of the Italian bourgeoisie who had been in favor of Italy's entry into a war supposed to be short and heroic, the discovery that it had turned into a senseless and endless slaughter was a terrible shock. He bore life in the trenches in silence, like so many others, convinced that he was fulfilling a moral and historical duty.

I do not have any of his letters from this period: he destroyed them all when he returned from the front. I doubt if he ever kept a diary as some of his cousins did. I am grateful to him for his modesty, because when I read the correspondence of other members of my family that found its way into the nationalist press of the time, I feel a deep embarrassment at the cloying banalities, the forced romanticism, and the spiritual emptiness concealed behind the literary efforts of people whom I respected and whose hospitality I had often enjoyed. Already many years before the Fascist racial laws, this type of war writing and memoirs showed up the empty public morality of a generation of Jews who had lost both progressive social conviction and genuine religious and cultural belief. The great flare-ups of patriotic sentiment that had driven Italian Jewry wholeheartedly to support the Risorgimento, and made them believe that nationalism represented the heroic epilogue of centuries of discrimination, had died down with the political achievement of Italian unity. Only in the schoolbooks had the new Italy remained the epic and pure country of Mazzini, Garibaldi, and Cavour; in practice it was a new, disorganized state, open to speculation and scandals. The Jews may have appeared less opportunistic than others, thanks to a certain reticence to exposing their financial success, due to their status as late arrivals. At least in our family, in spite of the break with our traditions, people still followed a style of life that united Risorgimento ideals with remnants of Jewish austerity.

During the war, however, I am convinced that for most of them Jewish sentiment often prevailed over other feelings. In my father's case this was certainly so. Facing death in the trenches, he tried desperately to reestablish contact with his Jewish origins. Among the books in his library I found one, torn and stained with sweat and mud, full of annotations, that clearly shows it was carried close to his skin for long periods of time. It was one of those books that the Italian rabbis of the time presumably thought could save Judaism through its linguistic tricks. Their idea was to revitalize the ancient Hebrew language through literal translations into Italian. In this particular book every word of the prayers written in Hebrew characters was divided from the following one by a stroke, and below each word, also between strokes, was the corresponding Italian meaning. How it was possible to pray with such a text is beyond my comprehension: Hebrew is written from right to left, Italian from left to right. The translated words follow each other not only imprisoned between bars but also in the wrong order. They looked like a line of ants with their front legs touching their neighbors and produced a visual and verbal discrepancy that made these texts look as though they had been composed for retarded stutterers.

Yet every page of the book had been annotated, underlined by my father as no other book in his possession. I often imagine him, sitting on a rock in a wet, muddy trench waiting for an assault, or checking his sentries, searching for courage and hope in the magic produced by this confusion of Latin and Hebrew characters. These printed words had lost their original meaning for him, and even if they had still retained something, the translation would have destroyed the rhythm they might once have possessed. But to my father, in those circumstances, they must have transformed themselves into mysterious links with an ancient and faraway world about which he was totally ignorant. Faced by a European civilization in the process of committing suicide in the mad war he had preached, that of his ancestors probably appeared to him as more solid and credible. One thing is certain: on Yom Kippur in 1916 my father rejected all attempts by his fellow officers to make him eat or drink before leading his platoon into one of the many deadly and useless assaults. He described that terrible day to me many times. Thirty men went out; six came back. His luck was rewarded by a brief spell of leave. He rushed back to his country home to find my mother had decided to become a Catholic.

Only after I returned from Palestine in 1945 did my father tell me the full story of this first attempt at conversion, about which I had previously acquired only fragmentary information.

My father, still amazed at being alive, had gone to the town nearest to the front to be deloused and had sent my mother a long, excited telegram to announce his forthcoming arrival. Therefore, he was quite surprised not to find her at the railway station; his blacksmith, too old to be mobilized, was waiting for him with a calèche. This blacksmith—Carlin was his name —born and reared on one of our farms, considered himself, and was considered, a member of the family. To my father, who questioned him anxiously about my mother's health, he was unable to give a satisfactory answer. He kept saying that Madamin had looked a bit agitated during the past few months; that she had been seen walking a lot in Annetta's company; she had spent long hours in church praying for his safety. The village clerk had shown him a newspaper that described the heroism of, and the terrible losses sustained by, my father's regiment. It must indeed have been a horrible day. It was certainly thanks to Madamin's prayers that he had come out alive. She was doing a wonderful job helping refugees and giving out a lot of money to the village poor, while spending most of her evenings sewing with the orphanage nuns. My father knew of my mother's religious bent but never expected that instead of welcoming him with the warmth due to a returning soldier, she herself, tense and excited, would announce to him her decision to become a Christian. He felt the most atrocious pain of his life.

He did not try to argue with this woman he loved. Wounded both in his masculine and his Jewish pride, he shut himself in his library for a day and a night, refusing, to Annetta's consternation, to eat in the dining room or to receive the friends and farmers who came to greet him. When he ordered the old gardener to hurry up and summon the village priest, the rumor ran through the village that something serious was taking place in our home.

The priest, a friend of the family with whom my father had spent many evenings playing chess and emptying bottles of wine, was the only person who had not yet come to welcome him back. My father trusted him fully and quickly understood that he was waiting to be called. Questioned as to what had happened in my father's absence, the priest gave him all the necessary information in detail.

With my father far away, my mother was even more bored than usual by country life. The assistance she gave to the war refugees, the knitting of vests, balaclava helmets, and scarves for the soldiers who were freezing in the trenches, was not enough to fill up the days of a woman who aspired to be involved in something different, more beautiful, greater. In the village, the war, with its unending slaughter, brought to every family with a relative in the front lines, a feeling of anguish, of terror, but also of anger and revolt against those who preached the war (and who now were more despicable than the workers who stayed home). The Jews, moreover, did not have special interests to defend in this conflict, as they did in the wars of the Risorgimento. They wanted to protect their newly acquired positions but no longer felt part of the country's elite. On the national scene there was no longer a Nathan, mayor of Rome, to shield Mazzini in his home, nor an Artom to work as a private secretary with the count of Cavour to unify Italy, nor an Ottolenghi, who, after serving as an officer with Garibaldi's troops, had been rewarded with a title and the war portfolio.

The Jewish community, from which my mother felt estranged in any case, had little to offer its members in those days. The synagogue imitated the church wherever possible, introducing, for instance, the organ on the Sabbath and High Holy Days, and dressing its rabbis in ludicrous black gowns and hexagonal hats. The patriotic rhetoric that these rabbis spouted from the pulpit sounded less convincing than the patriotic sermons of the priests in their churches. It was more difficult for a Jew than for a Christian to think of a Jewish soldier in the enemy camp as an enemy. The church, with its symbols of human and divine sacrifice, offered messages of faith and hope befitting the mentality of Christian soldiers. The synagogue, however, had nothing similar to offer its own faithful. The rabbis prayed for the return of Zion while Jews were asked to die for the recovery of lost Italian provinces; they exalted the Exodus from Egypt while millions of people knew that they would never leave the trenches alive. The war eroded, for everybody, moral values, the links between the classes, and the reciprocal feelings of respect and authority between them. My father, who had voluntarily chosen to share the horrors of that war, clutched at the meager advantages offered by the army: the authority of a military uniform that at last he could wear; the solidarity of the fighting men; the respect he aroused in others by his fatalistic approach to death;

his belief in the just cause of Italian arms; the simplicity of the choices facing him—recover Treno, Trieste for Italy—or death.

My mother, however, was seeing her *belle epoque* world crumble in an atmosphere of growing vulgarity and social promiscuity, in the dissolution of that aristocratic ambience—in fact already well and truly dead—that the Jewish middle class aspired to join like the rest of the country's petty bourgeoisie.

The war, viewed from the leisure of a quiet country life, increased her desire, indeed her need—more out of boredom than out of a sense of adventure—to go beyond good and evil. She felt herself swept away by events greater than herself, without support within the family, guidance in her religion, or advice from her friends. Desperately searching for values to hold on to, for occasions to feel different, she found in her brother-in-law someone ready to listen to her doubts and offer dispassionate counsel. Free—I have never known why—from military service, or perhaps serving locally, he used to visit her frequently, bring her religious books, and put her in contact with a friar gifted with eloquence and a desire to conquer for the Christian faith a Jewish soul so naturally prone to religious enthusiasm. This friar quite possibly thought he was acting in the same spirit as Italian soldiers conquering Austro-Hungarian positions in the front line. He had understood that my mother, separated from a husband who had preferred war to the boredom of country life, rich, without children, and searching for her identity, needed to do something exceptional, to make a gesture that might correspond with the general atmosphere of heroism created by the war. The church attracted her with its liturgy full of music, its paintings, its literature soaked in sacrifice and passion. It offered her an opportunity to realize herself, within a strong, confident hierarchy, capable of understanding, comforting, and bestowing social approval.

The village priest talked at length to my father. He did not

conceal the failure of his weak efforts to postpone, in time if
not in spirit, a decision that he thought improper for my
mother to make as long as my father was away from home.
But what could he, a poor village priest, do against so many
persuasive and influential people? There were also limits that
his cassock imposed on him in such circumstances. To save a
soul, to bring a lost lamb into the church, was a duty he could
not hinder even if he felt, out of friendship for my father,
unable to participate actively in such a mission. He had spent
many unhappy hours, he told my father, torn between his
religious duties and his human obligations. In the end he had
decided to withdraw from the whole affair. His conscience,
naturally, was not at ease. But who on earth could sleep
peacefully with what was happening in the world these days?
His eyes shone with unshed tears as he finished speaking. He
blew his nose several times into his big, red, snuff-spotted
handkerchief, shook hands with my father, and returned to his
parish after exchanging a few words with Annetta, who was
anxiously waiting to report back to my mother anything she
could learn about the meeting.

My father understood that in such circumstances there was
little to be done on the spot. He could not hope to persuade
my mother to return to an ancient faith about which he
himself knew so little. He could not expect, by his brief
presence, to neutralize the effect of months of persuasion by
so many missionaries. Without greeting my mother, he took
the first train to the city of Cuneo and asked to speak with the
bishop. They were not friends, but they knew each other well
enough for him not to be kept waiting. In any event, his
bearing was so stern that nobody dared to hold him up. In a
few short, well-chosen sentences he explained his problem to
the bishop. He told him that he was due to return to the front
lines and therefore could not care less how he would die. He
knew that the friar who had got into the habit of visiting his
wife belonged to the bishop's diocese. If he did not receive on

the spot a promise that no priest would be authorized to
baptize her before the end of the war or prior to his death, if
the bishop did not give him a formal guarantee that neither
the friar in question nor any other priest would enter his house
in his absence, he would look for the friar and put an end to
his life. Then he would decide what to do: commit suicide,
stand trial, or go back to the front lines and get killed. He had
already informed his lawyer, in writing, of his intentions and
prepared a communiqué for the press. Should the bishop refuse
his request, he would see to it that people would be informed
how the Church was stealing the souls of the wives of Jews
who were away from their homes fighting for their country.
He gave the bishop five minutes to decide.

Standing upright, with a theatrical gesture he took his
watch out of his pocket. It was a gold Longines, with the
monogram and the profile of King Victor Emmanuel II engraved inside the cover. He had inherited it from his uncle, to
whom the king had presented it in return for delicate services
performed for the "beautiful Rosie," the morganatic wife of
the king, when she was still the mistress of the monarch. The
watch, my father told me, showed ten past eleven in the
morning. With his eyes fixed on the hands, he stood there
waiting for the answer of Holy Mother Church.

I do not know what impressed the bishop most: the compressed fury of a man known to be one of the influential
notables of the province, or the threat of a scandal. He asked
my father to sit down. He ordered a very strong coffee. He
offered him a Tuscan cigar from a box well-concealed in his
table drawer. He tried to calm him down in every possible
way. Then he promised "to do his best" and in my father's
presence ordered the friar to be summoned to his office. My
father left the episcopal palace not entirely reassured but convinced that he had done his utmost. The idea of returning to
the front lines now seemed to him almost pleasant. Death
would free him from a painful situation, just as the conflict

with his wife was freeing him from the fear of going back to the trenches.

During the whole of his leave, he did not speak of religion to my mother and tried to enjoy as much as he could the warrior's rest. The detached behavior of a man who was ostensibly preparing himself to die probably made my mother hesitate to make the final decision. Before he left for the front, he learned from the village nuns that the friar no longer had the right to come to the village. Thus the conversion was postponed by twenty years to the day when, following the Fascist anti-Jewish laws and my departure for Palestine, my mother was again shaken by a violent religious crisis.

In the meantime, however, another factor helped to consolidate the religious truce between my parents—my father was in danger of being shot for high treason. Back at his regimental headquarters, he found an urgent call from the General Staff Office; they needed, he was told, a cipher officer in the personal secretariat of the king. The position was being offered to him on condition that he knew how to type. For an entire afternoon and throughout the night, my father worked unceasingly on one of the strange, new office machines. The following day he successfully passed the examination. Thus, he moved from the mud of the trenches straight to the luxury of a Venetian villa, in direct contact with the king and the top commanders of the Italian and Allied armies. This period of rubbing shoulders with the "top brass" he had so much longed to join probably influenced his opting for Fascism later. It also produced a valuable collection of photographs of the great personages of that time, which I have inherited and like to admire whenever I can, always asking myself how so many important and apparently honest and intelligent people could have allowed such a slaughter to continue unchecked for five years.

For my father the transfer also meant taking my mother away from the estate in Piedmont and bringing her to Udine, the nearest big town to the front lines. He obtained all the necessary permits for her arrival and chose appropriate accommodations for her. Then, just before her arrival, on a January night in 1917, he had to decode a personal message from Czar Nicholas to King Victor Emmanuel, in which the Russian emperor announced an offensive against the Germans. There was nothing strategically or tactically decisive in this action. The operation ended with a slight advance in the Riga area, during which the Russian troops, exhausted and already undermined by revolutionary propaganda, conquered a few German positions in the marshy area of Tircul. But for the Allies, pressed as they were by the armies of the Central Powers, this was excellent news. My father decoded the message and then made four copies, as was his procedure for top-secret documents: one for the king, one for the chief of staff, one for a certain General Porro, whose position at that time I do not know, and the fourth one for the file to which he alone had access.

I have heard the story so many times that I remember every detail by heart. It was January 4. There was quite a crowd of officers at the café in the Piazza dei Mercanti in Udine. A war correspondent approached a Russian liaison officer, slapped him on the back and said at the top of his voice: "At last you are moving!" People immediately crowded around the journalist, who retreated behind a mysterious smile, while the Russian ran to his office to report the matter. In the evening, while my father was busy at his decoding work, two officers came to his office, declared him under arrest, and took him straight to the commander in chief, General Cadorna, for interrogation. To whom, he was asked, did you reveal the contents of the coded telegram? My father did not know what they were talking about, but in such circumstances hypotheses were of little use. Since only four people could have known the contents of the telegram, and nobody could suspect either the king or the two generals, it was natural that suspicion should fall squarely on the fourth, the junior officer who knew the contents of the message.

By chance, a military police officer, in civilian dress, was present in the café when the war correspondent made his remark. He interrogated him and learned that he had entered the office of General Porro when nobody was there. He had cast an eye on the dispatches lying on the table, read the czar's telegram and been unable to stop himself from showing off.

However, it took more than two weeks for the matter to be clarified during which time my father was kept under house arrest. A court-martial was set up, and the danger of being sentenced to death became very real. Equally serious was the fact that a rumor began to spread that a Jewish officer had committed a serious crime. Jews who heard the rumor—and the many members of my family who were in uniform immediately became aware of it—thought a new Dreyfus case was being prepared. My father's brother, who already held an important position at GHQ, came to see him accompanied by one of Italy's leading lawyers.

Meanwhile, my mother had arrived in town, unaware of the events and totally confused by what seemed to be a major family, and perhaps national, tragedy. She knew my father too well to doubt his innocence. It was natural for her to come to his defense, to offer him her moral support, while finding in this affair an exciting diversion from her religious problems. For a few days the situation was serious. My mother, connecting her husband's troubles, through who knows what sort of logic, with her attempted conversion, already felt herself responsible for what was happening to him.

Then suddenly the charge against my father was dropped, official apologies were offered, and he regained the trust of the king. This happy ending smelled too much like a miracle not to be regarded by both my parents as a sign from heaven. And thus it was in Udine, a sleepy provincial town where many years later I would celebrate my bar mitzvah, that my mother promised my father to abandon the idea of changing her religion. It was a promise she kept strictly for more than twenty years and to which I owe the fact that I was born and raised a Jew. However, when the Fascist anti-Jewish laws were published and the world crumbled around my parents, my mother found herself once again isolated and unprepared to face events greater than herself.

My departure for Palestine, a country she could not even locate on the map, catalyzed her religious crisis. This time my father no longer had the courage nor the authority to dissuade her. His world, too, was shattered, the world of a Jew who had been a faithful servant of the House of Savoy, a Fascist and a confirmed Italian nationalist. He himself felt little comfort in the few Jewish rites he still observed, nor was he able to explain to himself the sudden social thunderstorm that was hitting him together with the rest of European Jewry. The only thing he could count on was the affection of the woman he loved. If the Christian faith—he explained to me—could comfort her in the midst of such a disaster, he had neither the right nor the desire to oppose her decision.

One day, when he was particularly open with me about these very personal matters, he told me what he did on the day my mother, on her confessor's advice, made a public act of repudiation of Judaism. The whole family (including those members who had already converted in secret) took this formal public statement very badly and denounced it as an act of treason, aggravated by the unnecessary publicity. But my father preferred to send to the convent, where she had retreated to prepare herself for her baptism, a bunch of red roses, like the ones he used to offer her on the occasion of their wedding anniversary. Then he went into the fields to prune his vines.

My mother saved two of these roses. She asked me to put one on my father's coffin, which she felt she could not follow to the Jewish cemetery in Turin; she took the other with her to Israel, where she went every winter after my father's death instead of going alone to the Riviera.

In Jerusalem, where everything was new and strange to her,

she seemed at last to find some peace of mind. On Sundays she used to go to mass, with great discretion, in a monastery where most of the monks were, like herself, converts from Judaism. With their help, she started learning Hebrew. One evening I surprised her teaching my son the same prayers that I had heard my father recite near my bed when I was a child. She spent long hours walking in the garden of the Convent of the Sisters of Zion at Ein Kerem, a convent built at the end of the last century by a rich French Jewish banker who converted to Christianity. In this place of peace and faith, she used to tell me, the little Judaism she had learned as a child revealed itself to her as the roots of the Christian gospel, while the catechism that the priests had taught her appeared to be dressed in Jewish robes.

Sometimes, in the afternoons when she looked at the shadows of the olive trees lengthening on the Judean Hills and the square stones of the convent turning first red then purple under the rays of the setting sun, she felt herself overtaken by a sweet languor. It seemed to her that time was melting her doubts, that the ancient landscape made her pains and anxieties minuscule in the face of the mystery that here, more than anywhere else, weighed on the conscience of the living and on the oblivion of the dead.

When she suddenly fell ill, she asked for and was given permission to be buried in the cemetery of the convent. The gravestone only bears her name, the dates of her birth and death, and a cross. Every year it sinks a little deeper into the earth, as if the body it covers is asking for a closer embrace. One day it will disappear, I imagine, sucked in by the soil perfumed by the winter rains, concealed like the other tombs by the broom and the wild gladioli that blossom in spring and disappear at the first sign of summer—the scratch left by a life on the face of eternity.

3.

My Jewish-Fascist
Childhood

I WAS born at the end of 1922,
a month after the March on Rome, and I lived for sixteen years
in Fascist Italy. Those years of Italian life were for me an
existence so regular, normal and carefree, so devoid of events,
that I would find it very difficult to say what was special about
Fascism.

Those who have experienced situations whose daily normality blurs the perception of their extraordinariness may perhaps
feel more keenly to the contrary. I never entered into the
Mussolini regime—I was born into it. As a totally assimilated
Jew and as an Italian raised under a political regime of which
my family and all my friends approved without any reservation, I, too, saw Fascism as the only natural form of existence.
I was not aware of its particularism, because I had no way of
comparing it with other political systems. It may sound incred-
ible, but the first time I heard socialism mentioned as a political
reality, not as a historical fact, was in 1939, in a kibbutz in
Palestine. As for democracy, I knew it was plutocratic and

decadent, and I did not understand (though the thing did not interest me in the least) how it could continue to exist.

This childhood experience of total adaptation to the environment allows me today to understand better situations that appear to be inconceivable to others: the ability, for instance, of the Israelis to lead a normal life, day after day, in the midst of an unending state of war; the ability of the citizen-soldier to bear and often enjoy military service provided that it lasts long enough to assume a regular rhythm; the ability of men and women to love, work, buy, and sell in a city like Beirut, ravaged by civil war.

The Fascist youth organizations to which I belonged from my earliest years—the Balilla and the Avanguardisti—were part and parcel of the school system. I respected them in the same way I respected my teachers at the Royal Gymnasium, but they did not interfere with my life. They wanted me for the end-of-year gymnastics exhibition, not for my ideas. In any case, my mother's "justification," written in her beautiful handwriting on handmade Fabriano paper with her name gracefully engraved on the top left-hand corner, was sufficient to free me at any time without question to go to the dentist, play tennis, or attend a Hebrew lesson. I do not remember, either in school or outside, one single occasion when I felt uneasy because I was a Jew. I was convinced that being Jewish was a treat no different from Cirio brand marmalade, the more so because I was the constant object of jealousy among my school friends for being allowed "for religious reasons" to be absent from the boring lessons of the Gymnasium priest.

The Judaism practiced in my home did not entail any special obligations. Except for the fact that I had to go on Thursday afternoons to the lesson at the Talmud Torah to prepare for my bar mitzvah, to be a Jew was not, in my case, any more inconvenient than being a Catholic or a Protestant. The Sabbath was like any other day: school in the morning and horseback-riding or fencing in the afternoon. There was no special food to be eaten or avoided at home or outside. As a Jew I was exempt from going to mass on Sunday mornings and free from the obligation to observe the forty days of Lent, but my mother took great care always to have fish on Fridays "out of respect for the servants." The Jewish High Holy Days of Rosh Hashanah and Yom Kippur usually fell at the end of the summer vacation. I spent them in the mountains playing cowboys and Indians. My father, secluded for the day in his library, used to read his big prayer book, translated into Italian; he used to call us into his room on the afternoon of Yom Kippur to read us the story of Jonah, and that was all.

At Passover, we ate matzoh, but naturally the servants always had their bread. I never attended a Passover seder until I arrived in Palestine. Of the other main Jewish holidays, Shavuot and Succot, I knew nothing at all. I was, however, well aware of a feast called Purim, the Jewish carnival, because my maternal grandmother used to bring us a round cake covered with glazed fruit, called *brasadel* in the Piedmontese Jewish jargon, which my mother tried in vain to imitate after my grandmother's death.

Hanukkah, the Festival of Lights, fell too near Christmas for me to be able to distinguish clearly between them. We used to celebrate both in the mountains. I attended midnight mass with my father and with my Christian cousins, all very excited by the long ride in the snow in the horse-drawn sleigh, skimming through the darkness to the accompaniment of the galloping horses' bells. We were aware (especially my cousins, who knew at the time that my uncle expected to be made a baron or a count) of our duty to receive with grace and reserve the greetings of the workers from the family estate. After singing the carols from the benches behind us, the workers formed a pathway down the aisle of the church for our passage; never did it cross my mind that the fact that they were Christians and I was a Jew might be considered peculiar. It was as natural as the pine trees around the church, the little cemetery and its crosses, the river bubbling by among the patches of snow, the old sawmill, the mountains, the wind, and the old cook who waited for us at home with mulled wine and biscuits.

Since I had no contact with the world outside Italy; since I read only school textbooks, adventure stories and, from time to time, the local newspapers to look up the titles of films or the sports programs; since I lived first in the gilded cage of my mother's estate in Piedmont and then in the cotton-wool climate of a Venetian provincial town in which my family occupied a certain position; since I had no political or social reasons to become interested in events or ideas beyond those of my daily routine, so full of small duties, of cycling and riding competitions, of social satisfactions, I lived in the belly of the monster, totally unaware of its existence.

The first sixteen years of my life were divided into periods of equal length—from 1922 to 1930 on my mother's estate near Turin, and from 1931 to 1938 at Udine, a small provincial town in the Friuli region. It was the nearest place with a high school to my uncle's fiefdom in the mountains along the Austrian and Yugoslav border, where my father worked after losing most of his fortune in the 1929 stock market crash.

After the publication of the laws against the Jews in July 1938, we returned to the Piedmont region and I went to live in my grandmother's house in Turin, one of the few cities in Italy where the Jewish community was able to organize secondary schools for students who had been thrown out of the public schools. Here I discovered for the first time a world different from mine; here took place the first brutal meeting with the particularism of my Jewish condition, my first contacts with a literature, a history containing ideas totally different from those with which I had grown up. In Turin I also met many people whose names have since been inscribed in the history of the Italian resistance movement and of the Jewish

tragedy: Leon Ginsburg, the Russian-born writer; and Eman-
uele Artom, the mathematical genius who was later tortured
to death by the Fascists; Franco Antonicelli, a future senator
and leader of the anti-Fascist Piedmontese resistance; Primo
Levi, the chemist whose account of life in concentration camps
would become a classic of the literature on the Holocaust.
However, I did not establish strong relations with any of them,
since I left almost immediately for Palestine in order to escape
from the new, and to me totally incomprehensible, situation
in which I suddenly found myself trapped.

I felt, indeed, like a fish out of water. I had never been a
Zionist, and I could hardly have become one since my father
strongly opposed the Jewish national movement, which to his
mind undermined the patriotism of the Italian Jews. I knew
that there existed strange boxes, blue and white in color, in
which my new schoolmates put coins on Jewish holidays. But
my father refused to have such an object in his house, even
after the publication of the anti-Jewish laws. I was also completely ignorant of Judaism, if one excepts the few notions I
had learned at the Talmud Torah classes while preparing for
my bar mitzvah. If, nevertheless, I was to be one of the first
Italian Jews to leave for Palestine after the publication of the
Racial Laws (after having tried without success and without
the knowledge of my parents to join the foreign legion in
France), this was only due to the attraction of romantic adven-
turism and to the hope of being able to imitate, in a country
that did not yet have a political identity of its own, some of
the deeds of Garibaldi. Unnoticed by everyone, I even tried
to teach myself to make candles as Garibaldi had done in Latin
America to make a living before joining the Italian legion,
fighting for the liberation of Uruguay. Feeling deeply
offended by the behavior of the Fascist party and the king
toward me and my family, I broke my ties with the Italian
nation in a series of secret, nighttime ceremonies, during the
course of which I buried, under the great cedar of Lebanon in

my mother's garden, my black Fascist dagger, a wooden toma-
hawk, and my collection of tin soldiers—the symbols of my
now-shattered hopes of joining the Royal Military College.

To the psychological shock caused by these sudden changes
(which were continued in Palestine with my passing—in less
than two years—from a kibbutz to an agricultural school, and
from that school to the British army), I attribute in part the
tenacity with which the uniformity of my life under Fascism
—the only normal existence I ever knew—has stuck in my
memory. It is as if my subconscious has refused to abandon the
illusion of the quiet, happy years of my youth and blocked all
attempts to look more deeply at those early periods of my life
that must, in some way, have recorded the events that shook
my family and the country of my birth during this time—for
instance, the stock exchange crash of 1929.

Of this event, which ruined my father, causing us to leave
Piedmont for Udine, and forcing him to work for the first
time in his life so that we became, in the eyes of our ramified
and still very wealthy relations, the poorest and therefore the
most stupid branch of the clan, I do not remember a thing. I
recall only some mnemonic flashes from the time just before
our move, completely detached from the events that were
shaking our family existence; for instance, a night drive on the
not-yet-asphalted road leading from my mother's estate, in my
father's 509 Fiat limousine, sitting next to the uniformed chauffeur, who allowed me from time to time to put my hands on
the wheel. I was full of excitement at the sight of the speedom-
eter needle jerking around the fifty-mile-an-hour mark, and I
kept turning around toward my parents to make them conscious of this extraordinary adventure. I could see them
through the movable glass partition that separated their seats
from that of the driver, totally indifferent to my enthusiasm.
They were talking to each other with agitated gestures that
seemed to mime the anguished movements of the two red roses
stuck in the silver vase next to the door. My mother, wearing

a big silver fox fur around her shoulders, crushed in her hand a handkerchief embroidered with her monogram and frequently touched her lips with smelling salts. It was the day my father, having lost all his money, understood for the first time that he was completely ruined. We were saved by a loan from his cousin's bank and by the job, offered by his brother, of running a chain factory somewhere in the Venetian mountains. To him this was the end of his world, of his material security, which for the last two generations had seemed indestructible; for me it was only a high-speed drive in my first—and last—private limousine.

Another clear memory of that time is linked to a rat. My sister and I were children prone to illness. She had had a mastoid operation; I used to progress from sore throats to bronchitis, which my parents tried to prevent by forcing me to drink great quantities of castor oil and by stuffing my nostrils at night with cotton swabs soaked in some strange and evil-smelling liquid. If to all this one adds my tendency to wound myself in the strangest ways (I once poured boiling water on my arms; another time I cut my scalp open with an ax, which I was using upside down to knock in the pegs of my Indian tepee), it will be clear why, as long as we remained in Piedmont, my parents preferred to have me taught privately rather than to send me to the public school. This resulted in my not studying anything seriously, not knowing boys my own age, and in living in the golden cage of a big country house among teachers, servants, and gardeners who, in the main, looked after their own affairs.

My mother's estate was surrounded by a long wall that cut me off from the mysterious world of the village. There was nothing much to see from three sides of the wall since it overlooked open fields, and agricultural life was far more interesting at home than outside. The farmers never objected to my joining them in their haymaking; whenever I asked they put me astride one of their big workhorses or allowed me to hold the reins of the two-wheeled Piedmontese carts, which looked to me like Roman chariots. Sometimes they even allowed me to steer the plow or shell the maize, or to collect frogs and snails from the ponds, which both they and my father liked to eat. From them I learned much more than from my teachers, and to them I owe the ease with which I was able to adapt to work in the fields when I reached Palestine.

The fourth side of the wall extended for hundreds of yards along the main road of the village, into which I was not allowed to go unaccompanied. I was only permitted to stand near the great iron gate at the end of the acacia-lined drive, to peer like a monkey through the bars into the world of free men.

The Via Maestra was narrow and full of life with two stone ruts down the center for cartwheels. To the left of the gate were some artisans' workshops, one of which belonged to my mother's cobbler, whose son eventually bought her estate. In these workshops wonderful things happened: from rusty pieces of iron there came forth delicate iron tracery; from masses of cane, all sorts of beautiful baskets; from big tree trunks, window frames, tables, and doors and—most important of all—my wooden shields and swords.

To the right of the gate one could see the beginning of a small winding lane, leading—so I was told in great secrecy by Cecilia, the kitchen maid—to a restaurant where one could rent rooms by the hour, which always seemed to me to be an excellent business. At the corner of the lane, soldiers of the local garrison used to wait in the evening for their girls, and women exchanged gossip during the day. The Via Maestra was crowded with carts, either filled with hay and corn, or empty with a farmer asleep inside next to a flask of wine, at the mercy of his horses' loyalty and sense of direction.

However, the most important things in that street for me were the parades organized by the local branch of the Fascist party and the processions of the local parish. They competed between themselves with their uniforms, their flags, their songs, their music, and the very impressive gestures that the participants made while walking—either raising their hands in the Roman salute or waving them in Christian blessing. My preference had been for the Fascists since the day my father, giving in to my insistence, put me between two of his militia-men in black shirts and armed with carbines and daggers, to march in front of the flag. I felt exalted and terribly important. Only many years later, when I saw for the first time a British regiment marching along with a goat as its mascot, did I realize that I had filled the role of the goat in my first Fascist march.

The Catholic processions were quite different. I was never given permission to join them and to swing the censers like the little village boys whom I so much envied. They succeeded, while marching and singing in unison, in raising white clouds of perfumed smoke, something I never could manage when I tried to send Indian smoke signals to my sister across the garden. The blue and gold garments of the priests, the crosses, the white, embroidered smocks of the choirboys, the white headscarves of the women of the Daughters of Mary, im-pressed me more than the black shirts of the Fascists. Yet an event once took place that created between me and the church procession that psychological barrier that still keeps me away from any form of collective liturgy.

It was a hot summer afternoon; the church bells had been ringing for hours; the Via Maestra was packed with people. The carabinieri wore their gala uniforms with blue and red feathers on their bicorne hats. The bishop was there, sur-rounded by priests, walking behind the statue of the Madonna with a golden crown on her head and a blue silk scarf draped around her wooden shoulders, carried by eight farmers dressed in their Sunday best. There were the boys from the elementary school, the Daughters of Mary, the canons and the clerks, and the association of ex-soldiers with their banners full of medals. There was the old soldier from Garibaldi's army with his red shirt, an antiquated military cap on his head, hobbling along with a walking stick. The smell of incense mingled with that of the hay still in the fields. The municipal band led the march, followed by my father, who had just been appointed mayor, wearing his tricolor sash of office and a black jacket, which had miniatures of his military medals pinned on the lapel.

Our farmers sat on top of the wall with their legs dangling near the heads of the passing crowd. My mother's maid and my French governess stood side by side near the iron gate. They gave me a special place at their feet; I sat on a little stool from which I could look down at the procession without getting tired. My sister, however, stood a few yards away under the last acacia tree of the avenue, next to the canal that crossed our property. Just before the bishop and his entourage passed in front of the gate, my sister let out a scream of terror at the top of her voice. Half a century later I still remember the scene: she stood petrified, pressing her little leg with both hands and screaming, "he's bitten me!" Her shrieks were soon echoed by the screams of the French governess, who was terrified of being thought responsible for whatever had happened.

The strange thing that was the cause of all this commotion stood motionless, like part of one of those still-life scenes that my mother used to organize in her sitting room among her guests when she felt that gossip and sweets were no longer able to keep people from yawning. It was a rat—to my eyes it looked monstrous—an aggressive sewer rat, not a field mouse, since it had the courage not to run away amid all the uproar. After having bitten my sister, it stood there looking at her and at the French governess with two small, red eyes and with tiny, bared, pointed teeth, which looked to me like elephant's tusks. The first to react was Gusto, the son of a tenant, who, swearing loudly, and with a hoe in his hand, threw himself at the rat but was not fast enough to hit him. The rat disappeared into the hay; my sister continued to scream and the French governess to cry. My father, who had recognized my sister's voice, rushed from the procession in the street and started asking worried questions from his side of the gate. The bishop, however, remained unperturbed and continued his march, only irritated by the fact that the people following him had stopped intoning and were asking each other what was happening in the farm of the Jews. I sat on my stool, in a way enjoying the whole scene through the legs of the people around me and outside the wall, but growing worried by the screams of my sister, which were mingling with the litany of the priests.

From that day I developed a great fear of rats, and the physical impression that life is a procession of mortals who pass by your anguish without feeling your existence.

During the eight years that followed our move from Piedmont to the Friuli region, my life went on, divided between school and holidays. Of the first class I attended in a public school in Udine I remember only the shining smile of my teacher, with whom I fell madly in love, only to learn later from my mother that she had false teeth. I was still not well enough to share in all the games of my new schoolfellows, and I spent most of the first year in our new residence in bed with fever. It was only in 1931, when we moved into a new apartment thanks to the growing income from my father's work, that I started living a normal life.

We lived in a large apartment, which my mother continued to describe in her letters to her relatives as "two rooms." Annetta, previously my mother's personal maid, was now the housemaid, and Cecilia remained as cook. We did not own a car, but for long trips we used the factory limousine. Usually my mother was "at home" on Thursdays, and on that day I was authorized to invite my friends to come in the late afternoon to finish up whatever cakes or sweets her friends had left for us.

My father lived apart from us in a mountain village, where he ran one of his brother's factories. We saw him only on

Saturday evenings when he came to town on the six o'clock train, only to go back to the factory early on Monday mornings, traveling second class, thanks to the special rate he enjoyed as an officer in the Fascist party. In the afternoon he used to take me to the cinema, sometimes even to see two films, one after the other. On Sunday mornings my father woke up at eight o'clock, and by nine was ready in his shining uniform of commander of the Fascist militia. He used to take out of a red cardboard box the black Fascist fez with its silk fringe falling to one side. He buckled the golden belt with his silver dagger dangling from it around his waist, and put on his gleaming boots with spurs, which Annetta had been polishing for hours, and which I had the privilege of carrying into his bedroom. In the cold weather he wrapped himself in a splendid gray-green cape that fell to his heels and left the house surrounded by an aura of authority and mystery, which many years later I suddenly recognized in the portrait of the *Fascist in Uniform* by Ligabue.

My mother, after much hesitation and pressure, finally agreed to become a patroness of the local Fascist party Women's Section. She hated wearing a uniform, even though her broad-brimmed black hat was always the most elegant among all the local ladies. At noon on Sunday she took the tram to join my father in the Piazza dei Mercanti for an aperitif. I, together with my school friends, had gone my way, dressed in the uniform first of the Balilla, afterward of the Avanguardisti, to the Sunday morning Fascist Youth meeting. These were horribly boring; they started and ended with a nominal roll call to check whether any of us had been able to disappear while the youth commander read the order of the day, gave the order to salute Il Duce, and made us march up and down in the courtyard of the school, which served as HQ for our youth organization's unit. I, too, wore my fez and carried a dagger, but both were infinitely less impressive than those of my father. I dreamed of becoming a section leader so that I could change my fez for an officer's cap and my gray soldier's uniform for the tight blue dinner jacket of the section leaders, which closely resembled the elegant dress of the Royal Naval cadets who courted my sister. It was the first of my unsuccessful attempts to rise in a military hierarchy.

Starting from the fourth year at the Gymnasium, we were forced to study Fascist culture and military history. Nobody took these lessons seriously since we all knew that our school fates would really be decided by the written examinations in Italian, Latin, and Greek, for which I took private lessons for years in preparation. My teachers were unanimous in thinking that I was "without a solid basis," and I am afraid that I have remained so to this day as far as academic culture is concerned. This intensive study did not prevent me from bicycling every day, fencing twice a week, going to Talmud Torah lessons on Thursday afternoons, skiing on winter Sundays, or from actively getting ready, psychologically and materially, for the school holidays.

The more I think of that period, such a happy one for me, the more I realize that I escaped the impact of the dramatic events already shaking the world and menacing the safety and unity of our family. The war in Abyssinia appeared to me to be a normal event, considering the fact that Italy controlled so little green space on the map compared with the red and blue patches of the British and French colonies. The war in Spain was too far away and too complicated to impress me. I did not meet any soldiers who had been involved in either war, nor school friends who had lost relatives in them. This was because most of the fighting troops were recruited from the unemployed, with whom I did not mix, or from the south, which for us northerners was beyond the pale. Indeed, when my father had to go to Rome to mount guard at the royal family tombs in the Pantheon, he used to announce his trip to my mother by saying, "I have to go south of the Po" (river), and would then send her a postcard from his military camp bearing the words "Kisses from the colonies."

In any case, I was convinced that Italy would always win any war, since the newspapers and our teachers spoke only of military successes, while the cavalry and air force officers I knew or who visited our house were young and eager to distinguish themselves in battle. Photographs of war horrors were not admitted into our home, and I was not troubled by the fact that I could not explain to Annetta why the Spanish Republican troops, which were obviously also Christian troops, took particular pleasure in killing nuns and priests. I was far more interested in collecting stamps from Abyssinia and Spain and learning about the Spanish Riding School in Vienna than in the political and military events that were preparing our ruin.

In 1935 there was a moment of agitation in our family when the police searched the house of my father's sister in Turin because of certain unclear relationships that my uncle, a well-known anti-Fascist (which meant that he had never registered with the Fascist party) had with political émigrés. Nobody was arrested. My father and his brother intervened "in the highest spheres," and things returned to normal. The only political incident I witnessed during the five years I spent at the high school in Udine was the beating up of a small boy in my class because his mother was Belgian, and Belgium had voted for sanctions against Italy. But, as in the films I used to see on Sunday afternoons with my father, justice quickly triumphed. As soon as the headmaster learned about the incident, he collected the whole school in the auditorium, brought the victim up to the podium and revealed to us that his father was an officer fighting in Abyssinia. With a rhetoric that moved most of us to tears, he promised to expel from the school and "denounce to the competent authorities" anyone who dared to bother the boy, whose only sin was to have a foreign mother.

It never occurred to me that if it were possible to beat up someone because his mother had a different nationality, it might also be possible to beat up somebody who belonged to a different religion or race.

To this very day I ask myself whence came my unshakable, irresponsible sense of security and my blessed ignorance, despite my being aware of the fact that I was a bit different from the rest of my schoolfellows. I did not attend the catechism class; my mother used to accompany me on Thursday afternoons to the Talmud Torah in the little synagogue, which was a transformed granary near the railway station. The rabbi who taught us, and who was to become a famous scholar in America and in Israel, was a Hungarian Jew, big, poor, and overburdened by a large family. Like the cantor, who was invited by our community for the High Holy Days, he wore a big beard and a stained black robe.

I knew that the rabbi and the cantor, despite their being Jews like us, were quite different. They were totally strange in appearance; they had to solve continuous problems concerning food and timetables, which I did not have; they were similar to those strange, bearded beings who from time to time used to ring the bell of our apartment and then stand immobile and silent in the doorway. Annetta, who usually opened the door in her white lace cap and frilly apron over her blue-and-white-striped uniform, used to leave the door ajar but with the chain on, to make quite sure that they could not get in. Then she would rush to my mother and tell her, in Piedmontese dialect: "Madame, there is one of those, there." My mother was always quick to understand her. Surprisingly for me, even if she were entertaining guests, she used to get up, go to her bedroom and open the cash box, taking out a small black silk bag that she had inherited from her mother and in which she collected large silver twenty-lire coins, with the head of Mussolini on one side and the inscription "It is better to live one day as a lion than one hundred years as a sheep" on the other. She would take one of these coins and go in person, to the ever-renewed astonishment of Annetta, who followed her closely for protection, unlock the door and put the coin into the hand of the strange being, who would receive it with an outstretched hand covered by a not-always-clean handkerchief. "They are dirty," Annetta used to comment. "Yes," replied my mother, "but they are very well educated, since knowing that, they cover their hand with a handkerchief." It never crossed her mind, even after she went to Israel in her last years of life, that orthodox Jews behaved in that way, convinced as they were that the women in a family like ours must surely have been impure.

Certainly some faint echo of anti-Semitism reached my ears, but it was the echo of the Dreyfus case, which was explained to me occasionally by my father, without of course any mention of the effect it had had on Theodor Herzl. They were far-off events, which some members of my family living in Paris still remembered, but which to me sounded like the deeds of Genghis Khan or Attila, reinforcing, through their unreality, my sense of security. At the Fascist party HQ in Udine, where my father had many contacts, everybody was openly opposed to the persecution of the Jews that had begun to take place in Germany, not because the victims were Jews but because the persecutors were Germans, hated by the local Italians. My father's brother, who continued to rise rapidly on the ladder of economic success, used to write to us, or tell us when we met him in the summer in his mountain resort, about his meetings with Mussolini. These meetings, always extremely friendly, never ended, said my uncle, without some allusion by Il Duce to the difference existing between the Italian Jews and those of the rest of the world. We were secure because we were different, and we could be different because we were, so far, secure.

In the military circles in which I roamed, either because my friends at school were the sons of officers or because around

Udine there were many military bases where I could ride at will, it was almost a ritual to show loyalty to the king and a detachment from Fascism, together with open hostility to the Germans. On such occasions I felt part of a quasi-secret society, since in the presence of my mother or father somebody always found a pretext to speak in favor of the Jews and against the Germans. The fact that in those years the colonel of the most prestigious cavalry regiment in town was a Jew, was enough to cut short on anyone's lips—in our presence at least—any criticism he may have had of the Jews. On Yom Kippur in 1937, when the cantor started singing the Kol Nidre prayer for the third time, three bareheaded youths entered our little synagogue with the obvious intention of disturbing the service. There was a moment of tension, even though the cantor continued singing the prayer. My father looked around him, and when he saw that nobody reacted, he left the bench on which I was sitting and with his tallith wrapped around his shoulders went straight to the intruders. Without a word, very slowly, he withdrew his wallet from his inner pocket and pulled out a document showing his position in the Fascist party. The three youngsters jerked to attention and left the synagogue. It was a small incident—one I still remember with great clarity. It confirmed, more than anything else, my feeling of total security, which was reinforced as in every previous year, by the life I lived during my summer vacation.

There were three different types of holidays, all of which were religiously kept by my mother, convinced as she was that the first two were indispensable for my health and the third for my father's psychology: a seaside holiday between June and July, a mountain holiday from July to September, and then a week or ten days back in Piedmont for the grape harvest.

The seaside holiday was the most boring period as far as I was concerned. I disliked swimming, I hated sailing, I burned easily in the sun, and I objected to playing chaperone to my sister, or as we say in Italian, "carrying the candle" for her innumerable admirers. In 1935 and 1936 the seaside holiday was replaced by two cruises in North and Latin America on board the big luxury liners *Saturnia* and *Conte Grande,* respectively, which transported, over and above many important people and rich tourists, a selected group of *marinaretti* (the maritime Fascist youth movement) belonging to families who were considered most loyal to the Fascist regime. Their task was to march in the streets of New York and Buenos Aires and promote the collection of iron and gold from the Italian communities of those cities in support of the Abyssinian campaign and as a gesture of defiance against the League of Nations' economic sanctions. I had no difficulty in being accepted for these cruises, and I was quite surprised to find that the percentage of Jewish *marinaretti* was much higher than the percentage of Jews in the Italian population as a whole.

It was during one of these trips that I delivered my first public speech, commenting on a speech by Mussolini that had been relayed to us over the ship's radio during the afternoon session of Fascist indoctrination, in which I did not usually participate because of seasickness. My speech was not a great success, partly because I spoke about the historical role of Il Duce while our commander, a teacher of calisthenics from Sardinia named Porcu (swine), was mainly interested in speaking to us about venereal disease and masturbation, which in his view were the main enemies of Fascist youth.

When we reached New York we found a very large deployment of foot and mounted police waiting for us, trying to keep away from our ship—moored to a quay near Grant's Tomb—a crowd of people shouting anti-Fascist slogans at the tops of their voices. It was a great surprise to me to discover that there were people who did not share the Fascist ideal and even more to hear for the first time some important Italian people on deck speaking openly about the connection between plutocratic communism and the Jewish International. But I quickly forgot the scene and the remarks because we were soon inundated by a much larger crowd of enthusiastic Italian-Americans who for the next three days did nothing but carry us from one feast to another, showering us with gifts and ripping from our uniforms whatever they could—stripes, medals, and so on—for souvenirs. The same thing happened in Buenos Aires. Here the highlight of the trip was a concert given by the famous Italian tenor, Tito Schipa, at the Teatro Colon. When we entered the auditorium in our bright blue navy uniforms, the people seemed to go mad with enthusiasm. I returned to Italy convinced that a military career was the one most suitable for me, although deeply upset by the fact that my stomach had proved that it would be unwise for me to enroll at the Naval Academy.

At the seaside resort of Grado, where we used to spend the first part of our summer holidays, I met the first Jewish re-fugees from Germany. I remember well a family by the name of Furst consisting of a distinguished elderly man, his wife, and their two daughters. They must have been quite rich and were staying at the seaside in Italy as tourists waiting for permission to go to Palestine. They used to tell my mother what was happening in Germany to the Jews, but never mentioned what they had personally suffered or lost. They listened, with inter-est but little belief, to what we used to tell them about the difference between Italy and Germany and the fate of the Jews in those two countries. They had not read the book by Ludwig on his meetings with Mussolini, so my father went to look for it in a library; before giving it to them he read to me some of the passages in which the German writer related what Il Duce had said to him about anti-Semitism and in favor of the Jews. The Furst family left Grado together with us, and a few years later I looked for them in Palestine without success.

In the mountains, within the large estate belonging to the factory that my father ran on behalf of his brother, the unreal-ity of my existence and my thoughtlessness were even greater than at the seaside. My uncle's factory was the main industrial establishment in the area; he owned a whole valley with several mountains, two small lakes that produced electric power for the nearby town of Tarvis, large patches of woodland, and an entire village, the houses of which he rented to his workpeople. It was, and to a certain extent still remains under my cousin's paternalistic rule, a kind of fiefdom, and at that time I was the son of the "overlord's" brother. It is difficult to describe to anyone who has not lived in such places and during those years what it meant to belong to a family that owned the land, the houses, the roads, the woods of an entire area; provided work for three hundred families and looked after their welfare through an old-fashioned system of charity for the needy; supported the small parish; was responsible for the local sports activities; and what it was like to live in a country where trade unions were illegal, strikes were punishable by imprisonment, and work was still scarce.

In the case of my family, there were also political ingredients that made our position stronger. The valley owned by the factory was a tongue of land squeezed in between the Yugoslav and Austrian frontiers. It had been allotted to the Italians after World War I by someone who apparently paid little attention to Wilson's principle of national self-determination, since the whole of the local population was Austrian and objected strongly to being under foreign, Italian, rule. In fact, when they were given the choice, under the 1939 agreement between Mussolini and Hitler, ninety percent of the local inhabitants opted for the Third Reich and went off happily to get themselves killed at Stalingrad or by Allied bombs during World War II. I imagine that their feelings toward the Jews were not very different from those of the Nazis across the frontier, but my uncle was their source of livelihood and my father, apart from being the manager of the factory, was the highest Fascist official in the area and was also responsible for the antiaircraft defenses of the whole border region. In other words, we were the object of their natural respect for the established authorities and of their fear aroused by the representative of the conquering power. The fact that we were also Jewish only made these circumstances more sinister in their eyes.

Of all this I was completely unaware at the time, despite the fact that the former Austrian burgomaster of the village, a nice, tall, old Carinthian nobleman, had from time to time tried to explain the situation to me. He lived next to the post office in a brick and wood mansion in which he painted and collected matchboxes, tram and railway tickets, dried flowers, and stamps. My passion for stamps had given me the courage to cross his threshold, which my father did not particularly like since he was convinced that at heart the old gentleman was still an enemy of Italy. In fact, he kept in his studio a very large portrait of a man he called his "uncle" but which was none other than Emperor Franz Josef of Austria. The burgomaster had painted elegant evening attire, complete with white tie and tails, over the kaiser's military uniform. When I stood in front of the portrait and gazed at it with admiration, my host would wink at me, his bushy white eyebrows beetling over the gleam in his eyes. It was a kind of silent secret ceremony we both enjoyed, after which he would take me into the sitting room where his maid had already prepared for me long slices of black bread spread with butter and honey. While I was eating he used to show me his war and peacetime decorations and tell me about his trips to Russia and England.

My father, as I said, did not like my visiting him, but my mother defended me, saying that the old gentleman was a polite and inoffensive person, that he had been living alone for many years with his housekeeper and certainly took pleasure in the visit of a person of my age. Better him, she would say, than some of the youngsters with whom I went fishing and who probably talked to me about unspeakably dirty subjects. She was right: the old burgomaster never spoke about sex or politics, nor did he ever mention my race or religion. He liked to recall the better service that the Austrian administration had provided in his time for the local population, and I listened to him as if he were speaking about an imaginary, lost continent.

During the months I spent in the mountains, my already carefree city existence transformed itself into a continuous fulfillment of childish dreams. I fished for trout; I accompanied the gamekeeper on his long walks to check the game birds; I was free to disappear from home for hours at a time, picking mushrooms and blackberries. My father's house stood in the middle of a large garden fenced with wooden stakes, which to us children served as a forest in the Old West. It was bordered on one side by a stream with one small island in the middle that had three tall pine trees. Here my sister and I built a permanent Indian camp, complete with tents, Sioux costumes, bows and arrows, and shields. It was linked to the mainland by a small drawbridge and connected to the house by an overhead cable capable of carrying a basket. We used this to send instructions to the cook, who promptly returned the basket full of provisions.

There were no service problems in the house since, in addition to the two maids my mother brought with her from town, there were those who attended my father throughout the year. The villa was always full of guests, especially during the summer military maneuvers. My uncle, in his rather imposing mansion on top of the hill, received officers from the rank of colonel and upward; my father, partly because of his lower social rank and partly because of my sister, was responsible for entertaining those from colonel downward.

The factory had a lot of cart horses that I could ride whenever I wanted. In the winter we harnessed them in pairs to the sleighs and spent hours galloping along the empty, snow-covered roads. It was a world of dreams, unreal and feudal, which I recognized many years later in some of the scenes from the film *Dr. Zhivago*. For me, however, it was absolutely normal and I accepted it without scruples or doubts because I knew no other. Into this world, unpleasant echoes from the outside could not penetrate, and if occasionally politics came up, they were always dealt with in a patriotic, Fascist, and triumphalist key.

The last week of the summer holidays was spent in Piedmont on my father's farm. It was a very small farm, the remnant of the huge estate lost in the wake of the 1929 stock market crash. But the house was—and still is—a large, eighteenth-century building, which my father rented out except for his library and a few rooms where he stayed during the period of the grape harvest. He was always very busy and happy in this village where he had spent the best years of his life. Apart from rents to be collected, there were always problems with the sewage, the roofs, and the garden, as well as an unending stream of farmers who came to ask his advice, mainly on legal and family matters. He was no longer the landlord, but the royal castle around which the village was built had belonged to his grandfather and his great-grandfather before him, and there were still many people who remembered when he had been the mayor. Quite a few of them had been his tenants; most had been his soldiers during the First World War. He knew every family, and people came bearing bottles of wine and baskets of fruit to ask him to read a contract prepared by a lawyer they did not trust, or for advice about their unending litigations. He received them, sometimes late at night, in his library, under a large reproduction of Rembrandt's *Rabbi*. I sometimes listened to their conversations, always carried on in Piedmontese dialect, but I spent most of my time in the attics among old trunks full of surprises. They contained monkey skins and gas masks from the Great War; medals and embroideries; ebony animals and tin soldiers. There were also strange objects, such as portable toilets in the form of imposing armchairs, stuffed birds, alcohol distilling apparatuses, and chalk reproductions of the Parthenon friezes. Most interesting of all were the family archives, full of old documents and photographs, especially from the First World War. In the photographs all the male members of the family appeared in uniform, and there were also pictures of King Victor Emmanuel, the Prince of Wales, General Kitchener, Clemenceau, the Duke of Aosta and his wife—all people with whom my father had rubbed shoulders in the service of the king during his years of military service.

In this village and in this old house I felt strangely changed —not into a Jew but into a Piedmontese, which was quite different from being an Italian or a young Fascist. To be a Piedmontese meant, for me, to belong to Italian national prehistory, to be a member of the people (in my imagination they seemed almost like a clan) that had made Italy. In that great mythical enterprise called Risorgimento, many Jews, my father among them, felt like the Pilgrim Fathers: they were, in a sense, their own ancestors. Italy, for the Piedmontese, was not a fatherland or a motherland: it was a geographical, emotional, political expression; an ideal that the Jews of Piedmont had helped realize and to which they had contributed more than any other group on the peninsula. In a way, they were the only true Italians, since they were born—as citizens—at the beginning of the Italian struggle for national unity. They could feel more Italian than the Italians because they were neither Venetian nor Florentine, not Roman or Neapolitan. They had no roots in any national identity that preceded the Italian one. Over and above this, we were also Piedmontese, part and parcel of the state that had united Italy under the House of Savoy. And to this house we Jews belonged more than anyone else. Before we had been emancipated and left the ghetto in 1848 (but who remembered those days anyway?), we were the king's servants, a strange kind of inverted aristocracy, lower than the local nobility in status, but higher than most of the king's subjects in wealth, culture, and influence. After the emancipation, we became the standard bearers of the Risorgimento, the most ardent partisans of a political Italian unity which, by destroying the power of the many minor Catholic princes and kings of the peninsula, had created a great secular state in which everyone was equal, and some—like our family —more equal than others.

I did not know much about being Jewish, but I knew that to be a Piedmontese Jew meant belonging to that special "sect" that had given Cavour his place in the Piedmontese parliament and had financed his wars through Jewish banks; it meant belonging to the people who had sheltered Mazzini, who had given the highest percentage of volunteers to Garibaldi, and who had fought for their king in every war of independence. It was natural that we should have a privileged position under the present regime. It was a position justified by our being an integral part of that village where my great-grandfather had bought the castle from the king's brother. My grandfather had lived in it until his death; my father had turned it into the village hall, the village school, and the seat of the local tribunal, and I still played in its gardens with a feeling of natural possession.

In the twenties, before we left for Friuli, I spent many hours during the cold winters in the cow shed of Annetta's nephews, sitting in the straw and listening to the stories of the villagers who had fought and died to make the king master of Italy. They all felt they had been robbed by the ungrateful Italians, those people living south of the River Po, to whom the Piedmontese had brought unity and freedom. And still they were proud to have been the driving force of Italian political renaissance. They never spoke Italian, and I had difficulty in following their singing, French-like dialect. But it was good to be with them, playing lotto for peas, shelling maize cobs, breathing in the warm, pungent smell of cow manure, and singing the nostalgic songs of the Alpine troops to which most of them belonged. On the kitchen walls, at the side of the great fireplace, were stained pictures of the king, Cavour, and Garibaldi, never of Mussolini.

Two of Annetta's nephews, who were sergeants in an aristocratic regiment of mounted artillery and therefore more royalist than the others, carefully avoided mentioning his name. When they spoke of him they would simply say "that one," and everyone understood. I, of course, did not, and in any case was not interested: what I wanted to hear were stories about the "lady" whom Garibaldi visited when spending a night or two in the village; about the pipe and walking stick that he had left in the local doctor's house; about King Victor Emmanuel II and Rosina, the beautiful girl whom he had married morganatically and whom Annetta's sister had known before she was made the Countess of Villanova.

My father and mother, always so particular about the people I mixed with, had no reservations concerning these farmers. My parents knew them all because they had provided the family with servants for three generations. They were part of "our people," and went to bed in winter like my parents with a warming pan between the sheets and had the same sticky flypaper dangling from their kitchen ceilings as we did. I knew that we were different, socially and religiously, in our dress and in our language, but I still felt that we were the same because we were all Piedmontese.

I do not know how many people in the village still feel that way today. Probably none. I doubt if they even know why the main road, Via Roma, is still called "Cornarea" by the old people. This strange name derives from the behavior of the gentlemen of the royal court who, staying in the village during the king's summer vacation, spent most of their time ogling the village maidens, making their fiancés or husbands grow "noble horns"—*corna reali*—on their heads. The mixture of aristocratic and popular blood presumably contributed to the fact that this small village of no more than seven hundred souls produced for over a century a considerable number of famous people, who brought honor to the village through their weapons, their robes, or their altars.

But already under the Fascists this compact agrarian society and its houses had gradually fallen into ruin and its institutions removed elsewhere. In earlier times the farmers' fear that a spark from a passing locomotive might start a fire in the corn caused them to write a petition to the king asking that the route of the railway be changed in order to protect them from the deeds of this new mechanical devil. The result now was that the village was not on the railway map; it remained cut off from the major road network and lost the battle to draw the new motorway nearer to itself. The local court was transferred to the nearby town. The church primary school has been replaced by a state secondary school that will probably close down in a few years' time for lack of pupils. The orphanage has already done so for lack of orphans. The great Seminary of Salesian Friars has been empty for many years, and so far no one has taken up the proposition to transform it into a hotel or dance hall, as some villagers have suggested. Only the old hospital, which has been transformed into a home for the elderly, is flourishing. The number of old people grows at the same rate as the number of vineyards left untilled by the young people who move into industry. Old men and their sons have certainly become richer through state pensions and industrial salaries—yet they look sadder because of their inability to keep the family together. The priests no longer follow the funerals singing litanies in Latin. The liturgy has lost its mysterious attraction because of the use of the Italian language, which the priest, walking before the coffin, broadcasts loudly into the air through a battery-operated megaphone hidden away under his robes with the microphone dangling like a cross from his neck. The church bells do not ring as often as they used to when I was a boy: nobody knows any longer, as they did in the twenties, when a dying man enters into agony, when the priest gives the last rites, nor the precise moment in which the soul of so-and-so, better known to everyone by his nickname, has started on its journey toward the Creator. The bells ring today during the funerals, clear and precise, carrying an impersonal message, controlled by the electrical mechanism of the bell tower, through the fields where tractors have replaced the big white oxen and the vines are dusted regularly by helicopters.

During the week of the grape harvest, when I accompanied my father to renew the yearly leases of the tenants, and my grandmother to do her "cure of the grapes," I used to go to the parish hall to look at the films that the priest showed twice a week. The films were only those approved by the bishop's office but they were preceded by documentaries made to exalt the deeds of Mussolini and the glories of the revolutionary Fascist party. Nothing could have been more boring than this politicized news, and we waited impatiently for it to end and the main film to start. However, from time to time these propaganda efforts also contained pictures of fashion shows or of seashore tourism through which the regime wanted to stress the normality of life in Italy. These pictures were unacceptable to the parish priest. He used to keep a stool between the two lanes of seats and would ask one of the young clerics to be ready to stand up on it whenever he told him and block the beam from the projector with a big handkerchief, usually the huge red one used after taking snuff. From the darkened hall rose shouts of protest, stamping of feet, curses, and allusions that were certainly more sinful than the innocent view of women he had censored. The priest was not moved by these protests: he was a man of few but clear principles, which he once summarized from the pulpit in a pithy axiom. Speaking of the demons that had invaded the village society after the Second World War, he denounced the use of motor scooters, shouting to his impecunious audience: "Mothers and fathers, remember that when your sons and daughters leave their homes on Lambrettas as a twosome, they usually return home as a threesome"—a historic maxim possibly, but of doubtful accuracy, considering that the population of the village was already clearly on the decrease.

The *maresciallo* of the carabinieri, too, had a way of his own of maintaining peace and order while being kept informed of everything that took place in the village. Until late in the 1950s there was neither terrorism nor abductions in Italy; open, vulgar violence was the monopoly of the Mafia in the south and the Fascists (as long as they were in power) in the rest of the country. But cow stealing was common, poplars and vines were often cut down in the course of vendettas, and corn sometimes set alight the day before harvest.

The head of the local security forces learned about all these deeds while playing cards in the local inn or when fishing on the river. It was a known and accepted custom for anyone wanting to tell him something confidential to do so while fishing by his side. As for the remaining security tasks, it was his wife who ran the show. The carabinieri went on daily patrol with their old, 91-type carbines slung across their backs, the black celluloid hat strap under their sweating chins. The *maresciallo*'s wife, however, sat at her window, or on sunny days on the balcony of her top-floor apartment, in the big house that served as the carabinieri headquarters and the permanently empty jail. I remember her knitting, or cleaning vegetables, apparently oblivious to the world around her. In fact, from her vantage point she could dominate almost the entire territory of the village. She knew better than her husband the routes the patrols had to follow and did not forget them for a moment. When she saw the two carabinieri on duty disappear for too long behind a house or a clump of trees, she blew on a big whistle she kept hanging around her neck, and the offenders against public order hastily reappeared upon the landscape.

Life in the village was certainly not as idyllic as it may have looked to an outsider. I knew of the many court cases in which almost every family was engaged, of the illicit affairs and the complex family feuds that dragged on for years around a patch of land, an inch of guttering, or an artesian well. Once I was told about a murder that had remained unsolved for years. Since it was a family affair, Annetta explained to me, even the carabinieri had no real business to intervene.

Today such a case would be unthinkable. And yet it was to this secrecy, to this sense of family and village honor, that members of my family owed their lives after the September 1943 armistice between Italy and the Allies when German forces occupied the area. Three years earlier, at the outbreak of war and after my departure for Palestine, my parents had left my mother's estate near Turin and had gone to live in the village where my father had been the mayor for so long, believing that it would be safer for them and that life would be less expensive. My grandmother went with them, and they took up their residence in one part of the big house, the remainder of which was leased to nuns as their summer residence. From the little land my father still owned in the village he was able to derive a large part of the food needed by the family. There were enough trees in the garden to provide firewood, and although in the valley below a big new airfield had been constructed, my parents felt secure in their old family home where everybody knew and respected them, and over which the Allied bombers flew on their way to bomb Turin, Genoa, and Milan.

War events and the tragic fate of the Jews did not touch them until one day in October 1943 when the *maresciallo* of the carabinieri came ceremoniously to tell my father, who was sitting as usual in his library, that he would be coming in the afternoon to arrest him, together with my mother and sister. He did not mention my grandmother since she was not in the local population register.

In less than three hours, my mother and sister, dressed as nuns, left for the nearby convent. My father went to the mayor's office, received false documents on the spot, and transformed himself into a peddler. He had foreseen the possibility of being arrested, and as an old soldier, was convinced that the best way of avoiding capture would be to adopt a profession that would oblige him to be constantly on the move. His disguise had been prepared long since and was hanging in his wardrobe. He put on heavy boots, filled a large, wooden, folding case with shoelaces, razor blades, toothpaste, small pieces of soap, and so on, and went out into the fields, spending the following eighteen months walking from one farm to another. He was arrested three times but was released after the mayor of his village confirmed in writing to the Fascist police that he was a well-known peddler, psychologically disturbed but quite harmless.

No solution could be found for my grandmother. She was already well into her seventies, completely sclerotic, and had to stay in the village. She was not even aware that a new world war had broken out. When she went out, accompanied by her old maid, Madeleine, to take the air in the gardens of the castle that had been hers many years before, she used to acknowledge ceremoniously the salutes of the German and Italian officers whom she encountered on her way, convinced that she was still living in the First World War.

This grotesque situation, which lasted until the end of the war, combined a deep sense of human solidarity with an equally deep hate for the Germans and the Fascist Republicans. It also gave an idea of the links existing between my family and the seven hundred or so villagers and of their ability to keep a collective secret that could have cost many of them their own lives. It was a situation in which, because of the war, but not only because of it, all social relationships and economic barriers were removed and replaced by a visceral, almost animal solidarity that I do not think existed, as far as the Jews are concerned, anywhere else in the Western world.

Such was the world in which I grew up, and it was difficult for me, even after the publication of the anti-Jewish laws in 1938, to feel marginal toward the Italian society. Through my relations with my new friends at the Jewish school in Turin

I was, indeed, beginning to detach myself from my Fascist background and become aware of the harsh fate of the Jews. Yet I could not emotionally break with the human realities of my father's village or my memories of my happy life in the Friuli. It was from this small, real, but at the same time imaginary, world that I left in 1939 for Palestine, a far off and completely unknown land. What made my father decide to give his consent to my departure was an event that took place in our family—dramatic but totally consistent with the type of life I had lived up to that time.

Even before the publication of the Race Manifesto in July 1938, the Fascist press had surreptitiously tested the reactions of the Italian public to an open campaign against the Jews. At the beginning of 1937, a book by Paolo Orano, *The Jews in Italy*, analyzed the Jewish problem on the basis of all sorts of contorted political and ideological arguments. It pointed out the difference between patriotic and unpatriotic Judaism, between Italian and Jewish nationalism, and it launched vitriolic attacks on Zionism, a movement that Mussolini in fact had supported not long before as being very good for Italian penetration into the Middle East. All this threw the majority of Italian Jews and the leading members of the central organization of Jewish communities of Italy (the highest administrative institution of Italian Jewry) into confusion and divided them. Naturally nobody spoke of all these things in my home, nor of the fact that at that time some members of my family were engaged in this communal and ideological struggle. The most active was my cousin, Ettore Ovazza, the only one of my close relatives to be killed, in a horrible way, with his wife and two children, by the Fascist Republicans at the end of the war.

Ettore Ovazza had always had literary ambitions. During the First World War, in which he had served as an officer with his father and two brothers and received great distinction, he had written and published diaries that today are astonishing in their emphatic banality.

After the war, my cousin, like my father, had naturally gone over to Fascism and founded a Jewish periodical called *Our Flag*, in which he expressed what he and many other Italian Jewish Fascists thought should be the political stand of the Italian Israelites: faithfulness to the ideals of the Italian Risorgimento and Italian unity; devotion to the monarchy; opposition to Zionism as far as the movement concerned Italian Jews, but not insofar as it offered a refuge against anti-Semitism; apologetic stressing of the Jewish contribution to the Italian cause and to Fascism; and criticism of the German racial laws but also of Western democracy and of liberalism, with which Italian Jews should not—in the opinion of the journal— meddle. It was a hybrid position, which became indefensible and unbearable with the development of the anti-Jewish politics of Mussolini. Yet at the end of 1938, when Italian Jews could no longer send their children to school and Italians could no longer use textbooks written by Jews; when civil marriage between Jews and non-Jews was forbidden (the Fascist regime could not interfere in religious marriages because of its agreement with the Vatican); when Jewish parents were legally losing their rights over children who wanted to denounce them to the authorities; and when Jews could not serve any longer in the army, there were still Jews who deluded themselves into thinking they would be able to ingratiate themselves with the regime through a public demonstration of devotion to Fascism and by detaching themselves from those Jews who were considered enemies of the regime.

My cousin was one of these deluded people. The Fascist press had been attacking, with ever-growing violence, the Jewish community's main organ, *Israel,* which defended with courage and dignity the position of Italian Jews, and in particular their right to be Zionists. My cousin thought that a "punitive action" against that periodical by Fascist Jews would demonstrate their patriotism to the government, and at the same time, be agreeable to the party.

On a cold, gray, autumn day, Ettore Ovazza arrived at my parents' home on my mother's farm near Turin, accompanied by two or three people I did not know. They had warned my father of their coming, whether by telephone or letter I do not remember, and he, contrary to his habit, had asked me to be present at the meeting. We received them in the dining room, with my mother in a state of nerves serving tea and small cakes, apologizing all the time for not having a maid (because of the "Laws"). After a while, with her eyes full of tears and fear, she left the room.

As soon as she had gone, my cousin explained his plan in great detail. The anti-Semites, he said, accused the Jews of being allied with the democracies. The number of anti-Fascist elements among the Israelites was unfortunately very high. The Fascist regime, because of its new politics, underlined this negative disproportion rather than the much larger and more positive one of the Jewish contribution to Fascism and to the Italian national cause. However, he said, in spite of the Racial Laws, Mussolini had not permitted the criteria of the Nuremberg Laws to be applied to the Italian Jews. Devoted and reliable friends who had direct access to Il Duce had told my cousin that Mussolini was irritated and sad at having to follow Hitler along the path of anti-Semitism. He had to do it for higher political reasons, but it was against his better nature and the very tradition of Italian Fascism. As proof of this, my cousin pointed out that the Fascist press had stressed that the battle for the defense of the Italian race was more political and ideological than biological and racial. The Nuremberg Laws found not an imitation but a limitation in the new anti-Jewish regulations. As former members of the Fascist party, and thanks to their military service, all our families had been "differentiated," that is, partially exempted from the new racial laws. But even for the common Jews life was better and more secure in Italy than in many other European countries. Even the new regulations facilitating conversion to Catholicism were a way in which the party showed the difference between Italian and German conceptions of anti-Semitism. In sum, said my cousin, it was clear that Mussolini was acting against the Jews with great personal reluctance.

However, the anti-Fascist Jews as well as the Zionists played into the hands of their enemies in the Fascist hierarchy as well as in the Catholic hierarchy by offering a reason to attack them, and through them the whole of Italian Jewry. One had to be honest and recognize that the Jews of Italy had made themselves too prominent; every issue of the *Review of the Race* (the new, anti-Semitic publication founded after the enactment of the racial legislation) underlined the numerical disproportion existing between Jews and non-Jews in the most important fields of life in the country. Just to mention the army and the navy, one could list scores of Jewish generals and admirals as against only thirty-six private soldiers. How right —said my cousin—were our forefathers who preached to their sons not to show off, not to boast of their new privileged status outside the ghetto. However, since it was no longer possible to go back in history, it was necessary to make a clear distinction between those Jews who had always been faithful to the Fascist regime and wanted to remain so and all the rest.

His proposal was as follows: in Florence the Jewish publication, *Israel*, which should be devoting its attention only to cultural and religious matters, had instead transformed itself into a mouthpiece for political ideas that Fascism could not tolerate. It claimed that greater Jewish solidarity and consciousness were necessary to compensate for the loss of that Italian identity being forcibly torn from the Jews. This thesis went against the interests of Italian Jews. To ask to be different in such a way and at such a moment meant detaching oneself from the national body, confirming the accusations of the anti-Semites who wanted to see Italian Jews as a foreign body. It was therefore important to show on which side the Fascist Jews, the patriots, stood. A punitive action, a minor pogrom, against the print shop and editorial offices of *Israel*, which in any case would sooner or later be attacked by the Fascists, could be an act more useful to the Jews of Italy than a thousand written polemics. The operation would also remind Mussolini of the heroic days prior to the March on Rome, during which the Jews had so ardently supported him. Such an action should be carried out by people of unstained Fascist faith and of recognized national stature. My father was one of these. By joining the punitive action, he would add luster to the initiative.

To me, so indifferent to political questions and so ignorant of what was happening around me, such talk was deeply disturbing. On the one hand, I was tempted to join in an action, during this period when I felt myself harassed without the ability to react. On the other hand, it seemed to me monstrous that at a moment when the Jews were trying to find new cohesion and had proved the strength of their communal ties by creating, in less than four months, an exemplary, independent, educational system; when everyone was looking for contact with the world outside Italy; and above all, at a time when the Fascist regime and the monarchy had betrayed the constitution, anyone could think of cooperating with our persecutors in such an explicit and unashamed manner. However, I felt it was a problem too serious for me to give an opinion before my father had replied. I looked at him and felt how difficult it was for him to take a stand because of his past, but also because he had no links with people outside the Italian national establishment—unlike me, who was now in touch with Judaism and had become mildly anti-Fascist through my school contacts.

My father took a long time to reply. He balanced his pipe in his hand, filled it with great care, and lit it as though nothing was of greater importance for him at that moment than the correct behavior of a smoker. I could see that these mechanical gestures helped him to formulate his thoughts. The others, too, kept quiet, and in the silence the tension grew. When my father began to speak there was no trace of emotion in his voice. He explained that it would be strange for a man like himself, so detached from politics, suddenly to join in an action of such gravity. Those who attached importance to his past links with the Fascist party or with the royal house were completely mistaken. He was by now no more than a poor Jew who would probably not be allowed in the future even to remain a poor farmer. But even if he had not been the unimportant person that in fact he now was, he would have refused to join them in their scheme. It was true that as Italians we had lost our sacrosanct rights inscribed in the constitution, but as Jews nobody could take away our sense of dignity and honor. To attack coreligionists in such hard times as those we were going through in order to ingratiate ourselves with a regime that had betrayed us was to act as slaves, not as free men.

He had spoken in a low voice, almost as though he was asking forgiveness for what he was saying. A long silence followed. My cousin broke it by saying: "As you like; if you change your mind, let me know." Afterward he inquired about my studies, about the farm, and about my mother's and sister's health. Before they left, my father offered them some magnificent pears. They took them, congratulating him on his life as Cincinnatus. A few weeks later they burned the offices and the printing press of *Israel*.

When my father heard about it, he called me into his study and told me that he agreed to my leaving Italy. It was not important where I went, but for a young Jew there was no longer any future or hope in Italy. When I told him that I had been informed that one could obtain a visa for Palestine against a deposit in an English bank of a thousand pounds sterling, my father, who knew very well the risk entailed in illegally exporting Italian currency, went straight to the chief of the Fascist police in Turin and asked him what he preferred: that the money be transferred legally abroad or that he (my father) should become a criminal. The party chief helped him to transfer the money, an act subject to the death penalty at that time. The fact that I emigrated to Palestine with the assistance of the Fascist regime still seems to me farcical, but also a proof of the unreal situation in which a Jew in Italy could still live.

In May 1939 Mussolini ordered large-scale military maneuvers along the French frontier. The mayor of our village called my father and told him that Il Duce would probably be passing through the Via Maestra and that it was necessary to whitewash that section of the wall on my mother's estate bordering the road. Because of its length and its even surface the wall was the most suitable place to be decorated with quotations from Mussolini's speeches. The mayor knew that my father was a Jew, but being aware of his Fascist past and his culture, decided to leave him free to select the most appropriate passages. My father chose the Mussolinian phrase "Many enemies, much glory." The mayor decided that it would be best to leave the wall bare and in the end, Mussolini, quite oblivious to all this, chose another route.

4.

The Tombstone

I INHERITED from my father a
burial plot in the Jewish cemetery in Turin and a farmhouse
in a small village near the town of Alba. Over the years the
value of the plot has increased, while the value of the house
has gone steadily down. I have received many offers for both,
but I have never been able to bring myself to sell them, even
though the money would undoubtedly be useful.

It is strange to see how in the Jewish cemetery of Turin a
community of dead Jews has within one century replaced a
community of living ones. Above the ground, the Jews have
spread themselves at an increasing rate, over countries, cultures,
and religions different from their ancestral ones. Under the
ground, their number increases year by year in an enclosure
that can no longer grow in size. Because of this, the prices of
cemetery plots are continually on the rise, independent of the
changing prices of real estate and oil, for which nobody in the
graveyard has any further need.

The Jewish cemetery in Turin is located next to the Christian one and is divided into two square compounds, the old and the new. In the former, many tombstones have sunk into the ground, the names are no longer legible, and the chapels perpetuate the withered glory of unknown families, once rich and powerful. Here are the tombstones of Jewish barons, consuls, bankers, army officers; people who, if one is to believe the inscriptions, all lived exemplary lives devoted to their families; people who drove out with a horse and carriage before switching to automobiles. Only the inscriptions and obituaries in old newspapers remain to prove that they really lived. Jews do not have the habit of remembering the dear departed with the oval photographs protected by convex glass so common in Italian Christian cemeteries. Our taboo on graven images is still strong enough to prevent this. But even without pictures, a date—1840, 1861, 1914—is enough to start the visitor pondering over the lives of these people, whose names indicate ancient and faraway origins: France and Corfu, Spain and Mantua.

Among the books I cherish most in my library is an "official and definitive" register of the Piedmontese noblemen compiled during the reign of King Umberto I, in 1886. The hundreds of names of dukes, marquises, counts, and barons include half a dozen Jewish aristocrats, all of recent creation, whose origin is given as "Palestine." Some of them are buried in the old Jewish compound of Turin. None of them seems to have been capable of transferring the title to succeeding Jewish generations for more than a century, whereas as simple Jews, their families had survived for over a thousand years. The glory achieved in the modern world outside the walls of the ghetto seems to have quenched forever their tribal Jewish vitality. The tombstones of these famous, affluent Jews left without successors have always seemed to me to mark a second death to be added to the physical one: a memento of the major contribution that the "dear departed" made to their "inconsolable survivors" has boiled down to the fact of removing themselves from the social competition. Thus, in the old cemetery, most of the tombs stand without a future: the descendants have been dispersed in the turmoil of life, usually beyond the wall that separates the world of the Jewish dead from that of dead or living Christians. The new compound, however, shows clear signs of life: graves are well tended, flowers are changed frequently in the vases, and one may even meet a relative coming to visit his dead "out of season."

I often visit this cemetery, but not exclusively for religious reasons. We Jews do not have a cult of the dead because, as the psalmist says, "The dead praise not the Lord." Before we are buried, we are laid on a marble slab and treated with alternate splashes of hot and cold water to make sure that we are not simply unconscious. Then, wrapped in a sheet, and for men, also covered by a prayer shawl from which the four knotted corner fringes, supposedly meant to remind us while alive of our duties toward God, have been removed, we are put into the earth. I have a marchioness cousin who does not believe me when I tell her that some of today's common habits are derived from old tribal customs: for instance, that of tying a knot in the corner of one's handkerchief so that one is reminded of something.

Naturally customs change with time and place. In Israel the last journey is made on a stretcher, carried by friends who take turns in this pious service. Other functions are carried out by the burial society (Hevra Kadisha), whose members thereby acquire merit for the world to come and financial gratification as long as they live in this world.

In Italy, where coffins are used, Jews travel like others, on a bier from which the crosses and other Christian symbols have been removed. It is a quick, functional method of transportation. These funerals have not yet reached the levels of death mystification practiced in the United States but considerably reduce the time devoted to burials, which once played such an important role in the society of the living. In our age, in any case, nobody dies any more; we disappear from the world through accidents that should never have happened in the first place. I remember the indignation of the surgeon who had operated on my mother when he saw her suddenly die. "I don't understand it," he said to me in perfectly good faith, "there was no reason for her to die."

In modern funerals I always feel the absence of an impressive bier, drawn by at least two black-draped horses with a band in front and some flags behind. These were the performances that I admired most in Italian villages when I was a child. If the departed was an important person, he was preceded by musicians, wreaths, praying members of religious confraternities, priests, and clerics. He was followed by crying relatives and a lot of people dressed in their Sunday best. "It was worth dying," my father used to say on these occasions. With Jews and Moslems, this pomp never existed. The body is not put in a coffin; the people crowd around the stretcher with a familiarity that does not diminish the horror of the sudden disappearance of the body, dumped into a freshly dug grave. *Memento mori* is the brutal message of these Semitic burials. I have often asked myself whether these differences in funerary styles have not given assimilated Jews an additional reason for changing their religion.

My family mausoleum in the new Jewish compound in Turin follows the local custom: it consists of a big, underground, waterproof vault, with thirty-two places neatly stacked one above the other around the walls. The upper part of the tomb was constructed by a famous architect in an elegant, modern style, and thick rosebushes climb up the decorative stone columns at the corners. It gives me a strange feeling, not devoid of pleasure, to sit on the large marble tombstone and look at my own name, the same as that of my grandfather, sculpted in iron letters, which has been waiting for me for over a century. Sometimes I trace with my finger the patina of these letters that confirm the earthly passage of an ancestor I never knew. The gesture reminds me of the pride that swept over me the first time I fingered the embossed title,

"Embassy Counsellor," on my newly printed visiting cards. My grandfather, a banker whose father still lived in the ghetto of Ivrea, might have dreamt of a diplomat grandson, but never of one serving a Jewish state. I know now that even the wildest fantasies can become reality, and yet, standing in front of my own name in my family tomb, I know with equal certitude that all realities turn sooner or later into dreams of the past.

Considering my parents' propensity for dissipating their considerable fortune on unsuccessful financial operations, our family plot testifies that at least on this occasion my father invested his money well. True, when he decided to build all these niches for his parents, sons, and grandsons, he was still convinced that he bore the responsibility for a large family, which has meanwhile melted away. Between conversions, dispersions, and mixed marriages, the mausoleum in the year 2000 will not host more than a dozen permanent residents—antecedents and collaterals included. As a result, I find myself the owner of a "residence," the value of which increases from year to year thanks to the requests I receive from strangers.

So far I have not sold to anyone, not even to an octogenarian lady who asked me to sell her a niche, convinced as she was that in my family tomb she would find better bridge partners than in her own. "It has been so difficult spending a whole lifetime with boring people that the idea of being bored throughout eternity terrifies me," she told me the last time we discussed the matter.

After having visited many countries in which the existence of the living is supposed to depend on the dead, I begin to believe that my friend was right. The break between this world and the next that marks the Judeo-Christian tradition is not a universal belief. In the country of the Hova, on the highlands of Madagascar, for instance, the richer and more important the departed, the more often his family feels compelled to take his body out of the tomb, to dress him in beautiful robes, and seat him at the center of a festive family gathering. Even if the French colonial legislation put an end to the custom of transporting—especially in the hot season—a dead grandmother on the roof of a bus, or a departed uncle on the handlebars of a bicycle, no respectable person in that country would dare to begin a speech without asking permission of the dead and apologizing in advance for any foolish things he might say.

We, on the contrary, have the habit of attributing to the dead, especially to famous people we have not known and whose ideas we have not understood, the strangest statements. It is a discourteous custom, particularly common among politicians and academics. They should learn from the wisdom of the Malagasy who, as soon as they had obtained their independence from the French, asked that the legal address of the living should be identical with the domicile of the dead. This would make the departed one still share with the living in the vicissitudes of life.

One does not have to go as far as the Indian Ocean, as I did, to find eloquent examples of familiarity between the living and the dead. It has always existed in my village in Piedmont. The most expensive graves in the cemetery are those that enjoy a good view of the surrounding vineyards, renowned for their excellent wine. This fine quality is thought to be due to the fact that once upon a time the land around the cemetery belonged to a doctor who, according to the villagers, contributed greatly to helping the living reach the world of eternal rest. Or take the case of the cardinal, a famous son of the village, who insisted, by virtue of his ecclesiastical rights, on being buried in the parish church and not in his local family chapel. To those who asked him with surprise why a humble man of great wisdom like himself should avail himself of an archaic medieval privilege, this prince of the church answered with perfect candor that throughout his life he had suffered too much from rheumatism to give up the right of resting in the warm, dry atmosphere of the church.

Luigi, my uncle's cook, would have understood the cardinal perfectly. Luigi was a much-traveled southern Italian who never felt perfectly comfortable with the alphabet. Unable to fill in the census form by himself, he once asked me to put his profession down as "sculptor in butter." He had a perfect right to this qualification, having spent a large portion of his life working in the kitchens of Balkan princes. In that volatile part of the world, which he observed from the depths of his pots and pans, he had reached some firm and wise conclusions concerning the powerful of this world who, on the upper floors of their palaces, disposed of the destinies of common human beings. He understood that food, like dress or hairstyle, is a form of language, without knowing how close his culinary-political experience came to Lévi-Strauss' ideas about the "raw" and the "cooked." Luigi had learned that the blows cooks and scullions could exchange over different types of borscht, or the fights over a description of coffee as Turkish or Greek, paralleled the discussions on principles, rights, and religions that the princes conducted in the conference rooms. He once told me how Romanian chefs at a certain diplomatic meeting had refused to cook chickens in Bulgarian pots, and the Serbian dishwashers had insisted that the Macedonians should clean the plates. Eventually the political agreement worked out on the upper floors drifted down into the kitchen on the basis of a compromise on the sauces and in the form of a large iced cake upon which each national flag was precisely reproduced in candied fruit. Luigi, who felt both neutral and superior to these squabbles, crowned the sweet political monument with a big sugar star, which nobody had the courage to eat, remembering the tragic consequences that another silver star—of the Bethlehem manger—had had on Balkan politics. They all read into the innocent, "sweet" message of Luigi (who, as a good Italian Catholic, had simply thought it proper to crown the diplomatic agreement with the star of Bethlehem) a deep, political meaning. After all, it was the stealing of a silver star from the manger in the Church of the Nativity that indirectly caused the Crimean War.

However, Luigi never accepted my historical interpretation: he was, in a way, an incurable romantic. That did not stop him from vigorously defending his privilege to receive tips from any guest who came to dinner, me included, while at the same time resenting the fact that I did not ask him for a loan when he saw that I was short of money. "I have given plenty of money to Michael," (the prince who twice sat on and then lost the Romanian throne) he used to say to me, "and he certainly needed it less than you," which was true. Only once, soon after the end of World War II, when I found myself in dire need of money to buy a wedding present for my sister, did I ask him if it was possible, with great discretion, to find somebody to buy the collection of guns that I had built up during the war years. "Of course," he said, "there is Prince so-and-so, from whom you 'English' have confiscated all weapons and who wants to rebuild his collection." I gave him two German Mauser machinenpistolen, a long-barrelled gun for precision shooting, and a P38. Luigi put them into his shopping bag and two days later brought me a roll of Italian bank notes. That was the only private arms sale I have ever engaged in in my life, and I still ask myself today whether it was an appropriate way to go about buying a wedding present.

Luigi entered my family when Mussolini asked my uncle to implement the policy of economic self-sufficiency by creating in Sardinia an imaginary Ruhr, called Carbonia. Unlike my father, who had studied agronomy and law, my uncle had no formal academic education. He had taken a course of commercial studies; had gone to Germany to learn the language; and had been involved in the early stages of the creation of the Fiat motor company, which he left when the future Senator Agnelli told him in good Piedmontese dialect that there was "no place for two cockerels in the same chicken run." He had already reached an important position in an

Italian bank when World War I broke out. Called up as an officer in the Engineering Corps, he rapidly scaled the military ladder; won a number of French, British, and Italian decorations; and got involved in drafting the economic part of the Peace Treaty with Austria and, later, in a great scandal linked with iron mines. All this helped to launch him on the road to economic success, and within a few years he was in control of an industrial empire with its head office in Trieste. For a long time he remained the most sought-after bachelor in that town. In my capacity as his only male heir, he immortalized me in a marble bust at the age of six. Later on he got to know a divorced Austrian Christian lady, whom he decided to marry at the age of fifty, and with the birth of his two children I lost my special status although I retained his special affection.

From the kitchen Luigi had followed my uncle's fortunes, producing an ever-increasing number of dishes for his political and financial banquets. From his stove he also observed with sadness but without surprise his master's fall on the eve of Mussolini's anti-Jewish laws. Neither my uncle's national and Fascist merits nor his late baptism succeeded in preventing the confiscation in 1938 of all the factories he had set up. For Luigi, who had seen the downfall of thrones, the loss of ten or twenty thousand workers a month was a natural part of the game played by all the great ones he had fed. My uncle's misfortunes only increased his devotion. "When everybody abandoned him," he told me once, in reply to my question why, despite the racial laws, he had continued to keep in contact with my uncle, "somebody had to cook for him."

When the Germans took over Italy in 1943, my uncle took refuge in Vatican City, from which he emerged when the Allied troops arrived in Rome, only to embark on a long period of agonizing illness. He died just before the end of the war and his family, waiting for the liberation of northern Italy to give him an appropriate resting place, buried him temporarily in Luigi's tomb at the Verano cemetery in Rome.

Some time before the transfer of the body to a permanent family grave, Luigi asked me to accompany him to take leave of his dead master. We fixed an appointment at the Piazza dell'Esedra, in a café under the pillared portico where he used to play cards with the servants of other Roman families. I was still wearing a British uniform, which made no impression on those butlers and cooks, experts as they were in liveries and accustomed to handing hats, gloves, and batons to generals. One of them asked me why I wore on my left sleeve a badge similar to the one the Germans had imposed on the Jews as a mark of shame. I explained to him where my regiment came from; how it was made up of Jewish volunteers from Palestine; and why we had chosen that badge, blue and white with a yellow star in the center, in honor of a certain gentleman called Herzl, a Viennese journalist who, half a century earlier, had had the queer idea of creating a state for the Jews and had designed a flag for them with the Star of David on it. That Mr. Herzl, I said, would be astonished to see how the Germans, whom he had asked for help in realizing his dream when the kaiser visited Jerusalem, had turned into the worst enemies of the Jews.

Luigi listened in silence. "Maybe you won't believe me," he finally said, "but I saw that Mr. Herzl in person when he went to speak with the emperor in Jerusalem." In his unconnected way, full of confused imagery, chewing his cigar stub, spitting from time to time on the marble pavement of the portico at his feet and carefully squashing the phlegm with his shoe, he told us how in 1898, at the age of less than twenty, he had been working as a dishwasher in the service of a German prince who accompanied Kaiser Wilhelm II on his historic visit to the Holy Land. In Jerusalem, Luigi, like all the other servants, was ordered to arrive on horseback so as to increase the number and impressiveness of the imperial escort during the kaiser's entry into the walled city of Zion. The sultan had ordered a breach to be opened in the ancient walls, near the Jaffa Gate, for the entry of the imperial guest, who refused to dismount in order to clear the gateway or lower his head decorated with an egret's feather—a dubious historical curiosity that Jerusalem guides still tell to tourists.

The trouble with Luigi was that he was no horseman. To avoid possible mishaps he was put astride a donkey that apart from being big and placid was also white. On this mount Luigi entered the City of David amid a cheering crowd, some of whom were shouting "the Messiah, the Messiah" and laughingly pointing at him. "I answered them by waving both my hands," concluded Luigi.

In the tram rumbling noisily along toward the Verano cemetery, I reflected on the little stories that form the texture of history. Luigi, dishwasher of an emperor who had thought himself the greatest ruler of his time, was now sitting next to me, an Italian Jew in British uniform. I was involved at that moment in some minor plots against the British in Palestine, a semicolonial regime that had first supported and later opposed the same Zionist dream that Herzl wanted to entrust to the Germans—those same Germans who, a few decades later, were to try and solve the "Jewish Question" in the gas chambers. Together Luigi and I were on our way to pay our last respects to the mortal remains of my uncle, who had tumbled from his exalted political and financial position because of a Jewish origin that no conversion to Christianity could erase. Ironically enough, he was now lying in the grave of his cook, who had survived him and the kaiser and the many great ones of the world for whom he had plucked chickens and concocted sauces.

Luigi was carrying with him a small package wrapped in newspaper. He held it in both hands as though it were a handwarmer. This made him look even more ridiculous, huddled in spite of the warm weather, in a thick black overcoat with velvet lapels, his homburg on his head, and with a small gray moustache that made him look like Charlie Chaplin in *The Great Dictator*.

When we reached the grave, he put the package down on the marble slab, which already bore his name and date of birth and awaited the date of his death. With controlled gestures he took out of his pocket a curved, silver-handled brush, like the one my mother used to keep on the lace-bordered table in her huge bathroom. The brush reminded me of the silver-framed mirror, held by two finely wrought screws, which I was forbidden to touch while my mother's hair was being dressed, because the slightest oscillation of the mirror immediately made her feel seasick. I used to stand motionless at her side, rapt by the sight of her beautiful face: it had nothing in common with the cancer-worn visage whose eyes I closed on a warm spring morning in a Jerusalem hospital.

The childhood image that always returns to my memory is of my mother, dressed in an evening gown, long and décolleté, with a silk rose (which I still keep in a sandalwood box) pinned to her breast with a sapphire brooch. That was one of the few occasions when my father was persuaded to wear tails and accompany her to a gala performance at the Regio Theater in Turin. At that time, a few years before my father went bankrupt, our coachman, now chauffeur, Vigiu, allowed me to sit on his knee and hold the steering wheel while waiting in the driveway for my parents. Of that 509 Fiat Berline, all that now remains is a mahogany box in which my mother used to keep a small brush with which she removed the dandruff from my father's collar before they left the car. Now Luigi was doing the same thing with the leaves that had fallen on the marble slab of the tomb from the nearby trees and with some grains of dust that only a trained eye like his could have discerned.

I felt a strong need to pray, but I could not decide in what language and according to what religion I should do so. I could not recite the Kaddish, the Jewish prayer for the dead, because I lacked the requisite quorum of ten Jewish males, which in any case could not have assembled in a Christian cemetery in honor of a converted Jew. I was unable to recall in Hebrew the words of the Pater Noster, that old Jewish prayer taken over by the Church, and felt uneasy, as a Jew, about pronouncing them in Latin. Finally, I decided that it would be best to leave religion alone and pay tribute to my uncle by keeping his image alive in my mind, remembering how he was always kind and jovial with me, while being so feared and envied by the rest of the family for his political and industrial power.

I had few memories of him to rely on. When we children were admitted to his presence, we were supposed to salute him politely and then disappear as quickly as possible so as not to steal one instant of his precious time from the adults. On these occasions, when I always thought that the grownups were unjustly robbing the children of their rightful proximity to the great man of the family, I observed with disdain the way in which they behaved toward him. If they followed him about while he was pottering among the flowers of his mountain garden, their real lack of interest in the art of gardening was more than obvious. If they played bowls with him, they could barely wait for the end of the game, which they often deliberately lost to please him, to get his undivided attention. If they admired, with exclamations of surprise, the latest addition to his collection of snuffboxes (one of the most beautiful in Europe, or so I was told), they could not conceal the envy in their voices. The hope of discovering a minor imperfection in the snuffbox was similar to the hope of finding reasons to criticize my uncle's social success. He liked to boast about his meetings with Mussolini, to describe in great detail a dinner in Vienna or a lunch in Paris at which he signed a new agreement, started a successful enterprise, or established powerful new friendships. From these conversations, which usually turned into monologues addressed by my uncle to the admiring family circle, there emerged a kind of gossip filter, made up of sentences such as "my brother says . . . ," "my brother-in-

law believes . . . ," "the commander denies . . . ," with which
not only my relatives but also the drivers, maids, and gardeners
built up their own reputations among their poorer relations,
perpetually in search of recommendations and jobs.

The first time I had my uncle entirely to myself was one
afternoon in early September 1939 in Trieste. I was due to
embark the same evening for Palestine on one of his ships, by
now already confiscated in accordance with the racial laws. My
father had accompanied me to my uncle's house but had gone
back immediately to Turin by train, with the excuse that the
midday express was quicker and more comfortable and that he
did not want to leave my mother alone. The truth was that
he no longer had the courage or the physical strength to wait
and see the ship sail, with the possibility of never seeing me
again.

We had left Turin the previous evening, riding second class
by virtue of the last reduced price ticket to which my father
was entitled as a reserve officer, but without any hope of
renewal because of the new anti-Jewish legislation. The loss of
this small privilege seemed to pain him beyond reason, since
he traveled very little. We had spent the night in a half-empty
compartment, not speaking about the problems that weighed
so heavily on our hearts so as not to reveal our race to the other
passengers, or the fact that I was going abroad. With a stern
and suspicious look on his face, the Fascist train police officer
who accompanied the conductor jumped to attention and
raised his arm in the "Roman" salute when he saw my father's
Fascist identity card, unaware that he was standing in front of
a second-class citizen to whom no respect was due. My father
returned his salute with a sadness that the other people in the
compartment interpreted as the feigned modesty of a powerful
member of the regime. A grotesque aura of respect thus accompanied our agitated slumbers during the rest of the journey
until dawn, when we changed trains at Mestre, after crossing
and recrossing the bridge linking the continent with Venice.

I remembered then the emotion and pride with which, in my third year at the Royal Gymnasium, I had recited in front of my class Fusinato's poem on the siege of Venice in 1848, when the city rebelled against the Austrians. I was praised for the "heart" I had put into my recitation, which was due to my father's explanation that the president of the embattled Venetian republic at the time was of Jewish origin. "Plague is rife/ bread is lacking/ on the bridge floats the white flag," said the poem. Now it was my father's turn, I felt, through my flight to Palestine, to raise the white flag over his broken Fascist ideals, over his pride as an Italian nationalist, over the ruin of all his family hopes. I had nothing to tell him, and he had nothing to tell me, as if we had both exhausted all topics of conversation.

I was grateful to him for not accompanying me to the ship, for cutting short the adieus, and for leaving me alone with his famous brother. My uncle treated me as his peer: he made me sit facing him at the long marble table around which so many great people had once dined. Now we were together, or rather he was alone with me, with a maid not yet taken away by the new anti-Jewish legislation serving us in silent precision as in the time of his greatness. Noiselessly, she kept changing fine procelain plates in front of me, with gloved hands, quick to disappear with a slight rustle of the starched white apron she wore over her black silk uniform.

My uncle made no comments on the political situation created by the war that had just broken out. He asked me about the agricultural school in which I had enrolled without ever pronouncing the word "Palestine." I answered him with the nonchalance of a spoiled youth on the point of entering a finishing school in England or Switzerland. From the window I could see the terraced garden full of flowers, with the replica of Rodin's *The Kiss* and the jet of water in the center of the pond where red, gold, and silver fish continued their lives undisturbed. Nothing had changed on my uncle's estate except for the feeling that both of us had been torn from the reality surrounding us, that we were strange travelers in a space ship of Jules Verne's imagining, in which the refined life of the past continued under the new, unreal dimensions of the present. For my uncle this may have been a surrealistic experience; for me it was a moment of total triumph, which I owed to the new Fascist anti-Semitism and which nobody could disturb. On the eve of my departure for a foreign land I had become, thanks to the racial laws, equal to the richest and most powerful man I had ever known in my life. The fact that this was due to his social and political collapse did not disturb me in the least. This was the first of many occasions when I realized that one person's good fortune is always linked to another person's troubles.

After lunch that afternoon my uncle took me to the home of Lionel Stock, founder of the famous distillery firm and a dedicated Zionist, to ask him for letters of introduction to some of his friends in Palestine. These letters did not help me in the least in a country flooded by immigrants looking for jobs, but I recall with deep emotion the meeting of those two powerful Jewish industrialists who had not, I believe, met for years.

Lionel Stock was dressed in a dark suit with a gold chain dangling from his waistcoat pocket. My uncle wore an elegant light gray suit, which was the only spot of color in the sober office we entered after passing through the factory courtyard. The two men represented different worlds in the social and ethnic mosaic of Jewish Trieste before the war: my uncle had come from Piedmont following the victory of the Italian army; Stock had stayed put after the collapse of the Austro-Hungarian Empire. One was the epitome of economic success in authoritarian Italy; the other the symbol of economic development in traditional Mittel Europa. One was baptized and a Fascist, the other a confirmed Jew and Zionist. The only thing they had in common was their Jewish origin and their interest in me. Conscious of my position, I sat silent between them like a laboratory animal, the focus not of an experiment but of a confrontation of ideas.

Lionel Stock was saying that no Jew could escape his destiny. My uncle answered that the storm would eventually blow over and that it was necessary to trust Mussolini, who had always been friendly to Jews on condition that they kept themselves out of the public eye. Stock said that we had no hope unless we stood as united as possible, that we could no longer rely on anyone, that we had to exploit the little freedom that was still left to the Jews in Italy to get away and to help as many coreligionists as possible to escape from the Germans. My uncle answered him that the Jews, as a separate group, were the agents of their own ruin. In order to reverse an illogical, tragic, unjustified destiny, he had married a Christian woman and had his children grow up in the religion of the majority, different from the faith into which he was born. Stock replied that this was perhaps a choice open to the individual, but not to the Jewish masses, and that my uncle's recent losses underlined the fact that even a powerful individual Jew who had been baptized could not escape his Jewish destiny. Since Hitler's decision to check the religion of the grandparents, we had reached a situation in which the lineage of Jews was examined as carefully as that of the nobility used to be. In the absurdity of the racial persecution it was necessary to accept the responsibility carried by this new type of negative Jewish aristocracy. I was wise to leave Italy because the future of the Jews was outside Europe, in America, and even more in Palestine, where a day would come when nobody would be able to contest their right to lead a normal existence like any other people.

My uncle insisted that the Zionist movement, even if theoretically rational, was politically illusory. It did not take into consideration the realities of the contemporary political world. England and France were two countries in full decadence. They were unable to stop the march of powerful nations like Germany and Italy, which were in the process of rapid demographic and military expansion. Possibly the destiny of the Jews in Palestine might have been different if Italy had been given the mandate over that part of the Ottoman Empire. Now, allied with the Arab world, Italy had less interest in Zionism than England, which had already betrayed the Jews of Palestine in order to capture the sympathy of the Arabs. He was convinced that I was not saving my skin but marching straight into a trap. He could not understand how my father could have failed to try to dissuade me, but we were living in times in which nobody, and more particularly the Jews, understood what was happening. Of one thing he was convinced: out of this war a new order would arise; woe to those who stood against it; they would be destroyed.

Stock knew that he could not sway my uncle. He listened without interrupting, sighing and shaking his head in sorrow. When we parted he said to me, with a note of hope in his voice, that he hoped to see me again in less troubled times so that I could bear witness to which of the two, he or my uncle, would be vindicated by the future.

It is remarkable with what clarity my uncle remembered this, for him, unpleasant conversation many years later. He was lying on a large bed in his apartment in Via Bruxelles, opposite the villa of Marshal Badoglio, in an area that was then one of the most elegant and quiet in Rome. The room was filled with the smell of death, a death my uncle had always dreaded and now accepted with surprising resignation—only from time to time he cried without apparent reason. The anxiety of recent years, his flight into the Vatican, his separation from his wife and children, all had shaken his physique more than his economic ruin out of which, however, he had saved a considerable sum that now served to pay the fees of the most famous Italian doctors. My aunt thought she could increase the efficacy of the medical care by winding around my uncle's neck a pair of white woolen socks that the family's confessor had obtained from Sister Pasqualina, Pope Pacelli's maid. It was said that the socks had been worn by the Pope himself and might, therefore, bring about the miracle in which the doctors did not believe. In my eyes, however, they made him look pathetic.

My uncle was happy to see me again. He wanted to ask me to leave the British army, with which I had come to Rome at the beginning of 1945, as soon as possible. I do not know whether he was fully conscious or under the effect of drugs, as he described to me in a gasping voice the immense new possibilities, political and economic, that would open up in Italy once it was free of the Fascist regime. From time to time he spoke about India, which he wanted to visit as soon as the war was over; about the forests he had lost in Poland; about past conversations with Italian politicians and international bankers; about the fleet of fishing trawlers that he wanted to establish as soon as the war ended; and of the importance of always having polished shoes because—he kept repeating—the shoes betrayed the man.

Once he described to me the frontiers of the financial empire he had created. They extended from mines in Lorraine to forests in Danzig, from food industries in Trieste to a hydroelectric plant on the Austrian border. The loss of all these riches seemed to have wounded him less than the rejection by the duchess of Aosta of a gift he had sent to the Castle of Miramar on the birthday of one of the duchess's children. The box, wrapped in shiny paper, had been returned with an icy letter of thanks. Even now, after the duke had died a hero's death in Africa, my uncle still suffered from having been considered, even at the peak of his power, a parvenu, a newly rich Jew who had no place at court. None of the many personalities he had known in Europe between the two wars—Paderewski and Balfour, Rathenau and Marconi, Balbo and Dolfuss—could compensate him for that snub, which he had been unable to erase since he had narrowly missed the opportunity of being made a count by Mussolini.

While Luigi cleaned the tombstone, I remembered the sudden visit that my uncle had paid to my mother in the winter of 1938. I had never seen him so happy, and his slightly mischievous smile seemed never to leave his lips. He gave me a big fifty-lire note, although he had sent me one shortly before, for my birthday. He asked my sister what she wanted for her birthday, in April, and then he retired to another room with my mother, surrounded by an atmosphere of great secrecy. When he left in the long, shining Lancia with his monogram on the doors, the chauffeur dressed in livery, he left behind him an aura of faint after-shave and strong mystery, which my mother immediately broke by telephoning my father while I listened at the keyhole.

He—Mussolini—had let my uncle know that he was prepared to support a proposal to the king to make my uncle a count or a royal senator. It was clear, my mother said over the telephone, that in the first place one should think of an appropriate coat of arms. It could not be anything connected with the "45" (a number used in the family in front of the servants to indicate that somebody or something was Jewish; the servants knowing no more than we that the Hebrew letters of the word *adam*, meaning "man" or "Jew," corresponded to the figure 45), but it would be nice if the coat of arms were in some way connected with our family. (This was not easy since it was only in 1849 that my forefathers left the ghetto of Ivrea where they used to sell rags, with special permission to remain outside the ghetto walls every Tuesday.) In any case, my mother went on, my uncle wanted my father, who was an expert in heraldry, to give some thought to the matter. It was a real shame, she continued, that the village in Piedmont where my grandfather had owned the castle and where we still had some property, was a fiefdom of the duke of Genoa. It would have been nice if the coat of arms could have been that of the village, with its cross and sheaf of corn, which was printed on the labels of the wine bottles my father prepared specially for my uncle every year. My father laughed at the whole idea. He was right, because before six months had elapsed, the new alliance between Mussolini and Hitler had destroyed forever the heraldic hopes of his brother.

With my heart agitated by these memories and my head empty of ideas, I now stood in front of the grave, following with my eyes Luigi's arthritic fingers struggling with the knots tied around his parcel. Eventually there emerged from the newspaper a small, round jar that might once have contained jam. Inside was a yellow liquid. Luigi, with a hieratic gesture full of respect, unscrewed the lid and slowly poured the contents onto the marble slab. A strong and pleasing smell of rum reached my nostrils as a puddle of liquid fizzed over the stone. With his cigar stub dangling from his mouth, Luigi murmured loudly enough for me to hear: "Commander, this zabaglione is made exactly as you liked it." With the back of his left hand, in which he held the lid of the jar, he wiped away a tear, turning his back to me in shame.

A slight breeze caressed the cypresses: I found myself thinking that they had nothing in common with those celebrated by Respighi. These were clumsy trees, powdered with dust, swaying above the yellowing grass at their feet. Indifferent to death and pain, they looked as though they were sucking up life from the graves, witnesses of everything and nothing, in a garden dedicated to nothingness and inhabited by everyone.

Silently we left the Verano, Luigi wrapped up in his black winter coat and I huddled in my badly ironed British battle-dress. The "Red Circular" tram was just coming. Without speaking we shook hands. Anyone witnessing the scene might have thought we were two mafiosi who had just completed a deal.

5.

A Fascist Cadet
in Zion

AFTER so many years I still laugh at the thought of my arrival in Tel Aviv. I was traveling on a small ship carrying a mixed cargo and about thirty passengers. I was sixteen and had a "capitalist" immigration visa, the type of visa that the British issued to immigrants with at least one thousand pounds sterling, which, in my case, my father had deposited in an English bank through the good offices of the Fascist party. I was alone in one of the six or eight first-class cabins. Traveling with me were some priests and a few Palestinian Jews making their precipitous return because of the outbreak of war. I was the only immigrant on board. The British mandatory authorities had by that time practically closed the door to Jews from Europe. With the publication of a white paper limiting Jewish immigration they had put an end to Zionist hopes of having a Jewish state in Palestine, since the percentage of the Jewish population had been fixed at one-third of the Arab inhabitants of the Holy Land.

My situation was thus particularly hybrid. I was a "deluxe" immigrant, due to join a kibbutz; I was the nephew of the owner of the ship on which I was sailing, but the ship had just been confiscated by the Italian government because he was a baptized Jew; I was under the personal care of the ship's captain at whose table I took my meals, and at the same time abandoned in every sense into the hands of an unknown fate. Nobody, and first and foremost myself, knew exactly who I was. Among the passengers, a beautiful lady seemed particularly startled by my presence. Wife of the owner of the then-largest textile factory in Palestine, she too was traveling first class, and we quickly became friends.

She could have been about thirty-five years old and told me she had a son not much younger than I. She did not mingle with the other passengers and spent long hours looking at the sea as if oppressed by nightmares. We used to take our afternoon tea together in long, quiet sessions—I too busy with myself to ask her about her troubles, she too plunged into her own thoughts. She must have left most of her family behind in Europe and perhaps had tried in vain to persuade them to follow her to Palestine. A tall, blond, sad woman, she listened to me with a strange look in her eyes, a look of curiosity and compassion. With considerable tact she kept warning me of the illusions I was weaving about the country awaiting me. I would not find anything remotely like Italy, she said, either in the landscape or in the people. It was not the physical toil that I should be afraid of but the cruelty of human relations. In Palestine the differences among people were greater than in other places because of the large number of immigrants. I would probably find myself lonely and misunderstood by other youngsters because of the type of world I was coming from. I would be caught up in a network of abrasive relationships among uprooted people who, because they were uprooted, were now busily engaged in building a world in which to forget their past. I should not expect compassion, pity, or kindness, though I would be able to rely on human solidarity. But it was a type of solidarity that shied away from privacy and individualism. Necessity and ideology privileged the group rather than the individual. For this reason it would be wise of me to find and adhere to a group as quickly as possible. I would suffer less than if I remained aloof. The price to be paid for acceptance would certainly consist of the loss of many of my dreams, not to speak of the tastes and habits I had brought with me from home, but nevertheless I should conform. The only other piece of advice she could give me was to try and develop thick callouses on my soul like those that would very soon harden the palms of my hands. Palestine, she kept telling me, is a land where caresses are made with sandpaper.

Naturally I was not convinced. Stretched out on my deck chair in the morning and the late afternoon, I enjoyed the infinite, changing blue of a bright, glassy sea—an atmosphere of well-being that made it impossible to imagine a future of pain and humiliation. The unreality that had always surrounded me was still there, even if different from before. World War II had broken out, but I was making my first cruise as a private person, free from uniforms, obligations, or discipline. I was a Jew, branded by racial laws, but served in style by Aryan waiters, protected by a captain who was perhaps wondering whether my uncle might not someday again be his boss. I was a refugee, an immigrant, a being in flight from a Europe that was tumbling into hell, but this did not prevent me from feeling free, fortunate, and happy at being able to run away from the war fronts, from college discipline, and from the oppression of Jewish life in Turin. I was full of hopes, without responsibilities, enjoying every minute of my life on board, which kept me busy from morning to night. I slept, I ate, I chatted; I read novels from the ship's library; I roamed freely around the ship, from the captain's bridge to the engine room; I talked to the boatswain, who demonstrated the knots he could make with a piece of string; I discussed the radio bulletins announcing German victories, and I was not— as I had dreaded—seasick!

During the crossing which, even near Crete, where the sea is often rough, was consistently sunny and calm, an abandon-ship exercise was carried out. The first officer called the passengers onto the top deck, checked the correct fastening of our life belts, explained the meaning of the siren blasts in case of danger, and took care to assure us that such danger was highly unlikely. Italy, he said, would remain neutral, thanks to the wisdom of Il Duce. Nobody would dare to provoke her in *mare nostrum*. Just the same, we should not allow ourselves to sink into a comfortable fatalism; not for nothing was England known as *perfide Albion*. Should we find ourselves in danger, we should face it with Italian, Aryan, and Fascist courage. The poor man, destined perhaps to die soon in some naval operation, must have learned his speech by heart. Facing a public composed mainly of Jews, his words sounded like a Marx Brothers' gag.

It was early in the morning when we anchored off Tel Aviv. To the right, clustered on the promontory of Jaffa, was a conglomeration of small houses, the bell tower of a church, and a large, castle-like building. Facing me, rising from an expanse of sand, were lines of flat roofs, colorless cement cubes with a splash of green here and there. A number of barges swayed on the water. The entire harbor consisted of a small jetty from which they shuttled back and forth to the few cargo ships waiting beyond the shallow water. An Italian priest, with whom I had gotten friendly during the trip and with whom I had discussed, for the first time in my life, the dogmas of Judaism and Christianity, explained to me that the only real harbor in the country was further north, at Haifa. The Jews had built the jetty in Tel Aviv and were handling their own cargoes because the Arabs of Jaffa had refused to unload the ships for them. "Jews and Arabs always quarrel," he said, "and they will go on quarreling for a long time to come if somebody does not put an end to the attempts of the Zionists to have a state of their own in Palestine." The war that had just started would certainly clip the Zionists' wings: the Jews were already not allowed by the British to immigrate into Palestine or to buy land from the Arabs. But after reducing them to a perpetual minority, the British government would use them to fight the Arabs, divide the country, and thus have a reason to remain *ad aeternitatem* in Palestine. In any case, he added, everyone was fighting everyone else in the Holy Land, which was supposed to be the Land of Peace. At the Church of the Holy Sepulcher the Christians quarreled among themselves no less than the Jews with the Moslems. If I visited Jerusalem one day he would be happy to take me to see it for myself. He wished me good luck and disembarked with the other passengers, including my beautiful lady companion, leaving me alone on board in the hands of the immigration authorities. They gave me permission to go ashore in less than half an hour.

As soon as the little row boat had taken me into the port, which consisted of a large shed for goods and a few hovels used as offices, a short, ugly, slant-eyed nurse got hold of me with the brisk authority derived from her white uniform and starched cap embroidered with a red Star of David. She took my temperature, measured my pulse, vaccinated me without a word of explanation, asked a lot of questions about my health and that of my family, and almost choked when I, in turn, asked her who the bearded gentleman was looking at me with sad eyes from the wall. "Theodor Herzl," she growled, "the founder, the prophet of Zionism." After which, stupefied and disgusted, she let me go.

Nobody, naturally, was waiting for me outside the port, and I wondered how to approach the passersby to get some advice. I did not speak a word of Hebrew, they would certainly not understand Italian, and I was ashamed to show how little French and English I knew. I was wearing a navy blue jacket, gray flannel trousers, a shirt with cufflinks and the detachable linen collar that dandies at that time sported in Italy, and a beautiful silk tie. To the people I saw outside the tiny port, open-shirted, perspiring, and scruffy, the men in sandals and shorts, the women in sandals and khaki bloomers hitched up to the tops of their thighs with elastic, I must have looked like the ringmaster of a circus. Next to me stood a big, leather-bound cabin trunk and a canvas bag. The trunk, a bar mitzvah gift from my cousins, was silk-lined and bore my initials; the canvas bag contained a collapsible camp bed and a small tent. These two objects were recommended items for immigrants, listed in the documents I had collected at the Palestine office in Milan. Among other useless pieces of advice, it suggested that one equip oneself with a Boy Scout hat. To find this headgear, my father and I had scoured half of Turin. Finally we came to the Borsalino shop in the station square, where we thought we had seen something like the hat in question in the window.

The shop assistant, after listening to our explanation of why we needed such a hat, told me that he still had some Boy Scout hats in stock. They had not been in demand for a long time, since the Boy Scout movement had been outlawed by the Fascist regime. He brought me a couple to try on—they were made of rich brown felt and shaped like those of the Canadian Mounties. The assistant assured me, in front of the mirror, that it fitted me beautifully. He said he was happy that I would be wearing it in a country where people could have uniforms without being trained for war. An immediate feeling of understanding and conspiracy was established between us. Hat in hand, we left without any further conversation, but I am convinced to this day that if I had stayed in Italy that shop would have become a friendly refuge for me, with the hat serving as a password for anti-Fascist action.

As soon as I landed in Tel Aviv I understood that it was safer for me to make the hat disappear. It was heavy and totally unsuited to the climate of the country. Worse, it made me look even more ridiculous than my jacket and tie in a world where women covered their heads with faded scarves of coarse blue cotton and men wore peaked caps of a Russian-Polish type. This latter fashion quickly disappeared in Israel, but at the time it symbolized adherence to Marxist principles, just as it does today, in a curious geographical development, on the heads of Chinese militants.

However, this was not the subject of my reflections when I went out under the blinding sun and stood alone, already without my jacket but still wearing a tie and a linen collar, next to my cabin trunk and canvas sack. I found myself suddenly faced with the emptiness of my future. For the first time, after months of excitement, enthusiasm, fantasies, and romantic projects, I was smitten by a feeling of utter hopelessness. In trying to analyze the cause after so many years, I probably tend to confuse the experience of that time with my present-day recollections. Yet that first fit of anguish left an indelible scar.

Leaning on my cabin trunk, which stood upright on the sand like a memorial column to my past, I did not understand the meaning of the new life facing me. But from the very first moment, I perceived the dessicated vitality of the place—the power of the people who, from ideological choice rather than from necessity, wanted to appear poorer and rougher than my father's peasants. They exuded an insolent misery; they displayed a life-style that signaled to me unequivocally I had fallen into a world of frenetic action, without reserves or counterweights, with no hiding places for the soul. It was a world devoted to deeds and burned by activism as the flat-roofed, peeling houses were burned by the sun. In the sudden, infinite emptiness of my situation, these houses seemed to eye me from across the street, graceless and only less frightening than the wooden barracks along the seashore, whose walls bore tatters of tar paper, which flapped grotesquely in the wind.

These shacks, perched on the dunes like witches' dens, looked down on the camel trains filing past along the shore. Laden with crates of sand, they made their way to invisible construction sites, their rhythmic pacing marked by the tin-

kling of the bells around their necks. From the lopsided veran-
das of some of the shacks, wash flapping in the breeze saluted
these indolent animals, pressing upon me the naked, miserable
reality of my new motherland, so different from that of my
dreams. I was unable at that time to perceive beyond the
poverty of the landscape the hidden meaning of the Zionist
adventure and the miraculous connection between the moribund Judaism of Europe and the acrid pride of a Jewish
nationalism in Palestine striving to create a new type of Jew.

In a confused way I felt that Tel Aviv had no personality
of its own, like some of the new towns Mussolini was creating
in the drained marshes around Rome. This burgeoning town,
in which a writer one day would say that people laughed in
Hebrew during the day and cried in many languages at night,
reproduced in microcosm the whole history of the human race.
It was a history of which I was totally ignorant and which now
paraded before my eyes in a living collection of tattered styles,
languages, costumes, and habits. It was a history that jumbled
together in a disorderly, unharmonic, unblended whole, the
passions, needs, and hopes brought here by fanatical idealists
and reluctant immigrants from the four corners of the earth.
In those short-long instants of my standing outside the gates
of Tel Aviv port, I experienced the first brutal contact with
infinite emptiness. But I also unconsciously perceived that
diabolical mirage that calls men to supplant thought with
action and to choke doubts with meaningful gestures: action
for action's sake.

A taxi driver, sitting in a dust-covered Ford, shook me out
of this nightmare. He was probably used to meeting stunned
immigrants like me. For a couple of shillings he offered to take
me to the bus station, the focal point where everyone seemed
to converge before dispersing into a new world that was, for
many, still without poles of attraction.

During that short trip I must obviously have absorbed
through my eyes and my pores the novelty of this ungrateful

landscape. Yet of those first visions of Tel Aviv I have almost no recollections. The shock must have been too strong for them to be recorded in my mind: this has not remained the only memory block I have experienced in my life. Anyway, on that particular morning my brain started functioning again only on my arrival at the bus station, if one can so describe the chaos of public transport that greeted me.

The vehicles of the Jewish bus cooperative—the main transport system then, as today, because the state only operates a couple of short railway lines—were parked untidily along narrow, unpaved streets branching off the main road named after Theodor Herzl. These squat, dusty brown buses had rows of hard wooden seats inside and dirty windows with wire netting on the outside to protect against the stones and sometimes the bombs that the Arabs had gotten into the habit of throwing. The streets were crowded with people dressed in every possible variety of Western and Eastern costumes and with carts pulled by donkeys or horses. I was struck by the fact that most of the latter had ulcerated skins and were not castrated. The fact that a badly cared for stallion could be harnessed to a cart seemed to me symbolic of a society in which human and animal energy kept pulsing in scarred bodies. But soon my eyes became mesmerized by an unexpected spectacle of popular magic: on one street corner a bearded man with a kind of turban around his head was making hieratic gestures while slaughtering chickens with a long knife. The sand soaked up the drizzle of blood under the attentive eyes of women carrying shopping bags.

Not far from there another man shuffled along in a pair of baggy, black Turkish trousers that fell onto his old, down-at-the-heel slippers. He carried on his back an enormous brass jar with an elongated, griffin-like beak high over his shoulder. A metal beaker dangled from three fingers of one hand; from the other was suspended by its handle a flat metal "basket" holding some dirty glasses. With the thumb and forefinger of the first hand, he drummed up customers by clacking metal castanets. "Tamarindi, tamarindi," he shouted, making his way slowly through the crowd. From time to time someone would hold out to him a coin with a hole in the middle. The tamarindi seller would then bend forward in a measured bow, allowing with the inclination of his back a yellow liquid to spurt out of the beak of the jar from above his shoulder. He caught the beverage in midair in one of the glasses that he had previously rinsed in water from the beaker. The customer drank and returned the glass to the tamarindi seller, who moistened it again with a little water, erasing with his thumb any trace left by the customer's lips. Then he moved off again to the sound of his castanets. He was an Arab, his head covered with a gray-white scarf. When he poured out the tamarindi for a Jew, standing in front of him in a peaked cap, his sunburned, hairy legs sprouting out of his faded shorts, they looked like two bizarre animals exchanging silent messages through the colored bottom of the glass.

I was also feeling thirsty, and since my cab driver had refused a tip, I invited him to have a drink. He took me to a restaurant called Istanbul where, sitting at a shaky, oilcloth-covered table, I received from this good man my first lesson in the comparative history, geography, and psychology of the country in which I was to become a citizen.

The driver wore a khaki shirt and shorts and, like the bus drivers who went to-and-fro in the restaurant, he sported knee-length socks and brown shoes. Unlike some of the others, he did not have a Mauser automatic pistol dangling from a holster strapped across his chest, nor did he wear, strapped to his belt, a strange gadget to dispense change. This odd apparatus consisted of three metal cylinders of different diameters, each with a spring pushing up a round plate the size of a particular coin. The drivers, who also sold tickets, slid the coins they received into these cylinders or took them out by a pressure of the thumb to give change. My father had a similar instrument, smaller and box-shaped, in his study. Inside were two cavities, each with a spring in the bottom, in which he used to keep golden sovereigns and half sovereigns. He took this box with him when he went to Monte Carlo to play and once described its use to me as though it were already an archaeological relic. Under the thumbs of the bus drivers, without dandified refinements, I now watched silver shillings and perforated tin piasters sliding in and out from these gadgets.

They bore the word "Palestine" in English, Arabic, and Hebrew. After the Hebrew word was a bracket enclosing two letters of the cuneiform alphabet, which the Jews had brought back from their exile in Babylon: an *aleph* and a *yod,* the initials of the words "Eretz Yisrael" (Land of Israel). My taxi driver held one of these coins under my nose and explained its political significance. The Arabs, he said, had refused to allow the Jews to have the words "Land of Israel" fully inscribed on the coins. The Jews, for their part, objected to their ancestral land being called only by the Arab name "Falastin" (that is, the land of the Philistines) which, quite apart from contemporary political considerations, was, in my driver's opinion, an anachronism, since the Philistines had been massacred by Samson a long time ago. The British, however, Solomonically added the brackets with the *aleph* and the *yod* after the Hebrew "Palestine." It could be pronounced "Ai!" and this cry of trodden-on corns was, according to my impromptu teacher, a perfect description of the situation now facing the Jews.

The driver was born in Russia and had emigrated to Palestine with his parents after the revolution. He spoke Italian and a few words of Ladino—the Jewish-Spanish speech—which he had picked up on his summer trips between Salonica and Venice. He had been shuttling back and forth on that route, engaged in a very special trade—pro forma marriages with Jewish girls who had been refused immigration certificates by the British. By marrying him, a Palestinian citizen, a girl could enter the country by right and then, through a quick divorce procedure, proceed to join her real fiancé, if she had one, or look for a husband locally. The British had eventually caught on and forbidden this type of arrangement, and he had thus lost the opportunity of making free summer trips to Europe, where because of Hitler and the war, people were now, he said, in deep trouble. Fortunately it would not last long; he knew France well, and the French army was the strongest in the world. The Nazis would be beaten after breaking their heads against the Maginot line. Meanwhile life for the Jews in Poland was turning sour, he went on; one heard terrible stories about their fate. Yet they had asked for it; they could have come to Palestine during the years when immigration was free, but they had chosen to stay among their enemies.

My man was particularly hard on the religious Jews who believed that Zionism was the work of the devil. Now they were tasting hell, he said, and could see for themselves what it meant to pray three times a day for the return of the Jews to Zion and yet stay put in their quarters in Lodz and Warsaw. They could at least have emigrated en masse to America! Instead they had waited till the Germans arrived. Like the Jews of Western Europe they felt secure because the goyim (Gentiles) had passed laws giving them legal equality. "Pieces of paper," grumbled the driver, sipping his lemonade. "Pieces of paper which all the governments will eventually tear to pieces as has already happened in Germany and Italy." The Jews of Europe now found themselves trapped with their money and their houses full of possessions that they could not get rid of. Instead, had they had a bit more *sechel* (common sense), they might have been able, with a bit of that money, to buy villas and orange groves and build factories and theaters in Eretz Yisrael, helping Zionism while saving their skins. But that's what Jews are like, he sighed hopelessly; I would find that out for myself very soon. Jews, he explained, were clever but not wise. A clever man is the one who finds ways out of an unpleasant situation into which a wise man would never have got himself. I should try to be wise, not clever, he advised me, because just by looking at me he felt that I would never have any success among the clever.

Anyway, now that I was safe I could start a new life. But to succeed in it I should turn my back firmly on the past. There was no way back for the Jews: the war would sever the physical links that still existed with Europe, and Zionism should cut the cultural and spiritual links with it and put an end to the mentality of the Diaspora. From this war the old continent and old Judaism would emerge in shambles. The Zionists, like Cortés' Spaniards in Mexico, could only go forward, in spite of the opposition of the British and the hostility of the Arabs. They should transform themselves from refugees into conquistadores. Jabotinsky (the nationalist right-wing leader) and his Revisionist party were right—one could not build a state, as the socialists were trying to do, just by adding one cow to another cow, one dunam of land to another (bought at a "golden" price from the Arabs). Only strength would permit the Jews to live in security in Eretz Yisrael. The Jewish Agency (the Zionist administration in Palestine) and the world Zionist movement were wrong in believing that it was possible to pacify the Arabs by practicing *havlagah,* the policy of self-control that authorized only to reply to attacks but never to initiate them. On the contrary, it was necessary to be the first to attack, to show one's teeth, to frighten. The Jews of Eretz Yisrael must convince their enemies that they were no longer the Jews of the ghetto; they were the new oriental barbarians, the new Hyksos. Mohammed, with four hundred riders, had destroyed the Byzantine Empire; four thousand Jews could shake the British Empire.

There was something fascinating in his words. In my imagination I saw bands of Zionist Arditi, the Italian storm troopers whose exploits in the Great War had so often been taught us at school, dressed in shining armor, galloping with flying banners to the conquest of London. But as soon as I returned to my senses, my eyes fell on the flies sipping the drops of lemonade bubbling on the table. No war cries came from the street but only the clucking of chickens and the braying of donkeys. Unknown people, looking most unwarlike, chattered around me in incomprehensible idioms. The landscape was that of a small, dusty, provincial town, of the dirty corner of a market from which the smells of cooked food and rotten vegetables rose into the air, displacing all fantasies of glorious conquest. What I saw was a perspiring and agitated humanity, not a phalanx of martial warriors. The crude white light leveled all objects into an unending succession of black and white shapes. Nothing could be further from a battleground than this inordinate ambience, in which all living things searched for cover in the miserly shade of noon.

I looked at my jacket, creased by the chair back. I had already undone my collar and tie and turned up the sleeves of my shirt, which sweat had glued to my spine. I felt undressed, dirty, defenseless, immersed in the still air of surroundings made up of sand, noise, shoving, and shadows.

My driver had to go. He helped me carry my luggage to the edge of the dirt road from which the bus to my kibbutz was supposed to depart. He assured me that I could leave everything unguarded; no one stole in the only totally Jewish city in the world. He shook my hand, wished me luck, and left in his dusty Ford, unaware of the help he had given me and for which I would never have the opportunity to thank him.

The trip to Kibbutz Givat Brenner was uneventful. I expected stones or bombs to be thrown at us and for our driver to fight off enemy attacks with his pistol, as in a Western, but nothing happened. We drove through areas of Jewish settlement, alternating with Arab villages and large tracts of empty sand. On the road we passed small groups of Arab peasants astride their little donkeys, followed by women carrying bundles of greens or firewood on their heads. The landscape was exotic but poor and the dimensions of everything were miserable.

As we left the outskirts of Jaffa, we passed in front of the bell tower of a Russian Orthodox church, standing almost opposite the minaret of a mosque. Around both buildings I could see low, flatroofed, crumbling mud houses and crowds of barefooted children. Their faces were covered with flies, their clothes consisted only of dirty nightgowns falling to their feet. There were scattered palm trees, some vineyards, and many orange groves, whose brilliant green contrasted vividly with the sandy, dusty monotony of the surroundings. Squatting women baked bread in ovens of stone and dried mud. Here and there, in the courtyards or on the flat roofs, apricots, tomatoes, and bunches of peppers were drying in the sun. In front of these hovels and under thatched roofs, groups of Arabs eyed us, sucking at their water pipes. By the doors stood water jars and bundles of sugarcane. From time to time a slow-moving, skin-ulcerated camel slowed the bus down. Chickens darted out from all sides amid the howling of skinny dogs. It was an ugly and impoverished world, from which one had to lift one's eyes to the sky, limpid and blue, to recover hope.

Next to me sat a fat, perspiring woman with a basketful of vegetables on her lap. Encouraged by the other passengers, she questioned me about my origins, my age, the family I had left behind in Italy, the people awaiting me in the kibbutz, my father's business, how much he had earned, why I had not gone to America, what I thought about Tel Aviv, why I had chosen to go to the agricultural school at Mikveh Yisrael instead of the one at Kfar Tabor, which was much better and which was where her uncle had studied. She gave me a mass of unasked for advice; inquired about my political views and offered her own in exchange; discussed my case with a man sitting in front of us; made sure three times that the driver knew where I was going; and finally got off at Rehovot, today a great science center but at that time just a spot of green and a cluster of white houses between two stretches of sand.

After a while we entered the kibbutz grounds through two revolving, rusty iron gates standing wide open over a shallow concrete ditch full of whitish water. The bus moved slowly into the water to disinfect its tires against "foot and mouth" disease, which, unchecked among the Arab herds, also caused considerable mortality in the Jewish cattle. A road of beaten earth wound through a thick orange grove leading to a bare, stony hill covered with buildings.

On the way we encountered first, on the right-hand side, workshops full of machinery under repair, welding equipment, and men dressed in grease-stained blue overalls. Next came the chicken runs and the stables; higher up, laid out in semicircles, stood three types of dwellings: there were two-story, rectangular blocks with an outside staircase in the center and two balconies, one above the other, providing access to a row of four rooms each. The balconies sported broom handles, flowers in petrol tins, and wooden crates used as cupboards. Lower down the hill, in no clear order, were many wooden huts, also divided into four rooms, with an open veranda serving as a storage space for brooms and buckets, makeshift cupboards for work clothing, and gaping shoes covered with mud. Here and there one could see large crates transformed into "private houses." Some were painted outside; one had a curtained window and looked like a doll's house; another was surrounded by a small path lined with white-painted stones and rows of flowers. Finally, there were a lot of bell tents, supported by central poles, with their flaps rolled up to allow air to circulate, revealing iron bedsteads and untidy blankets and sheets hanging to the ground.

It took me some time before I realized that this distribution of dwellings indicated a precise social hierarchy. The older kibbutz members, who were usually married, occupied rooms in the two-story cement blocks. The unmarried young people and the new immigrants lived in groups of four or six to a tent, men and women separately. Some married newcomers occupied the crates in which they brought their own or their friend's furniture to Palestine, while less senior kibbutz members lived in the huts, two to a room if they were married, four if they were single. Near the top of the hill, a spot of green on one side surrounded the children's house. Separated from their parents, they enjoyed conditions of order and comfort far superior to those of their elders.

At the very top of the hill rose the water tower, under which were situated the post office, the auxiliary police guardroom, the infirmary, the administration office, and, at some distance, large huts used as a dining room, kitchen, and clothing store.

I had brought with me from Italy a small tent, quite welcome to the kibbutz administration since the bachelor quarters were overcrowded. They allotted me a small piece of ground between the infirmary and the showers and in this way, without knowing it, I excluded myself from the social hierarchy of the kibbutz habitat.

I learned my first lesson in collective life from the latrines and the showers. The latrines were easily identifiable in daytime by their kennel-like, elongated form and their wooden doors banging in the wind. By night they indicated their position by the smell of sewage mixed with the stronger and more acrid one of Lysol. Within these constructions, partitioned inside by jute curtains, crude wooden seats standing on the slatted floor permitted the free fall of metabolic products into the trench below. In a land where water and manure were in short supply, it was a logical and economical system. Next to the seats were containers for used paper. These primitive, smelly latrines, together with the showers, fulfilled a social-cultural function no less useful than their hygienic one. Since toilet paper was a luxury the kibbutz could not afford, everybody used old newspapers. The latrines thus turned into extemporary reading rooms with the help of crunched up pieces of publications reporting local and foreign events, some of them well in the past.

I soon learned to accumulate stocks of printed papers in French and English. Since I did not yet know Hebrew and could not find reading material in Italian, these scraps of old news added a dimension of intellectual relaxation to my bodily one and represented moments of comfort in the crudity of the situation. In these latrines I could offer my body, untrained for physical labor, moments of delightful relaxation for my aching muscles, while the bits of news I read without fear of being disturbed transformed themselves into a multiplicity of links with the external world. Through the jute partitions one could naturally perceive signs of the existence of other human beings nearby. But once one had latched the door on the inside one could feel absolute master of one's own space. Furthermore, because collectivism dominated almost all other aspects of life in the kibbutz, nobody in the latrines tried to violate the exclusive privacy of his neighbor by talking. If two people were walking together to this place of reflection engaged in a hot philosophical or political debate, they cut short their conversation as soon as they reached the latrine doors, as though every link between them had been suddenly severed. Compelled by bodily needs, secluded in wooden and jute cubicles, each one would find himself temporarily free from the communality that continuously shrouded him elsewhere in the kibbutz. In this thinking place, as happened to Luther, great ideas and hopes may have germinated. Here, in any case, sitting above the disinfected excrement, people felt free to sigh more deeply than in the silence of their nights. Here, having abstracted themselves for a while from group life, individuals could bare their bodies and souls without shame. Today no trace of these latrines remains, but I do not think it is possible to describe the atmosphere of those days without taking into account the role they played in the collective society of the time.

On the kibbutz showers much has been written. As far as I know, however, no one has stressed their social role as opposed to that of the latrines. The two institutions, located one in front of the other, one long and low, the other squat and high, acted as two poles of the same communal dynamo, energizing the entire community through a kind of point and counterpoint of promiscuity and privacy, of biological individualism and ideological collectivism.

One entered the showers after having abandoned one's dirty, sweaty working clothes in a wooden box on the veranda. With a towel draped around the hips, feet pushed into wooden clogs (I thought they were a Zionist invention until the day I found a pair in a bathroom in Berlin), one then teetered along toward the purifying water, carrying the soapbox, toothbrush, and the dental powder supplied by the kibbutz in one hand and, if one could afford it, a second towel slung over arm or shoulder.

The kibbutz showers were the daily scene of an important social rite, as much as a center of hygiene. Between five and six in the evening the entire population of the kibbutz changed through this rite from one of workers to one of intellectuals. This transformation reminded me of Machiavelli's letter to Francesco Vettori, which we had to learn by heart at school: "As the evening comes . . . on the threshold of my house I divest myself of my daytime wear, full of mud and dirt, and don royal, ceremonial robes." Here a similar but reverse ceremonial process was taking place: we shed our working clothes, "full of mud and dirt," and stood in Adamic dress under the steaming water, the women on one side of the wooden partition, the men on the other. The ambience was certainly not ideal for nurturing what Machiavelli called "that food which is only mine," namely one's philosophical and political writings. Yet it helped to strengthen the psychological tissue of an egalitarian society, which aspired to create a new man in an old land.

Naked as worms, but socialized, looking forward to an evening and a night free from the biblical curse of manual toil, we appreciated the shower as a powerful means of reinforcing the links of our proletarian brotherhood. Refreshed by water that everyone knew was precious, often warmed by ideological discussion, we lingered on the humid, slippery benches to talk politics while washing our feet; we exchanged quips and darting comments through the steam that blurred the contours of our bodies; and we dried away the dribbles of water on our skin, together with the tears that sometimes overflowed unseen from the depths of our hearts.

In this daily rite the hedonistic pleasure of ancient Greeks and Romans mingled with a modern desire to overcome our Freudian complexes. In the process there was also an attempt to align the different components of the elitist and egalitarian society of the kibbutz: the strong with the weak, the introvert with the extrovert, the ambitious with the humble. There was an implicit offer of familiarity that ceased at the threshold of the showers as one left, but that made it possible, inside them, to initiate difficult conversations, admit doubts, overcome timidity, feel defenseless without shame. From the showers one emerged clean in body and renewed in spirit, feeling the impalpable flux of ideas and hopes that later, in the dining room and the "House of Culture" (the room where books and current newspapers were available), turned into endless intellectual debates, ideological quarrels, military planning, and political conspiracies. It was in that complex, watery atmosphere that I sensed the possibility of becoming freer by giving up a part of my own freedom.

Looking today at photographs of forty or fifty years ago, which every kibbutz keeps in its archives, one wonders how these collective villages were able to undergo such radical changes in such a short time. Families today live in small apartments with one or two rooms for the children, well-furnished, often air-conditioned, with private showers and kitchenettes, full of more or less useful objects and gadgets produced locally or imported. The communal dining halls are often more elegant than those of a first-class hotel. The kitchens, totally automated and deodorized, equipped with the most modern labor-saving devices, are still visible from the dining room. But bars, little taverns, reading and music rooms, game clubs, and swimming pools shaded by trees and beautified by flowers are today an integral part of the normal standard of life of a collective village.

Nobody goes anymore to a common shower or latrine. Along the cement paths winding coquettishly through the mown grass, far from the workshops area and the smell of chicken runs and cow sheds, people walk or ride bicycles with the elegance and ease of an elite that has fully accepted its new status as a rich and secure class. Whether the kibbutz members are happier today than in the past I cannot say. Happiness is a state of the soul, not a function of the environment. Something has certainly been lost with the disappearance not of a certain austerity but of the tension created by the daily contrast between collective labor and individual freedom, conformism and rebellion. Machiavelli would not have been able or willing to live in a kibbutz, but he would have had no difficulty in understanding the political role of these free communities nor in identifying them as the most original, populist aristocracy of the modern world—an aristocracy without princes, still solid and active today in spite of incipient signs of corruption, social hardening, and ideological sclerosis. When I knew it, almost half a century ago, the kibbutz was still an enthusiastic experiment threatened by external dangers but consolidated inside by the austerity and moral standards of its members.

The physical and economic hardship of those days—work was barely sufficient to cover the subsistence needs of a community constantly increased by the arrival of new immigrants —was a spur to the vitality of the kibbutz. One of the strangest and liveliest discussions at which I happened to be present, for instance, was on the moral, philosophical, economic, and biological right of the community to fix the number of children a couple could have. This right was never conceded by the "comrades" to the general assembly, but the debate showed both the difficult, material conditions at the time and the honesty and intellectual rigor with which they were faced.

It seems to me that, denuded of its ideological elements and extemporary necessities, the principal strength of the kibbutz in that difficult period (and probably still today) was its capacity to bring together, behind an image of equality, people of profoundly varied capacities and cultures. The strongest personalities could lord it over the others without appearing to do so or bearing external signs of power; the weaker ones could accept the security offered by the group without feeling humiliated and without having to carry responsibilities for which they were unfit. But for people like myself, who stood in the middle because of their cultural mediocrity and ideological indifference, the collective life of the kibbutz had the attraction of a convent and the repulsion of a discipline deprived of style and spiritual tension. It seems to me, however, that the main reason why so many young people born and reared in the collective villages of Israel today leave them at the end of their military service is that biological links within a self-conceived elitist community are not sufficient to fill the need for new spiritual challenges or compensate for the moral and psychological void of a righteous conformism that has turned into an aim in itself. Thus, many young people who discover that they are not weak enough to identify with the group, nor strong enough to emerge within its façade of false equality, opt for the life of the town. The appeal of privacy and the lure of individual success often seems more attractive to them than the monotony of a disguised upper-class existence in which they have to share the results of their work without obtaining visible rewards for their ambitions.

Nobody I knew at Givat Brenner was more conscious of this tension to come, between idealism and reality, between image and content, between aspirations and daily realities, than Enzo Sereni. Sereni was born to one of the oldest Italian-Jewish families. On the Via Appia one can still see the remains of an ancient shop belonging to a certain Serenus. Possibly one of Sereni's ancestors, he may have sold wine and food to the Roman legionnaires on their way to Judea to put an end to Jewish independence in 67 A.D.

Sereni had come to Palestine at the end of the twenties with his wife, who also belonged to an old Roman-Jewish family, impelled by the same spirit of revolt against Fascism that had made his brother one of the historical leaders of Italian communism.

In Sereni a strong vein of religious passion also colored his philosophical rationalism. Alfonso Pacifici, one of the leaders of Italian Zionism and later an exponent of the strictest religious anti-Zionist orthodoxy in Israel, once told me that Sereni in his youth had gone through a profound religious crisis. He had confessed to Pacifici that he had been on the point of converting to Christianity because of the fascination monastic life exercised on him and his need for inner search. Anti-Fascism and the austerity of socialist Zionism had thus combined to attract him to the pioneering life of the kibbutz. There his political acumen, his socialist faith, and his witty realism made him not only the uncontested leader of the small group of Italian Jewish immigrants to Palestine but also one of the country's emerging labor leaders.

Small, plump, nearsighted, gifted with a sparkling intelligence and a monumental culture, Sereni did not at first sight convey the impression of being a political man. He looked rather like a schoolteacher, slightly inhibited in his movements and permanently uncomfortable in his clothes. He reminded me of the portrait of Silvio Pellico, the Risorgimento patriot imprisoned by the Austrians, whose diary we used to read aloud at school with much pathos and emotion. But as soon as Sereni opened his mouth, in public or in private, this romantic image disappeared, chased away by the immediate psychological tension he always created in his interlocutor. More than by the logic of his thesis, more than by his humanistic culture, one was fascinated by his humanism and his messianic vision of Zionist socialism. Compressed like a coil within a Greco-Christian mold, his Judaism possessed the passion, the rigor—but also the humor—of the neophyte. He himself drew, like Anteus from the earth, renewed strength from the daily contact with the awesome problems of constructing the new Hebrew society in Palestine.

Numerous books and articles have been written about Enzo Sereni. I feel disinclined to read them because of the remorse and sadness I still feel, after so many years, at having developed with him only relations tainted by antagonism. A more serious and deeper contact with this extraordinary person would certainly have enriched me and perhaps changed the course of my life. In part, however, my reluctance to know more about him is due to my desire not to spoil the image—certainly excessively personal—that I have constructed of him and that is so different from the one described in these publications. It is the image of a prism, exposed to the ever-changing realities of a very complex life and reflecting onto others the disconcerting light of an ambiguous personality. This is, as I said, a very personal and probably wrong impression, which I have carried with me since the only occasion I had to talk with him at length, without quarreling or having to listen in enraged silence (because of feelings of inferiority he always induced in me) to his scintillating ideological harangues and his, to me, irritating ideas.

I had recently arrived at Givat Brenner. During the New Year holiday a fit of nostalgia induced me to look for a place where I could attend a service as we did in Italy. I found myself sitting next to Sereni one late afternoon near a wooden shack, which served as kitchen and synagogue for the elderly parents of kibbutz members. They were a small group of decrepit people who, unlike their children, continued to follow the "superstitions" of Judaism and for this reason had permission to cook in a separate kitchen according to biblical dietary rules.

It was sunset, a time that, especially in those circumstances, invited melancholy reflections. We were waiting for the arrival of a few more Jews to make up a minyan for the recital of the evening prayers. Sitting on a wobbly bench outside the shack, with an old Jewish *babushka* wrapped in her Eastern European clothes peering suspiciously at our uncovered heads, we were talking in our native language, trying not to disturb a few old men reciting psalms nearby. All around us, the kibbutz activity, barely reduced because of the holiday, gave us a feeling of temporary exclusion.

Sad and thoughtful, not in his usual optimistic mood, Sereni was quietly thinking aloud about the incumbent tragedy of European Jewry. He had been on a mission to Germany, and only his Italian passport had saved him from trouble. Anticipating the disaster that was about to overtake our people, he felt the immense responsibility that we, the Jews of Palestine, bore for the rest of the nation. He was asking me, or rather he was asking himself in a monologue that I dared not interrupt, in what way we might associate ourselves with the fate of millions of humans trapped by the Nazis in Europe only because they were Jews. It was true that they had not believed in the Zionist message; it was true that they were now paying the atrocious price of their social choices and lack of decision. But we, wiser, cleverer, or just more fortunate, were, in our turn, in danger of becoming the parasites of our national tragedy by remaining spectators of their destruction. What could we tell our sons in the future? That because we were protected by the British we had been able to survive in order to record what European anti-Semitism had done to the Jews? In that case there was a good chance of our young people regarding Hitler and Mussolini just as historical figures detached from reality like Genghis Khan. They might think that our fate was that of just another people, descendants of a race whose destiny was changed by the simple fact that their parents had emigrated to Asia, just as English criminals were deported to Australia, or like the Spanish conquistadores who had gone to America. If we became unable to teach them the meaning of Judaism, they would never really know why their parents were called Zionists.

The working hypothesis of many Zionists was no different from that of the assimilationists, who thought that there was an excess of Jews in the world and an excess of tradition in Judaism. But if the body of the nation was going to be physically destroyed in Europe and if the ancient soul was to become dried up by the passions of the non-Jewish ideologies, what would remain of the fragile Jewish civilization that we wanted to revive? The secularism of socialist Zionism made him fear the creation of ghettos, of Indian-type reservations for the religious Jews in a Hebrew Palestine, in which people would be the object of ethnological curiosity rather than the guardians of one of the most ancient national identities.

In those days Sereni was engaged in an effort of persuasion with the new immigrants from Italy, some of whom wanted to leave Givat Brenner, convinced that life in a socialist kibbutz was a new form of assimilation—a society of Jews who had intentionally ceased to be Jewish. For these newcomers, who were assimilated Jews like me, and mostly former members of the GUF (Fascist university youth), the racial laws proclaimed by Mussolini had brought a sudden need to emigrate and an incentive to search, in Palestine, for the ancient roots practically destroyed by the emancipation for most of the Italian Israelites. They had not yet decided to move to a religious kibbutz, as many of them later did, but Sereni could feel, through the often confused expression of their doubts, that the national-Marxist alternative they offered the socialist movement, and to which he had devoted all his strength and intelligence, could not meet their spiritual needs. He was not interested in gaining more "souls" for his party, being satisfied that these Italian Jews had taken, through their immigration to the ancestral land, the first essential step on the road to "Zionist" truth. What seemed important to him was to convince himself that the ideological road he had chosen was not an erroneous one, that it would not lead some time in the future to a dead end through the creation of a new Jewish Golah (Diaspora) in the Land of Israel.

On the eve of that religious festival, near that decrepit synagogue which, as I said, also served as kitchen and dining room for a miserable bunch of human relics escaped from the moribund ghettos of Eastern Europe and whose sole apparent link with the kibbutz was their biological relationship with some of its members, Sereni argued with himself about the problems that would one day obsess the Zionist state, namely whether the state of the Jews would be able to remain a Jewish state without losing the pluralism that constituted its strength. He was asking himself whether the price of national rebirth might not be paid with the destruction of a traditional collective consciousness, which we would one day increasingly need so that the Land of Israel did not become a land of refuge instead of the promised socialist land. This was, I believe, the first time I heard anyone formulate the idea that the Zionists represented for Judaism what the barbarians had represented for Roman civilization: an instrument of physical regeneration through a process of moral barbarization; a forced passage into normality in order to recover the strength necessary to defend one's uniqueness in a world bent on destroying that embarrassing uniqueness. He hoped, though he did not seem very convinced, that this role could be undertaken by Zionist socialism. He conceived of it like the roots of an old tree from which new shoots of hope, of social and moral progress, would spring up, and not only for the Jews. Jewish socialism, unlike Soviet Marxism and Fascist nationalism, in which Sereni could nevertheless see certain similarities with Zionism, might one day develop the energy of both. It could become, in his view, what Mazzini's version of the Italian Risorgimento had failed to be: a national faith conceived on the basis of man's duties, not of rights; a new approach to old problems; the transformation of the weakness of an ancient race into a new, civilizing force.

The workshop in which this new moral and collective movement should be forged could only be, for him, the kibbutz. But it would not be easy to make the Jewish refugees from Europe, brought to Palestine less by idealism than by the need to escape anti-Semitism, understand that the kibbutz was a kind of new, secular monastery through which the old-new Israel could face the challenges of destruction and rebirth. It would take time, and time was running dramatically short.

I had the impression that afternoon of listening to the abbot of a not-yet-founded monastery, the inspirer of a new monastic order who would have liked to transform Givat Brenner into a Jewish Monte Cassino or a Hebrew Abbey of Cluny. I never had another opportunity to check whether this impression was correct or not. Absorbed as we both became, he in the vortex of political action, I in my romantic dreams, we only had brief and unpleasant occasions to meet afterward. From these encounters I got the impression, probably wrong, that Sereni had developed unfair, preconceived ideas about me. I felt that he despised me for my refusal to remain in the kibbutz and for my emotional attachment to a bourgeois world from which I was still unable to free myself. Among the new Italian immigrants at Givat Brenner, I must have seemed to him the least prepared and the most immature. My ignorance never ceased to astound him. When seated on the grass in front of the "House of Culture," he used to lecture us on socialism, speaking about Labriola and Lasalle, Marx and

Rosa Luxemburg, Engels and Lenin; he could see from the expression on my face how strange and meaningless these names were to me.

He used to explain on those occasions the evolution of the labor movement in Palestine, the moral and political problems created by our coexistence with the Arabs, and—a topic I remember more clearly than the others—the illegitimacy of commercial competition. "We cannot have peace in the world," he argued, "if even we socialists pray for frosts to destroy the orange crops of Spain in order to survive in Palestine." He would then throw himself into complicated explanations on the questions of worker exploitation; of *plus valorem;* on the capitalists who had taken the place of the feudal lords; on the Arab landowners who, without being bourgeois, were assuming in Palestine the historical and political role of the European bourgeoisie; on the British who were liberals at home and imperialists abroad; on the Fascists who, with their secret agents, were trying to persuade the Arabs to support their late colonial expansionism.

I listened to him, often without understanding a word of what he said. The other Italians competed among themselves with questions and comments to prove they knew the texts on which Sereni was speaking and could follow him in his historical and dialectical intellectual games. I kept apart, silent, totally lost and confused, filled with the rancor of the ignorant who would like to discuss something he does not know. At the time I was unaware of the fact that no intellectual and moral idea is more useless than the one offered by others to free one from his doubts. In a confused way I perceived that there was something false, uncertain, unclear in all this verbiage about absolute social values, brotherhood of workers, superstructures, conscious and unconscious complexes, historical materialism, and national myth. It was enough to see how Jews spoke to and looked at the few Arabs who came to the kibbutz to understand that human relations could not be easily categorized. But I could find neither the words nor the ideas to refute them. To my Italian kibbutz comrades, as probably to Sereni, I must have appeared a superficial, aimless youth, reared in an atmosphere politically and socially perverted, who needed to have his "dog's legs straightened," as the Italians say, and his character reinforced by ideological discipline and hard physical work, two things from which, as everyone knew, I intended to escape. In sum, I was, or at least I had the impression of being, a lost cause, on which others in the kibbutz had neither reason nor desire to waste their time. The kibbutz was doing me a favor by letting me pay three pounds a month (a considerable sum in those days) for my food, a daily Hebrew lesson, and four hours of work in the chicken run and, later, in the vegetable garden.

The isolation caused by my violent transplantation into a society so different from that in which I had grown up became deeper day by day because of the indifference and imaginary ostracism with which I felt I was surrounded. When I returned at dusk to my tent, so low that it looked like a dog's kennel (and indeed, I did once find a large bone at the entrance), I was torn by opposing sentiments. I wanted at the same time to adapt myself and to run away from the new society in which I was living. I suffered atrociously because of my ignorance, which made me look childish in front of the others, while possessing an instinctive, animal perception that the perfection of the ideological systems to which I was asked to adhere contained invisible flaws. The less I was able to analyze Sereni's arguments, the more indigestible they were made by these contradictions. I had the constant impression of taking part in a play of the absurd from which I tried to escape, mocking everything I did not understand. The result was a split in my psyche soon manifested by a stutter, which I tried to overcome by going into the fields to declaim Italian poems by Carducci at the top of my voice, or, after I joined the British army, by shouting army commands out loud.

The state of anguish to which this stammering was linked has not yet disappeared. I often find myself speaking aloud to myself or underlining my thoughts with vulgar barracks oaths that I murmur under my breath, hoping nobody will overhear. A difficulty in expressing myself also overtakes me when I have to speak in public, especially in Hebrew. Perfectly normal, my psychologist friends keep telling me. Yet I cannot conceal the fact that the need to repair a crack in my young personality has driven me, and still drives me, to try to find compensation in action for my spiritual and cultural needs. In this prolonged debate with myself, the lure of activism has certainly interfered with an orderly crystallization of habits and a more meaningful accumulation of experience. As a result, I have found myself for years fighting against another, imaginary self, who refuses to accept the realities of life and age and succumbs to the fascination of adventure and change. The dichotomy between my two selves has often made me appear to others and to myself as a bluffer, a "seller of smoke" as we say in Italian, even when time and events have proved me right.

Today I know that my mistake has been to try to force events prematurely, to try to realize projects for which I was not morally prepared or intellectually and culturally ready, though I do not regret that, having just one man's span of life to live, I have tasted many lives. But I also know that this impatience with timetables and realities, this need to overdo things, this passion for change and adventure, is not peculiar to me. It is characteristic of the whole Zionist movement and of the State of Israel, in which, pressed by necessity and inexperience, people have wanted to achieve too much too fast and without being prepared or willing to pay the price that time imposes for what is done without it.

Perhaps there was no other alternative for the Jews of Palestine who survived the Holocaust. The Jewish population, writer S.Y. Agnon makes one of his heroes say, "has suffered

so much that it has lost the patience to wait for the Messiah."
The result, according to Agnon, has been that in the attempt
to build up its own messianic era, the people of Israel have
postponed the arrival of the Messiah. This poetic interpretation
seems to me an appropriate description of the socialist Zionist
epic I witnessed and which is in a way reflected in my own
experience. The price we all seem to be paying today in Israel
is that of an unsuccessful attempt to catch the Messiah by force.
Yet without this arrogant effort, our drama would have turned
into banality, a situation in which Jews have never particularly
liked to be.

After almost a hundred years, Zionism, a movement supposedly meant to "normalize" the Jew, continues to struggle
between exile and the promised land, between the Holocaust
and Hitler, between the vulgar and the sublime, without
finding a middle path—the path that Maimonides called
"golden" and that a famous Hasidic rabbi, the Rabbi of Kotch,
"reserved for horses." The break between the real and the
fantastic, the possible and the impossible, the serious and the
fake, which caused me such great pain in conditioning my
character, seems to me today to be part of a larger situation,
a reflection of an inescapable condition, a manner no less
genuine than others of ultimately sharing the singular fate of
the people to whom I belong.

Now that passions and ambitions have been put to rest by
age, success, and disappointments, I feel at ease with the fact
of having felt, probably earlier than others, in exile in the
motherland to which I had chosen to return. I am no longer
alone in realizing that the State of Israel—a natural but imper-
fect incarnation of a splendid ideal—has transformed itself into
one of the many Jewish Diasporas, morally distant from, even
if physically closer to, the historical and cultural cradle of
Jewish civilization. Partly because my familiarity with Italian
fascism has immunized me against the more vulgar and grotesque manifestations of Israeli nationalism (which, like the

Italian ones, I know to be the transitory and infantile maladies of an ancient people), I am able today to taste the sweetness that a hard, exciting, contradictory experience offers to people like me: the opportunity to make of the art of living—for lack of other talents—a living *commedia del l'arte*.

6.

Smell and Fear

For a long time my relations with other Italian Jewish immigrants to Palestine were determined by my stomach. Even today, when I think back to this period of my existence as a young immigrant, I can clearly recall the smell of the kitchens in the houses that hosted me, the boredom of the conversation and of the prayers that I had to bear before and after meals in order to satisfy my appetite, the irritation that I had difficulty in concealing from those hosts who did not realize rapidly enough the reason for my visit. Two kitchens, however, never attracted me: that of the various kibbutzim in which I happened to stay and that of Mrs. Levi in Tel Aviv—but this was for completely different reasons.

The kibbutz kitchens at that time dished out plates of glued-together spaghetti, probably invented by admirers of the Borgias. They sweetened their poisonous food with vanilla-scented sauce, which I always thought was the product of a sublimation of Jewish suicidal complexes. Meat, in that first year of the war, was rare. Potatoes, which Palestine had just learned to grow, were scarce. However, semolina, olives, and tomatoes were plentiful. Together with slices of black bread spread with margarine and jam, they helped to stay the pangs but left the mouth dry and the stomach empty.

Mrs. Levi's kitchen, on the contrary, offered dishes that had nothing in common with those of the kibbutz. But they were so expensive that it was impossible for me to enjoy them. I still feel melancholic when I remember the hours of unsatisfied hunger I spent in her ground-floor apartment on Karl Netter Street, a street in the heart of Tel Aviv, short and silent even today, and which acted in those years as a welcome harbor for many Jews who had escaped from Italy.

Mrs. Levi was a widow. In 1939 when I first met her, she could not have been very old because one of her sons was still at school. To me, however, she looked decrepit: small, slim, with an angular face, she possessed a shrill, metallic voice that struck fear in my heart. Always dressed in black, tidy, and with a carefully made-up chignon on her head, she seemed to me like the incarnation of a lady director of a reform school. She never offered me anything to eat but showered me with compliments. She had known my mother in her best years, and she used to describe to me her beauty, her grace, and above all her wealth, which had all but vanished. Mrs. Levi, who knew personally almost every Italian Jew in Palestine and a considerable number of those who had stayed in Italy, seemed curiously ignorant of the economic situation of my family. She kept addressing me as though I were an affluent immigrant, impressing upon me, in her own way, my duty not to forget my past. She showed great interest in my agricultural studies, about which she spoke with the respect due to an already famous researcher. In her dining room there was a sofa under a bay window, on which she ceremoniously used to invite me to sit down and accept a lemonade or a small cup of coffee. On these occasions she entertained me with mannered conversation about how painful and unusual it was for her to keep a pension. But she carried on with a dignity that did not allow concessions, economizing on every possible expense but maintaining a culinary standard that on the only two occasions I scraped up enough money to appreciate it, seemed to me miraculous when compared with that of the restaurants I normally frequented. Among my acquaintances she was the only one to assure me that I would certainly reach the top of my military career when I told her of my intention to join the army. She proved wrong, as in most of her other judgments concerning me and my family, but that prognosis at the time gave me tremendous pleasure.

Mrs. Levi had two children. The younger one became in time a respected member of the kibbutz movement and later a teacher of social sciences. The older one, a graduate in agriculture, possessed great talents as a musicologist and a journalist but was destined to suffer increasingly from mental troubles, which finally ruined his splendid brain. At the time his occasionally queer behavior had already marked him as an eccentric among the Italian Zionists.

Many stories circulated on his account. In June 1940, when the British arrested as enemy aliens, for short or long periods, any holder of an Italian passport, this Levi found himself deposited by the British police in the central prison of Jaffa. The place was far from pleasant, but Mr. Levi was shocked mainly by the fact that some of his best friends were missing. He gave the British a detailed list of the people with whom he wanted to share his bedroom, and they were only too pleased to oblige. No wonder that some of these friends remained cool toward him for a long time to come.

Years earlier Mr. Levi had also been imprisoned in the Turin jail on suspicion of being an active anti-Fascist. On that occasion he created some notoriety because of his beard. He had started by refusing the services of the prison barber who had come to shave him on the Sabbath, a day on which, he rightly claimed, Jews do not shave. This happened in September, a

month in which the second visit of the barber brought no
result, because Mr. Levi, calendar in hand, proved to him that
it was not permitted for a Jew to shave on the two days of
the New Year, which fell just then. The director of the jail
himself, so the story went, summoned Mr. Levi to his office
in order to reach an agreed date when, according to the
Gregorian calendar, there were no religious Jewish obstacles to
the barber's working. Mr. Levi gracefully chose one day, but
when the appointed time arrived, again refused to be shaved.
"A Jew," he argued with reason and conviction, "is never
allowed to shave."

At the agricultural school of Mikveh Yisrael, where I
started to study, Mr. Levi acted as instructor, political commissar, educator, and confessor to a group of religious Italian boys
brought to Palestine by the Youth Aliyah, the youth section
of the Jewish Agency. With these youngsters, we students who
had enrolled privately in the school and paid full fees for our
studies and keep, had few contacts. They lived in huge dor-
mitories located over the kitchen. We lived four to a room
on top of the granaries and the oil press of the school farm in
the French colonial style buildings constructed at the end of
the last century. They followed a strict religious discipline; we
enjoyed the free life of unbelievers. They were all destined to
join a kibbutz; we were free to dream of any future activity
or career we might choose. We met in classrooms where we
shared some of the lessons, in the fields where we worked and,
from time to time, on Friday evenings when I used to join
them in the school synagogue. I liked the cozy atmosphere of
that old building, also in French colonial style, with its red and
blue painted ceiling, its stained-glass windows and the marble
slabs in the wall commemorating benefactors and fallen students.

But in general the two groups kept apart, also because the
quarters of the "private" students were divided according to
secular party affiliations. I had chosen to sleep in the quarters

of the General Zionist party because it was the political movement that required the least ideological involvement. The
immediate result of my political choice turned out to be the
stealing of my wallet with many personal mementos I had
brought from home. It was quite a shock, for which the lack
of obligation to attend long, boring political meetings never
fully compensated. The long-term result of this choice was that
I became as separate from the most active elements in the
school as—for reasons of college snobbery—from the Italian
boys belonging to the religious movement. With these estranged schoolfellows one of my only links was our common
fight against bugs, about which we exchanged daily information. We were never completely victorious in spite of the huge
quantities of petrol we sprinkled over our straw mattresses and
the empty bully-beef tins full of kerosene in which we put the
legs of our beds.

Mr. Levi was conscious and resentful of this "class" distinction. Every time we passed each other on the school grounds,
he made pointed remarks about my feudal attitude and that of
my roommates. Sometimes he would sit with me under the
trees that surrounded the grave of the school's founder, Karl
Netter, the father of Jewish agriculture in Palestine. The cenotaph dedicated to him and two little boys who had died,
apparently of typhoid, in the 1880s stood in the middle of
cascades of bougainvillea at the heart of a eucalyptus grove.
The sandy path leading to it seemed to go to the end of the
world: here, silence was broken only by the buzzing of insects,
by the whirring of birds' wings, by the faraway braying of
unseen donkeys, by the rustling of the leaves in a subdued
symphony of nature's orchestra. We used to sit on the base of
the cenotaph and talk quietly with long, silent pauses. I do not
remember what we talked about, and I do not think his
arguments impressed me particularly. But thinking back to
those meetings, so different from those I had later with Pavese,
the great Piedmontese writer, sitting on the slopes of the hills

of Turin, I cannot help being struck by how similar they were, too. I was introduced to Pavese by Professor Monti, an outstanding figure of the Italian resistance movement, soon after my demobilization from the British army. As with Mr. Levi in Palestine, I went on talking for hours in Italy with Pavese about war and God, women and religion, democracy and anti-Fascism, the false hopes the war had raised, and the anguish of people like us, who witnessed the passing of history without being able to take part in the realities borne out in our dreams.

In both cases—with Levi and Pavese—I was struck by the frustrations of two brilliant minds, so different from each other but equally unable to express their talents in the ways they would have liked. Pavese committed suicide; Levi ended up in a psychiatric hospital, where the brightness of his mind slowly dimmed into paranoia. Pavese reacted against the banality of life with the sadness of his writing; Levi brought the impatience of his mind into collision with the inertia of daily life and sought notoriety with clownish actions and eccentricities.

One of the stories, probably apocryphal, that was told about him, concerned his collaboration with a cabalist determined to hasten the coming of the Messiah. This rabbi had conceived a plan to sacrifice an animal on a certain day and in a particular spot in the Holy Land. According to his cabalistic calculations, the sacrifice should take place at dawn and the blood of the animal should be sprinkled on the top of a deserted hill located in the middle of an Arab zone where it would not be safe for Jews to go. The solution was found with the help of a small airplane and the substitution of a strong cock for the sacrificial camel. Mr. Levi was charged to perform the ritual slaughter, while the rabbi coordinated time and space according to his mystical signs. Mr. Levi, however, delayed the arrival of the Messiah by his inability to overcome the reaction of the cock, which refused to keep quiet in the small hired plane, insensitive to the exhortations of the rabbi who, in despair, kept comparing his map with the flight plan of the impassive British pilot. As I said, the story was probably apocryphal, but Mr. Levi's extravagances turned into legends with the passing of time. I witnessed only one of his eccentricities.

On a cold winter's day I went to pay him a visit in the small hut that served as home and workshop for making *grissini*. The hut stood in the outskirts of the town of Ramat Gan, now part of greater Tel Aviv but then separated from the city by a few kilometers of open ground. The idea of introducing this delicate type of Piedmontese bread into the pioneering Jewish society of the time and in the midst of war rationing came from Levi's wife. With her already large family, she was struggling hard to make ends meet by all sorts of activities, among which her handmade bricks were not the most successful. The production of *grissini* was also imperiled at the outset by the smell of petrol acquired in the process of baking them in an improperly functioning oven. The day I went to visit them, the two Levis were about to leave for Tel Aviv, using their children's pram as a means of transport. Mr. Levi, on the basis of his mathematical calculations, had persuaded his wife they could both reach the city with less fatigue if they took turns sitting in the pram and pushing the other along. I saw them leaving on this commercial journey, he with his black beard floating in the wind, his sandaled feet protruding from the pram and the packets of *grissini* in his lap; she, with dignity and energy, pushing the vehicle almost collapsing under the weight, followed by the stupefied eyes of the passersby.

In Ramat Gan there lived a group of Italian Jews whose behavior was the very opposite of the Levis. With few exceptions they had all been members of the Fascist party, out of inertia rather than conviction. This was not their main characteristic. What distinguished them within the Jewish society of the time was the care with which they preserved, in a pioneering socialist country, the life-style of provincial Italian bourgeoisie.

Most had immigrated to Palestine with means, and those who lacked them quickly enriched themselves in the burgeoning war economy and later in the rapid development of a society to which they contributed with hard work. Their numerous sons and daughters participated in the subsequent military conflicts with the Arabs. In their homes, full of solid furniture, bibelots, miniatures, lace runners, and fine tablecloths, there prevailed the same ordered and cautious atmosphere one would find in Venice or Florence: a patriotic mood, devoid of ideology but full of suspicious respect for the establishment. Industrious but mean, dignified but inelegant, they were proud of their newly acquired status of anti-Fascists but strongly attached to the class prejudices that had contributed to the rise in Italy of a regime against which they had never fought. They were boring and banal people, entrenched behind religious rites, concealing a profound ignorance of Judaism; they had transformed the Italian synagogue service into a kind of clannish bond and sign of social distinction. Moderate in every way, from the love of food to political passions, they were happy to have found in Zionism the solution to the problem of their own physical survival and of their own spiritual anemia. Listening to their chatter at the kiddush parties after the conclusion of the Sabbath service in one of their beautiful homes, I wondered how they managed to share in a double, contrasting process of assimilation: that of Italian nationalism, which had betrayed them, and that of the new society of Palestine, which was now called upon to absorb the remnants of a moribund Jewry together with its folklore and liturgy. The result was a switch from one nationalism to another with the same prejudices—the romantic patriotism and the social conformism that they had brought from Italy.

In this minuscule, pretentious, prudent Ramat Gan society I felt at ease only with a Milanese family of Greek origin. Deprived of their own children, they adopted any young person in need of permanent or temporary shelter. At their table, even when their tight budget forced them to cut back the portions, I always satisfied my hunger without shame. In that house I also learned to appreciate, not just understand, the meaning of the blessing for what I had received; I spent here the least sad vacations from school and army. Here I gave free vent, without fear of being laughed at, to my dreams, my hopes, my pains, always finding a comfortable bed, a hot shower, and a clean towel. Only those who have known the pangs of hunger and social uprooting, the shame of a dirty shirt in the middle of well-dressed people, the sleepless rest on a bed without mattress or sheets, the shivers of an icy shower in winter and the thirst of a summer without shade can appreciate a hospitality offered without reservation, understand the longevity of resentment, unjust in my case, borne from help not received because I was too proud and too shy to ask for it.

The house of this Italian-Greek family was built on a small hill, now completely devoured by city blocks, on which a mulberry tree proudly stood for many years. Sitting under its branches in the heat of a summer Sabbath, I would often see a strange person crossing the street below me to enter a wooden hut used as a synagogue. He was a young man in his twenties, tall and suntanned. He wore his hair shoulder length and a long, dirty, white shirt outside his trousers, torn at the hem. He was called the "Messiah" because of his blue, watery eyes looking into infinity and a queer behavior that made him seem like a harmless lunatic. One day, in the middle of the war, he disappeared. Some people said he had been arrested by the British, who had discovered him to be a dangerous terrorist. Others said that he had been run over by a car; others that he had been confined to a mental hospital. In any case, as long as he roamed around in the Ramat Gan streets he attracted me with a strange, inexplicable force.

He was certainly mad. But he shared, or rather epitomized, a type of madness that in various forms circulated during those years like a collective narcotic in the veins of most of the Jews of Palestine. Like them, the "Messiah" seemed touched by a kind of apocalyptic mania. The war that was tearing the world apart was that of Gog and Magog. The Jewish tragedy, of which all the horrors were not yet known, looked like a divine punishment for the assimilation of the Jews to the political and social idolatry of Europe. The White Paper with which the British shut the doors on Jewish immigration and tried to put an end to the hopes of the Zionist movement was a devilish plan; it would eventually be thwarted but at the same time should also be taken as a heavenly warning to the Jews not to misbehave. To the "Messiah," as to many orthodox Jews, misconduct meant the substitution of secular ideology for the Covenant with God, the replacement by human political pride of confidence in Divine Providence. Whatever happened, he preached, the Land of Israel would always remain the land from which God "never turned away His eyes." The faithful Jews, those who—in his words—formed "the personal body-guard of the King of the Universe, Blessed be His Name," would overcome all tests and eventually witness the great portents to come.

England was the ultimate Rome, the "unclean beast" destined to die. The Arabs were the enemy brother. Jews must struggle with them not out of hatred but with understanding of the mysterious fate, decided upon in heaven and linking forever the descendants of Isaac and Ishmael, of Jacob and Esau. In every generation, Jews and Arabs would battle for a common heritage, which made difficult, if not impossible, their coexistence in the same territory.

Seated on a shaky bench with peeling paint, his back against the tar-papered wall of the synagogue hut, the "Messiah" threw himself into dissertations of metapolitics, always starting from a particular problem of Talmudic casuistry—for instance, whether it was permitted to tie a knot on the Sabbath using the fingers of both hands. From this type of question, for me totally unreal, the "Messiah" went on to discuss—with

arguments supported sometimes by the simple displacement of
a syllable in a word from the Bible—the duties of man toward
animals or the responsibility of the citizen toward the state. I
had the impression of standing in front of a political conspira-
tor disguised as a dervish or a prophet's apprentice. His face,
surrounded by a thick black beard, turned livid and tense. As
he developed his ideas, it looked as though all his blood and
the energy of his muscles concentrated on an invisible point
of his interior passion. His long-lashed eyelids closed to a slit.
From his pupils a sharp, manic gleam darted out, more expres-
sive and frightening than any words. It was the look of a
tortured, possessed man, detached from the world and at the
same time fully conscious of its existence and totally involved
in its reality. A world in which the substance of the body and
the substance of the soul—so the "Messiah" explained—were
mysteriously joined at their base and their apex with the
substance of worlds different from but no less consistent than
ours. Man was the crossing point of these invisible junctions
that determined the existence of everything in creation. Man
could exist only because the Divine has in a way withdrawn
into Himself and "left open" a space for His creatures. Only
many years later I realized that the "Messiah" was drawing his
theories from the Kabbalah. But what I was witnessing then
was the running of trickles of ancient, esoteric Jewish thought
over the seeds of political messianism, which in time would
grow and cover an increased portion of the ground of secular
socialist Zionism.

In those first years of war there were no Jewish political
successes that would justify the slightest optimism. Everything
in Europe and in Palestine seemed to be militating against the
establishment of a Jewish national home. It was only natural
that in a politicized society like the Yishuv, the Jewish community of Palestine, there began to circulate ideas of national
religious mysticism which, forty years later, would openly
challenge the legitimacy of secular Zionism.

To this possibility, of course, I never gave a thought. Nor did I understand the meaning of certain news items appearing in the papers and relating to the activities of "fanatical Jews." They were ready, the papers said, to collaborate with the Nazis in order to destroy the British mandatory power, because it had cynically shut the doors of Palestine in the face of desperate Jewish refugees fleeing from Europe. I did not understand why "religious madmen" were joining with "secular bandits" —as the papers said—to reject the authority of the Zionist national institutions and throw themselves into "insane and irresponsible" terrorism against the British government and the Arabs. But in fact I also cared very little about it. So that when I read in 1942 (I had already been in the army for a year) that a certain Abraham Stern, a student of the Hebrew University of Jerusalem, had been killed by the British after having carried out many acts of banditry, I paid no attention to this news. I certainly did not connect it—an event that looked to me like a plain criminal act—with that Jewish resistance movement which, a few years later, would challenge and jeopardize British rule in Palestine.

The "Messiah" was probably affiliated with some of these new secret sects. When he suddenly disappeared, strange things were told about him. But neither these rumors nor the political ideas I heard him propound in the little synagogue in Ramat Gan had any impact on me. Quite the contrary. I was only struck by his theories on angels and devils which, according to him, each of us creates with his own acts and thoughts, sacred or profane.

In some of my waking dreams I witnessed, impotent and terrified, the furious dances of the beings I kept generating with my words and my fantasies, my fears and my repressed ambitions. The angels were few and looked quite feeble; the devils, however, deafened me with their shrieking cries, their accusations of cowardice, and their denunciation of my indifference to the convulsions of our burning world. During these nightmares I had the impression of levitating over masses of tears and blood; they suddenly transformed themselves into papier-mâché figures, similar to the Doré illustrations of Dante's *Inferno* that my father kept locked up in his library. Chased by devils and steered by angels, I floated like a kite on the current of my dream, diving suddenly toward the world of humans, which appeared to me like a succession of sharp edges and pointed angles. All around me people who had called for my help were turning their backs to me, moving away in orderly and disciplined ranks toward a labyrinth of faiths and opinions, of passions and interests, the access to which was closed to me. I saw clusters of people passing by without looking at me, old schoolmates dressed in Fascist Youth uniforms and new comrades from the kibbutz in British military garb. I called them by name, but they did not seem to hear; when they opened their mouths, I did not understand what they were shouting at me. I was standing alone, kept waiting without explanation. Then suddenly I felt condemned by the voice of the "Messiah," who proclaimed that observance of eighty percent of the Sabbath was equivalent to desecration of the Sabbath; or by the voice of a tutor at the agricultural school, who explained why joining the British army was an act of concealed prostitution; or by the voice of the driver who had picked me up at Tel Aviv Port, now murmuring that there was no salvation in political compromise. It was not only a question of nightmares. For someone like me, freshly arrived from a world of compromises and social conformism, the strange behavior of the "Messiah" and the less extravagant but equally rigid behavior of many other people seemed like a spasmodic effort to keep action perpetually aligned on radical ideology.

Nowhere was this more true than at the crossing of Rothschild Boulevard and Allenby Street in Tel Aviv, where I sometimes stopped to buy a glass of orange juice at a kiosk and where one could hear in the street the arguments overflowing from the open terrace of the nearby Café Atara. This was a meeting place of well-dressed gentlemen and shirtsleeved activists. They discussed the future of the world at the tops of their voices in German, Polish, English, and Hebrew, sipping tea and iced coffee. They knew everything, predicted everything, had a ready-made, authoritative, logical answer to every question. They were all prophets, issuing verdicts out of personal beliefs and individual ignorance without listening to other people's arguments.

They were not alone. Discussions of this type often kept me awake all night when, lying on the prickly straw palliasse of my bed, I could hear the aggressive statements of my roommates or those in the adjoining rooms. They went on for hours, usually without reaching agreement: every speaker had his own ideas on how to defend the Jewish people, how to contribute to the war effort, how to win over capitalists to Marxism, how to deal with the Arabs, how to convert the British to the idea of a Jewish state, how to exploit the need of the Allies for our cooperation, how to create a new type of Jew in Palestine.

I found myself immersed in the oppressive climate of these unending discussions without feeling part of them, without sharing in the tension created by continually opposed beliefs, personalities, and cultures. I knew that I should feel involved, if for no other reason than the fact that my family in Italy was by now entangled in the tragedy of the Jewish people. But these impassioned speeches contrasted not only with the memories of the padded world from which I had come but also with the boring routine of agricultural college life, regulated by the sound of the school bell. It woke us up at a quarter of six in the morning and called us to class at eight. It gathered us, famished, at noon in the dining room, dispersed us, lazily, in the afternoon to work in the fields, and invited us to silence at ten at night. That was the time when many of us started talking to ourselves.

The nights I still vividly remember were all made up of skies dotted with stars. A velvety obscurity, refreshed by breezes, caressed my face. The rustle of the eucalypti was broken by the howls of jackals; the sound of a nearby harmonica contrasted sometimes with the call of muezzins from the minarets of Jaffa.

On those nights, when melancholy memories and the pain of work-stiffened muscles joined to make sleep difficult, my mind swung undecided from the knots that could or could not be tied on the Sabbath to the horses I had ridden on the Sabbath in the green fields of Piedmont; from the bullets that we could or could not fire according to the Jewish principle of self-restraint in the case of an Arab attack to my dog Bizir, who was sent to guard my uncle's home in Trieste in the wake of my father's bankruptcy. In those nights I felt my personal dilemma—the inability to forget my past, accept without reservation the present while dreaming of an impossible future —becoming acute and confused. I searched in vain for success among contrasting loyalties, for an escape from our college routine through the uncertain fortunes of war. At the same time I craved for a corner where weeping was honorable, for plains on which to ride silvery steeds. I dreamed of being lulled by the hands of beautiful women, of facing imaginary enemies dressed in full armor, of declaiming patriotic poems in Italian without feeling ridiculous, of playing again with my dog without the constraints of a fatherland, a family, a flag. I dreamed of being asleep for the rest of my life, next to my mother dressed in her red evening gown, the big silk rose on her bosom, her neck adorned by three strings of pearls, with the rest of humanity, the good and the bad, the Jews and the goyim, the living and the dead, evaporated into the air.

During those nights when, perturbed to tears, I got up from my palliasse and sat on the parapet at the top of the granary, I chanced to meet a modest schoolmate one year older than myself. He used to read his poems to me. They were in Hebrew and Polish. They spoke of the vigor of Israel and the forests of Silesia, of the blushing of virgins, and of famished wolves, of glory and of love, of men who turned into gods and gods who turned into men. These images had nothing in common with the earth we hacked by day or the muddy brown water we channeled among the orange trees. It was a language of dreams, of hopes, of repressed fear, which had much in common with my growing sensation of having become a sparrow in a cage. On those occasions, Kantarovitch—that was his name—went on for hours, reading and pausing, reading and staring with me at the starry sky. Once I heard him sigh softly, "Why were we born Jews and not Bulgarians?" Neither he nor I had any answer to questions of this sort. I would have been unable to answer anyone who might have asked me what I thought about the British and the Arabs, the two realities ever present in our daily existence and at the same time distant and hostile, mysterious and evasive, as if they were living on another planet.

Until 1941, when I joined their army, I had no direct contact with the British. A few days after Italy entered the war in June 1940, I had been called into the office of the school director to meet with a sergeant of the British CID accompanied by an NCO of the Jewish Auxiliary Police. They had come to the school to check up on me as a citizen of an enemy country. They probably did not know that a few weeks earlier the Italian consul in Jaffa had sent me a note to inquire whether I wanted to avail myself of the facilities provided by the Fascist government for the repatriation of Italians. As a member of a family that had "deserved well of the regime," I could be included in a list of "Aryans." If the British had known about this they would certainly have interned me temporarily, since they had interned many other Italian Jews with fewer "qualifications" than mine. The British sergeant, after asking me a few questions, polite and sarcastic, allowed me to return, confused and perturbed, to my class. He must have come to the conclusion that I did not constitute a danger to the security of the empire and that as a minor I did not fall into the category of those who had to be automatically arrested.

From this short meeting I derived a fleeting impression of the British mandatory power and of its representatives. Contrary to what the Hebrew newspapers—which I had begun to read—were writing daily, I did not find anything cynical in this behavior of a quasi-colonial administration, which had closed the door of Palestine in the face of Jewish refugees. I realized, of course, that the British were reneging on their promises to the Zionist movement, but apart from the fact that I had no idea what this meant in terms of the future of the Jewish national home and of the Diaspora—since I had not been a Zionist and had no idea of the plight of the Jews in Europe—I did not feel that they behaved toward us as if we belonged to an inferior race. I had never had occasion to meet English people; I had never been an object of their maltreatment or spite. It was also difficult for me to understand how we could—as we were taught at school—fight Hitler as if the White Paper had not been published and fight the White Paper as if Hitler did not exist. Furthermore, what impressed me and attracted me toward them was the feeling of total security and superiority that somehow physically emanated from them even when patrolling the streets. Later, after I came into close daily contact with the soldiers, recruited from all strata of the population of the United Kingdom, I would quickly discover that the British were far from being demigods; they were human beings like anybody else, affected by the same fears, and the same meannesses, and conditioned by the same level of culture as Jews, Arabs, Italians, or French of similar standards of education. However, at the end of the thirties most of the British personnel serving in Palestine still belonged to a generation, now completely vanished, of colonial administrators. They acted at all levels with a great sense of duty and were conscious, sometimes overly conscious, of their imperial responsibility. The fact that they were few—at the outbreak of war the British garrison in Palestine was less than ten thousand soldiers—increased their prudence.

Whatever their feelings toward the Jews, they made a point of behaving, at least outwardly, with great correctness. I was impressed by the distinction of their carriage, by the detached courtesy with which they treated us common mortals when we happened to approach them in the street or in an office to ask for information. The courtesy and authority that were expressed in the way they dressed, spoke, smoked, and behaved became ever more evident when compared with the efforts the "natives" made to imitate them. The social aping in Palestine was then common to all levels: from the "British" moustaches sported by the Jewish and Arab policemen to the smoking of pipes, from the hats of the ladies to the affected pronunciation of those who tried to speak English "better" than the Englishmen. This native version of the language of Shakespeare had become so ridiculous that a special word was created to indicate this type of speech. It was called "Pinglish," a contraction of "Palestine English." A humorous dictionary of this language was compiled by a Jewish lord living in Palestine. What he forgot to tell his readers was that Spanish and French were also languages born out of corrupted Latin, the imperial language of the past. Indeed, when I observed these modern imperial representatives from a distance, it came naturally to me to associate them with the ancient Romans. I realized that in their manner resided part of the secret of their political and moral power, a power that in Italy the Fascist Youth had taught me to deride but that here one could breathe in the air.

Their hidden strength attracted me in a different way but just as strongly as did that of two other groups of inhabitants of Palestine: Arab peasants and orthodox Jews. Totally different, one from the other and both from the British, they seemed equally similar in their social impermeability to foreign influ-

ence, the originality of their dress, their social solidity, and
their apparent indifference to the world around them.

With the Arabs I had no contact whatsoever. I passed them
in the street on my way to the Italian Consulate in Jaffa—as
long as it existed—or to the central post office where one
could buy international postal certificates to be used for corresponding through the Red Cross with relatives in enemy
countries.

At the time Jaffa was, and to some extent has remained, a
kind of municipal rubbish dump. Dirt accumulated on the
sides of unpaved roads, dogs scavenged through the oil drums
full of refuse, horses spilled fodder out of their nosebags, and
animals stood among clouds of flies sucking their blood and
feeding on their excrement. Equally dirty and miserable were
the barefooted Arabs shuffling aimlessly in the streets, badly
lighted at night by electric wires hanging loosely from poles
and between houses built of limestone blackened by smoke.
Jaffa at the end of the thirties thrived on a confusion of trades,
vices, and rivalries concealed behind the apparent idleness of
men sitting in cafes, sucking their water pipes and watching
with bored satisfaction, through half-shut eyes, the passing of
strangers and of women hiding their doubtful beauty behind
their yashmaks.

At the end of King George Boulevard stood a tall building
with two black, cavernous entrances. It served as a brothel, first
for Arabs and later for Allied troops. When passing in front
of this building, throwing quick glances at the women in the
windows—all fat and blowsy—I shuddered with horror and
curiosity. I did not stop or show my face to them, less out of
shame than out of an obsessive impression of being followed
by thousands of eyes. When strolling through Jaffa I always
expected to be met by sudden explosions of violence like those
—we were told at school—that burst out in Hebron and
Jerusalem at the end of the twenties, in the course of which
hundreds of Jews had been massacred. Nothing ever happened

to me, not because of my luck but because the situation was absolutely calm. The British, after three years of guerrilla warfare, helped by special Jewish auxiliary units, had succeeded in defeating most of the bands engaged in what the Arabs called "revolt" and the mandatory government called "disturbances." The main troublemaker, the mufti of Jerusalem, Amin al-Husseii, was thousands of miles away, exiled by the British before joining the Germans. The departure of many German and Italian agents in the wake of the outbreak of war, and the change in political attitude of most Arab governments toward Britain as a consequence of the conflict and of the presence of powerful armies, had put an end to all kinds of violent expressions of defiance against the mandatory administration. I never had occasion to encounter any Arab hostility, and I was always surprised by the kindness with which people in Jaffa answered the queries I addressed to them in my poor English, when asking for directions in the street or how to find a shop where I could buy the sesame sweets I liked very much. Yet I could not help breathing more freely when I saw a policeman appear around a corner or another Jew wandering like myself in the streets of this miserable city, of which Tel Aviv had been for many years a Jewish residential quarter.

I drew a quite different impression from the Arabs who passed in front of the school gates or who used to come inside the grounds to offer us their produce or their services. They were peasants and bedouin and to me looked immensely grand. At night, when I was on guard duty along the school's fenced perimeter, first armed with a stick and later with a heavy Enfield rifle with only ten rounds of ammunition, I watched these Arabs, singly or in groups, swarm on the road to Jerusalem, which passed in front of the school. On foot, on horses and donkeys, in front of their women who followed them carrying bundles on their heads and runny-nosed babies on their backs, they looked like mysterious and unapproachable figures chiseled against a landscape of oriental poverty and exhaustion. We could hear them coming from a distance in the silence of the night. I looked at them, filing past with muffled footsteps without looking at me, aware of my presence but acting as though I did not exist. The black and silver caftans that the men hitched up to their belts, the baggy black Turkish trousers tied to their ankles, the *keffiya*—a black-and-white or colored scarf held on the head by the double ring of the *abbaya* —gave them a noble deportment that Jews, especially those of recent immigration, markedly lacked. Contrary to the debased merchants I saw sitting in their shops in Jaffa, some made more vulgar by their unaesthetic mixture of European and oriental clothing, these peasants, and in particular the bedouin, had the carriage of princes. I envied them their horses, which I would have liked to ride, their way of life, which seemed to me so harmonious and romantic, their apparent imperviousness to foreign influence. This was of course pure imagination, derived from my total ignorance of their language and my absence of contact with them. Yet I felt gratitude toward them for being faithful to themselves.

My feelings toward orthodox Jews were quite different. In Tel Aviv at that time one did not see many of them. At our agricultural college the "religious" people belonged to a youth movement called B'nei Akiva. Their motto was *Torah ve'Avo-dah* (Law and Work), a slogan that sounded to me like the *Ora et labora* of the Benedictine monks. Monks these companions of mine were certainly not. But they worked harder than the "secular" students, in order, I believe, to overcome a feeling of inferiority toward the secular Zionists, who at that time ruled the Yishuv, and were proud of having succeeded in freeing themselves from the yoke of the Lord.

The problem of the B'nei Akiva in my school (and later of the religious Zionists in Israel) was thus to prove to others and to themselves that they could successfully compete in everything with secular Zionists: they could build collective villages and join labor unions, handle weapons as well as plows, discuss

Marx and Roosevelt no less than the Bible and the Talmud. Yet in their efforts to imitate the others, in the wake, as they were, of the Marxist currents then prevailing in Jewish Palestine, these young religious Zionists felt uneasy, in some way marginal, and in many instances acted with an arrogance equal to their uncertainty.

Not so the orthodox Jews. Their love of Zion was not the result of nationalistic ideas imported from Europe; their presence in Palestine was not a reaction to Fascist anti-Semitism. Their ambition was not to transform the destiny of their people and create a new type of Jew in the land of their ancestors. The Mosaic tradition was the alpha and omega of their existence. It expressed their collective identity; it answered every problem. Tradition was the golden and unchangeable rule to be followed in the service of the Lord. It began before they were born, in their mother's womb, and did not end for their souls after they had shed their mortal coil. The world could persecute them but not make them change their self-righteous, elitist views. Their duty was to improve the unfinished work of creation through an unending process of sanctification of every moment of life, of every gesture, according to a code of behavior that everyone had the duty to learn through continuous discussion but that only their savior could interpret. They did not pay much attention to current affairs, not because they were blind to daily events but because they firmly believed that they understood better than secular people—deluded beings, blinded by earthly passions— the essentials of life. Like true aristocrats who, even if boiled alive by cannibals, cannot help looking down on their torturers, the behavior of these orthodox Jews toward political power—British, Arab, or Jewish—was one of willful detachment and social indifference. A rabbi, invited to give evidence in front of the Royal Commission, which the government in London had set up to inquire into the problems of Palestine after a recurrent outbreak of violence, exemplified the intellectual position of these orthodox, anti-Zionist Jews when he reminded the members of the commission, in Hebrew, that the Israelites had created a highly civilized society in Palestine "one thousand years before your ancestors came down from the trees." This sentence was translated by the Zionist lawyer acting as interpreter as—"The rabbi has expressed some personal considerations of historic interest on the past of the Jewish people."

In spite of my ignorance of Judaism I perceived in these Jews, totally indifferent to the frivolities of the world, piled up in their shabby neighborhoods, overflowing with nervous, animal mysticism, a sense of continuity, a dignity stronger than in any other group in the country. I felt the same about their women, who first shaved their heads out of modesty and then covered them with wigs or ridiculous shawls like the Daughters of Mary congregation in my village, and their children, bundled up into trousers inherited from older brothers and with angelic expressions on faces surrounded by earlocks dangling under stocking caps—all strange, fascinating, repulsive, agitated inhabitants of the orthodox world of Jerusalem. From outside I observed this closed, perfectly integrated milieu with a curiosity made up of admiration and aversion—a milieu from which I felt excluded more than from that of the Arabs, the British, or the Zionist activists at school who enraged me with their ideological atheism.

Between the loyalists of the God of Israel and the modernizing rebels, between the Jews who waited with anxiety for the Messiah and those who, having lost their patience and capacity to suffer, had decided that Jews no longer needed a Messiah, there existed a common denominator of culture that was alien to me. Walking in the alleys of the ghetto-like orthodox quarter of Jerusalem or sitting in a political seminar, peeping through the shutters of miserable Talmudic schools into which I dared not enter, or marching in the fields to the rhythm of a song whose Hebrew words were adapted to the music of

Russian muzhik, I always felt like an intruder, ashamed of my estrangement as well as of the uneasiness expressed by my body language. I knew that I belonged to none of these groups, neither to the Jews nor to the Arabs, not to the religious or to the secular, not to the socialists or to the nationalists, not to the Italians or to the British. This solitude of mine in the lack of privacy of college life, this loneliness, being part of a foreign society in which I could not find a place to retreat, rendered my search for a point of support more pressing and painful than ever.

In this search I switched from feelings of sudden dislike to those of violent attraction for this or that person, from transient ideological enthusiasm to deep reservation about any political trend. This made me suspect, ill-tolerated, and often derided by my schoolmates, better integrated than I in sports teams, youth movements, paramilitary activities, or religious coteries. Forty years later, their faces, some of which have become internationally known, have faded away like the problems that seemed so obsessive to me at the time, leaving only bursts of olfactory memories sterilized by time: the smell of garlic that socialist activists blew into other people's faces with the violence of their argument; the musky smell of charcoal that the Arabs carried in their clothes and that hit the passersby in their villages; the smell of rancid oil frying in the public canteens; the smell of *yash*, the strong eau-de-vie, and of the Sabbath "kugel" in the synagogues at the end of the morning services; the smell of sweat and menstruation of some women on the buses or in the evenings that more piercing and perturbing smell acquired through immersions in the ritual bathwater.

In a hot country where the majority of the women with whom I came in contact did not use any perfume and washed themselves with hard laundry soap, these natural feminine odors that insinuated themselves into my conscience, sexually inexperienced and religiously ignorant as I was, created a permanent tension about which I bragged to my mates and sometimes attempted to speak about in oblique ways with my English teacher.

I was preparing with her for the London Matriculation, which I never managed to complete. I unburdened myself of my dreams and my olfactory experiences through essays, full of spelling and syntactical errors, which she used to correct without ever seeming to notice the allusiveness of these messages. I had established with her—a quiet beauty, much older than I—a halting dialogue made up of broken sentences, rough-cast speeches, and imaginary stories. At the most difficult moments of our lessons, when I tried to conceal the tears in my eyes by looking at the flight of a bird or at a cloud sailing in the sky, I perceived how sensitive she was to my repressed emotions. On those occasions she suggested that I read aloud some poetry or try to declaim some passage from Shakespeare that I had learned by heart. I gratefully complied, aware of the reserve with which she touched the hollow of her throat to make sure that her shirt was buttoned up.

One day, at the end of the summer of 1940, while we were reading a passage of *Othello* together, a solitary enemy plane suddenly dropped a cluster of bombs on Tel Aviv. One fell in front of her apartment, where we had our lessons. It was the first air raid I had ever experienced. I clearly remember the sound of the explosion and the heat of the gust, the rattling of the windows, the crash of the door uprooted by the blast, the sudden sensation of emptiness in my stomach, which afterwards I had so many other occasions to experience. We rushed downstairs where a small crowd of terrified people had already gathered in the basement.

That was the first time I experienced the splitting of my personality, which would accompany me throughout my life at moments of great stress: I saw myself as though from the outside, uttering inconsequent phrases to people from whom I tried to conceal my physical fear and the far greater fear of showing my fear.

My teacher sat in a corner of our improvised air-raid shelter in a state of abysmal detachment, wholly engaged in observing with blissful surprise the cacophonic scene surrounding her. When the sirens sounded the all clear, we rushed out into the streets, which were quickly returning to normal. Lying on the ground was a horse, his gray coat spotted with blood, his tongue hanging out between two rows of long yellow teeth, his body twisted in the harness of a cart, which seemed to look at his death through the shafts sloping down to the road. It was a macabre scene.

People eyed it sideways without stopping. I was fascinated by it because I had never experienced such a vision of violent death. The air was still full of the smell of the explosion, but the birds had started to twitter again in the trees. My English teacher put her arm around my shoulders—many months later she told me that she had noticed my trembling—pushed me gently up the stairs, sat me down in a chair in her blown-up apartment, and offered me a cup of tea. I drank it, leaning on the table from which she had just removed fragments of glass. She stood in front of me. I noticed that my hands were still trembling and that she discreetly feigned not to see. After a long, tense, mute colloquium, she barely opened her mouth to murmur: "There is nothing wrong in being afraid." Her eyes were misted with tears, but perhaps it was only a reflection of the light. I felt a joy mingled with shame when she laid her hands on mine. We stayed like that for a minute. Then I got up, managed an apology and a smile, and turned to the door to leave. She remained leaning on the doorway, following me with her eyes until I vanished down the stairway, her head slightly bent, forgetful of her unbuttoned blouse. That day I began to think seriously about leaving school and joining the army.

7.

The Court-Martial

THE court-martial took place in
Ramle, in a bungalow built in the colonial style imported by
the British into Palestine from India, together with Indian
penal law procedures, the topee, and polo. It was a wooden,
E-shaped structure, with four rooms in the central row and
two more on the wings to accommodate the guard and the
toilets. The veranda, its wooden railing coated with burned
black oil to keep away lice, had two cascades of red and purple
bougainvillea at the corners, giving some color and beauty to
this building planted in a landscape of thistles and sand.

Nothing in Ramle was pleasing to the eye. The few administrative buildings erected by the British next to the older
ones built by the Turks made the other small, shabby houses
—some made of cement, others of clay—look even more
miserable. It was difficult to believe that this had once been the
capital of an Arab kingdom fighting the Crusaders. Of the old
grandeur nothing remained except a high, rectangular tower
hidden among the orange groves. Called the White Tower, it
rose majestically on the postage stamps of the mandatory

administration, but seen at close range its arches seemed to stare at the plain as if through empty eye sockets.

The passing of the train momentarily distracted the flies from their massed attack on the backs of the donkeys and camels. There was a continuous battle between them and the rosy cheeks of the British soldiers, between the sweat of bodies and the starch of uniforms carefully pressed by Sudanese boys, between the rhythmic swish of the animals' tails and that of the command sticks that the officers held clamped under their armpits.

Sitting on a wooden bench near the end of the veranda, I reflected sadly on my military situation, so far from what I had aspired to when I first joined the army. More than anything else I was perturbed by my trousers. While the British wore shorts carefully measured to show off their sporting knees, regimental colors dangling from the elastic bands that held up their long socks, my lower limbs were encased in two degrading tubes of khaki cloth that made me look like a circus clown. These were a type of colonial shorts that the quartermaster's service had designed in one of those flashes of ingenuity encountered only in the military. The idea was to save money and at the same time fight malaria. In order to maintain some kind of uniformity in military dress by day and to protect the legs from mosquito bites by night, we were issued this versatile specimen of military fashion instead of two pairs of trousers, one long and one short. This "divided skirt" was intended to be turned up and fastened with four metal buttons during the day (sewn two outside and two inside the thighs) and let down to the ankles at sunset. The buttons did not fulfill their function. Those on the inside were torn off in the simple process of walking; those on the outside of the thighs resisted longer —with the result that the trousers permanently dangled between the legs. To walk during the day with those swinging tubes continuously falling toward the ground was a spectacle, specially devised, it seemed, to make a visible distinction between servants and masters, between colonial and metropolitan soldiers. I suffered more keenly from this tacit discrimination than from the official prohibition that separated officers', NCOS', and enlisted men's latrines, or, in order not to irritate the Arabs, from the British enjoinders against our wearing the blue and white Zionist colors on our sleeves when serving within the boundaries of Palestine. I was struck by the irony of the situation: my family in Italy might by that time have been obliged to wear the yellow star, while here was I, prevented from displaying the badge of my race on the degrading military uniform I had eagerly donned to fight for freedom and to escape the routine of the agricultural college.

For nine months I had been mounting guard around depots where only the British had the right to enter or escorting convoys of food and ammunition through monotonous, arid landscapes in Palestine, dotted with clusters of miserable houses and the occasional bright patches of orange groves and irrigated fields of the kibbutzim. The great event about which we spoke for weeks in the other ranks' mess had been a trip to Damascus, where once I got a faraway glimpse of the Abbasid capital from a dusty transit camp where we spent a night.

It was not yet eight o'clock in the morning and the air still held some of the dewy freshness of the night. The judges in the court-martial to which I had been summoned as a witness would certainly not arrive before ten o'clock. I had plenty of time to taste my freedom from oppressive garrison duties, at the expense of an accused comrade-in-arms. Opposite the veranda was a small, sparse lawn, on which an Arab soldier squatted on his heels. He had arrived straight from prison, dressed in khaki overalls stained with oil but girded with an army belt and shiny buckle, a side cap dangling on his freshly shaven head. A Scottish corporal, his topee sitting straight on his head, his dark green flannel shirt bright with campaign ribbons, the red and brown kilt of the Cameron Highlanders circling his hips like a peacock's tail, and the leather sporran firm on his belly, asserted all the elegant superiority of the imperial power over my ridiculous colonial trousers and the stained overalls of the Arab.

The Arab was not handcuffed but guarded by two soldiers belonging to his unit. They were moustached and imperious, conscious of the superiority their rifles and their task gave them over another human being. The scabbards of their bayonets shone in the sun. They had, I thought, probably soaked them overnight in a bucketful of urine, then dried the black leather in the shade to avoid wrinkling. They would then scrub them with Kiwi polish diluted with saliva, polishing the scabbards for hours with a red-striped five-by-two-inch piece of white flannel, which I knew was intended only for cleaning the rifle barrel. I had been through this procedure myself and had learned the tricks of the trade upon which our forty-eight-hour leave often depended. This was all that remained of the splendor of a military life that I had dreamed would sweep me away to the battlements of a fort in the Himalayas or to the cloak-and-dagger depths of the heart of Africa. Instead, here I was in Ramle, bored to death and ashamed of my ridiculous trousers, waiting to be called in to bear witness to a sequence of events that I would be forced to lie about.

The idea of swearing on the Bible and then bearing false witness had been tormenting me for a week. It seemed that the act I was on the point of committing for Jewish patriotism and barracks solidarity was the last step along the road of my aborted hopes. My first year of war had not seen one single military action, only a succession of ascents to the corrugated iron roofs that we regularly had to camouflage with mud against improbable air attacks of the unseen enemy. Our Welsh sergeant major, a lanky fellow plagued less by the drudgery of commanding Jewish recruits than by the ulcer that tortured him, liked that corveé the best; the painful contractions of his stomach translated themselves into our Sisyphean work. This consisted of kneading the red earth of Sarafand

with water, handing bucketfuls of this mixture to the soldiers
on the roof, spreading the mixture on the hot corrugated iron,
and then waiting for it to dry and the wind to blow it away
so that we could start all over again. The technique must have
been invented by the Egyptians for the benefit of our pyramid-
building forefathers, although our sergeant major never
stopped reminding us that it helped to win the war against the
Nazis.

We reaped our revenge by working to the rhythm of
impromptu ditties in Hebrew that heaped scorn on our Welsh
tyrant. They were usually inspired by a fellow soldier who had
trained to be a diplomat in his native Austria. A strange man,
this composer; his new Hebrew name, Ben-Yosef, concealed
a past that deeply marked his thoughtful face. When we served
in the same platoon of the Palestine Buffs, he had not yet
grown the beard he wore when he was killed in the defense
of Kfar Etzion, a religious kibbutz near Jerusalem, a few years
later. A burst of Jordanian machine-gun fire ripped his stomach
—so the legend says—as he was playing the accordion. This
accordion, carried in a big wooden box, was part of our unit's
equipment. On it he composed some of the best-known war
songs of that period. Indeed, he was one of the last true bards.
I asked him once what the kind of music he composed meant
to him. "It soothes the pain of a soul wounded by memories
of a beautiful time which none of us will ever know again,"
he answered.

By now the Arab prisoner had shifted his position. He was
standing up in the middle of the lawn, mechanically massaging
his thighs as if to rub away the oil stains on his overalls. Like
me, he had noticed a car approaching the bungalow and
thought it might be the judges. But it was only the duty officer
coming to check whether everything was in order for the
court-martial. The Scottish corporal brought us to attention.
We stood upright for a few minutes and then fell back into
our own thoughts and affairs. I left the veranda to go and

urinate behind a eucalyptus tree near the railway line. To satisfy my bodily needs without shame, scaring away an ant into a safe crack of warm ground with the stream of my water, gave me a sense of freedom totally absent in the garrison latrines. At the big Sarafand base, as I have already pointed out, status and race were to some extent linked to human metabolism: there were latrines for enlisted men, for NCOs, and for officers. There were also separate latrines for whites and blacks, for men and women, and for civilians and military personnel. Equality was expressed by their identical, long rectangular shape, with the same wooden planks found in the kibbutz, and the occupant's being protected from indiscreet eyes by jute partitions. Since these flapping curtains did not reach the ground, passersby could view a selection of boots and shoes of every type and from every outpost of the empire. Woe to those who entered the wrong compartment; the military police, with their white-painted belts, shiny buckles, and red caps, seemed to have nothing to do but lay ambushes for those who missed the right address. Only the Australians acted as if they lived beyond good and evil. Off duty they did not bother to salute the officers; they ran their own units as if they were autonomous communities of giants in uniform; they were always happy and insolent. After losing a protracted battle against the bugs that infested their barracks, they set fire to a wooden bungalow. When we rushed to the spot together with the army firemen, they told us to keep away. Sitting on the ground, they drank beer, happy as children at the sight of the giant bonfire they had created.

We Jewish Palestinian recruits quickly developed a deep admiration for these Australian soldiers, hoping one day to create a national army as carefree and undisciplined as theirs. Meanwhile we were just a platoon of green recruits waiting for the arrival of additional volunteers to form a Jewish company, which in time would become a battalion of that fighting brigade the Jewish Agency wanted to create as a nucleus for the future Jewish army, and which the British opposed for exactly the same reason.

At the time I understood little of the political problems in which I had become involved. Back on my bench on the veranda of the court-martial bungalow, I recalled ruefully how I had enlisted. It all started on the day the radio announced that the Germans had bombed Belgrade. The news reached us at the railway station of Binyamina, a village near the coast, built by the Rothschilds, where we had been waiting for a train to take us back to the agricultural college. Among my schoolmates was one of Yugoslav origin, who was later to become chief of staff of the Israeli army. He kept explaining to our teachers the reasons for the attack and its probable consequences. The Serbs and Macedonians, he said, would fight against everyone; the Croats and Slovenians, however, would join the Axis. Yugoslavia would eventually be divided among Italy, Hungary, and Germany.

Listening to him, I thought of the valley in the Carnia region where I used to spend my winter and summer holidays, of my walks along the Yugoslav frontier, of the visit I had paid with my father, when he went to inspect the paramilitary units under his command, to the underground defenses that protected the road leading from Tarvis to Zagabria. Names of faraway places well-known to me were now chasing each other around Binyamina railway station like the pieces of newspaper the wind was whirling through the air. Sitting in the shade of a eucalyptus tree, I followed them with my eyes, wondering what might have been printed on them. A stronger gust of wind lifted one piece of paper high in the air, carrying it first in the direction of the vineyards stretching endlessly at the foot of Mount Carmel, then turning it back, first right, then left, and finally landing it on the sandy road to the village. A gray donkey with its head bowed to the ground and its long ears twitching away the flies, waited patiently for someone to pay attention to him. A barefoot Arab, the corner of his tunic raised and tucked into his belt, looked at us with disinterested eyes from the trunk of the dead tree on which he was sitting.

I kept forcing myself to think of the Wild West, trying to imagine myself in a frontier station among cowboys and Indians, waiting for the arrival of a herd of cows announced by their thundering hooves. Everything was still around me, the silence broken only by the voices of my companions, busily refilling their water bottles at the station's water tank, tired and sweaty after the long march that had at last come to an end, discussing the latest war news and the results of our examinations.

With my head leaning on my rucksack, I reflected on the three-day march we had just completed. The hike at the end of the semester was supposed to complete our military training and acquaint us with our surroundings. The British did not like these school marches; twice on the road from the village of Zichron Ya'akov to Megiddo they had stopped us to inquire about the purpose of our trip. As our papers were in order, they let us go, knowing that we would not dare to walk through an Arab area unarmed. The Mauser pistols were indeed with us, dismantled and concealed in pouches tied between the legs of two or three girls, chosen because their demurely braided hair and innocent faces aroused no suspicion. These girls could have been betrayed to a more discerning eye by the fact that they were the only ones wearing "capitalist" skirts. However, the British closed at least one eye. The outbreak of war had created a fragile and turbid collaboration in Palestine among them, the Arabs, and the Jews. It was a peace without social contacts or agreements, full of suspicion—each side knew that the others were preparing for the fight that would inevitably come. However, that was not the only reason why we felt secure and cheeky. It was the thoughtlessness of our age and the unjustified righteousness of our belief that our own strength would ensure us a better fate than that of the Jews of Europe. Their tragedy was a direct consequence of their refusal to come to Palestine when it was still possible; our good fortune was a confirmation of the correctness of Zionism; our self-confidence due to our naive belief in the fact that our strength, not that of the British Empire, protected us from the Nazi extermination machine.

Oblivious to the horrors of war, we swung along, singing to fight off heat and fatigue, on the road of the Apocalypse, which ran from the sea to Megiddo, the site of Armageddon. The acacias and fig trees in the fields bent their leaves toward the hot ground. The wheat stood high and ripe in the small patches of earth, separated by stone walls, in which the Arabs toiled with wooden plows pulled by a mule or donkey yoked together with a small, emaciated cow. The harness, made of rope, often cut ulcerous wounds into the animals' skins, at which swarms of flies came to feast. It was a world real but remote, which met our arrogance with a silence charged with suppressed hatred. This, at least, was how it seemed. I was probably wrong—the Arabs probably felt nothing toward us but fear and embarrassment. They preferred not to look at us. When we met them suddenly at a bend in the road, driving their herds of goats, they squeezed to the sides to let us pass. Those who suffered most from these encounters were the sheep and goats, pitilessly beaten by the shepherds to make them move out of the way faster. Occasionally a goat, less politically sensitive than the others, lost itself among our ranks, refusing to react to the furious barking of the dog. We received it with enthusiasm and mad laughter since it broke the monotony of the march and filled the void of our minds.

We had spent one night at the youth village of Shfeya, perched on top of the only wooded hill in the area. In the afternoon we had been training with wooden rifles, learning to judge distances, to use a compass, to acquire some notion of topography. In the evening after supper we had gathered in the dining room to listen to a speech by the head mechanic of our school. Usually we saw him busy with tractors, his hands covered with grease, his blue overalls oil stained, his sleeves rolled up over his powerful arms, totally immersed in the work for which we all envied him. Here in Shfeya he was transformed into an officer of the Hagana, the Jewish Agency's clandestine military organization. He stood before us dressed in a uniform without badges of rank, but clean and starched, almost as elegant as the British officers, surrounded by a deep aura of respect enhanced by our surprise at the sudden revelation of his true identity.

He delivered a short political speech. We must prepare for the war against the Arabs that would certainly break out once the war against the Germans and Italians ended. The battle of Britain had been won; the battle of the Middle East had not yet started. The Germans and Italians were trying to provoke an Arab revolt against the British, who would not allow any disorder during the period of emergency. If the British could have got rid of the Zionists they would certainly have done so with pleasure, but they could not because of America and because of the moral and political obligations they undertook once they decided to fight Hitler. They had also discovered that they needed us more than they thought. For this reason they had reluctantly accepted our collaboration in fighting against Vichy France in Syria and against the pro-Nazi revolt in Iraq. They appreciated the fact that all over the Middle East Jews were able to collect more information than the entire British secret service put together, but they did not like to admit it. They wanted the collaboration of Jewish individuals without building up a debt to the Jewish institutions. Because of this we had to work together in common schemes authorized by our own authorities. The war would be long—not months but years. Millions of soldiers would pass though Palestine from every corner of the empire. They would need food, uniforms, medical services, and every other kind of supplies from needles to vehicles. Palestine did not possess raw materials, but the Jews were the only ones in the whole Middle

Eastern area who were able to offer the British the fruits of their skills and their agricultural and industrial experience. It was imperative that we exploit this wonderful opportunity the war was offering us to create the basis for a modern Jewish economy capable, once the war was over, of supporting our own fight for political independence. From this war, he said, we would emerge either stronger or with our national hopes shattered irreparably.

It was a serious, precise speech, without rhetoric and without illusions. It gave me a wider vision of what we should do; it showed me that there were possibilities of action other than the agricultural schemes exalted at school. I felt that I could be associated with a task of wider scope with a place and glory for everyone. Lying in the shade of the eucalyptus tree at the railway station, apart from my companions who were, as usual, discussing the prospect of life in the kibbutzim, which they would be entering at the end of the school year, I kept thinking of the Hagana commander's speech, and I was overwhelmed by a sudden secret joy. At last I was going to make the first free decision of my life: to enlist in the British army in order to train for the war of the Jews for the Jews, as the Italians of Garibaldi's legion had done in Uruguay. By leaving the college, I hoped to crack the shell in which I had lived up to that time, to break out of the suffocating atmosphere of boring agricultural studies and of a collective society for which I felt no empathy. By enlisting, I kept repeating to myself, I would fulfill both my national duty and my own destiny. When the train puffed into the station I felt like another person, different from the other inhabitants of my little school world and from the youngster who had left Italy less than two years before without really breaking with his Italian past.

The day the Germans put an end to the Serbian kingdom of Karageorgevich, I swore allegiance to the king of England, emperor of India, and defender of a faith that was not mine.

In exchange he gave me ten silver shillings, a uniform of khaki drill, a topee, a pair of boots, three pairs of woolen socks, a little pouch containing a piece of soap, a toothbrush, a few needles, some thread, a few metal buttons, and a packet of gauze for first aid.

"Ten-shun!" shouted the Scottish corporal. Like an automaton I found myself snapping to attention in front of the three senior officers comprising the court-martial, who were followed by judges, their black gowns over their arms and their wigs in their hands, ready to dispense justice.

The Arab prisoner and his two guards were also standing at attention on the small, yellowish grassy patch. A little further away, a van escorted by military police was disgorging other prisoners, obviously more important than the Arab since they had been granted the right to a defense. Among them stood Corporal Attiah of my company, a twenty-four-year-old brute, looking as elegant as usual in his freshly ironed uniform, his black hair slick with brilliantine. His arrogant smile always irritated me but served him as an infallible weapon for conquering the hearts of shop girls. He passed in front of me, perfectly sure that I would lie in his defense, throwing a glance at me that appeared impudent and scornful.

Since the day I joined his platoon I had hated him for the tricks he played on me as my squad commander and for his jokes. When I was promoted to lance corporal he shouted in the middle of the other ranks' mess that I should replace my stripe with macaroni. Everybody laughed at me. I had not reacted because we were engaged in a war against "macaroni" Italy, and I could not defend her. Now I preferred not to think about it; if I allowed old rancor to overcome me I might not be able to lie convincingly as I had been ordered to do. Attiah disappeared with his escort and the other prisoners into the guardroom. I went back to my seat on the bench, waiting to be called and free meanwhile to plunge again into my reveries.

The British army had not treated me badly. It had not imposed any inhumane discipline on me; it had not given me rags to wrap my feet in, as was common in the Italian army. At the camp in Sarafand we slept six to a room in clean bungalows with warm showers and latrines less smelly than those in the kibbutz. The bed consisted of three movable planks lying on two wooden horses. They were not unduly uncomfortable once one learned how to stuff the mattress cover with straw. True, we had to fight invasions of insects, some of them undoubtedly direct descendants of those brought into Sarafand by the imperial armies of World War I, but they were less annoying than the mosquitoes, against which we vainly fought by spreading eucalyptus oil over our skins at sunset and by using the nets that dangled from the roof over each of our beds.

I loved that net. It was made of a fine white mesh, which allowed me to see what was happening in the room without being seen myself. It gave me a feeling of protection, of privacy and of luxury, which compensated for many of the discomforts of a recruit's life. Neither the physical effort, nor jobs like carrying buckets of excrement or cleaning huge cauldrons full of smelly grease bothered me. What I could not bear was the monotony of colonial garrison life, which killed every dream of adventure and glory I carried in my heart.

In our camp, after half an hour of morning PT, they made us march back and forth on a cement square to train us in close-order, like Napoleon's troops, as if the battles of the twentieth century should still be fought in closed ranks and with fixed bayonets. When we were on guard duty, even in the middle of a sandy waste, we were told to take three steps forward before shouldering arms so that the barrel of the gun would not hit the imaginary roof of an imaginary sentry box. This is what was done in London; this was what all His Majesty's soldiers had to do everywhere in the empire: truth does not change with geography.

Twice during the first three months of our training they took us to the firing range. I was a keen marksman and did not need lessons from my corporals on how to hold a rifle and hit a target. I was complimented by my British officer but offended by the fact that he personally counted the bullets we used, before and after the exercise, to make sure that not one bullet was stolen from the royal armory. In a military camp inhabited by Scotsmen, Australians, Gurkhas, Bantus, Senegalese of de Gaulle, Boers from South Africa, Arabs, and Indians, we, the Jewish members of the Palestine Regiment, were—and felt ourselves to be—more strangers than anyone else in our country, and they, the British, felt that we were not like the other soldiers. The color of our skins placed us among the whites, but the political geography among the colonials; our Jewish race made us natural enemies of England's Nazi enemy, but our origins were in the Axis countries. We were the only military personnel to have a religion as the basis of our national identity and to reject it in favor of a new secular identity, which left the British mystified.

A few days after my enlistment, our Jewish sergeant informed us that we were going on strike. He had informed our British sergeant major that we would refuse all duty, stop eating, and go to prison if necessary, if we were not given bacon for breakfast like the British soldiers instead of other food in the name of "special religious treatment." We were not to be treated like Muslims, or Indians, or any other "bloody natives"; our rations should be exactly like those of the British because we wore the same uniform and fought (at a distance) the same enemy. We were Zionists, not ghetto Jews, and it was not for the British to decide which of our religious superstitions we should follow. Obviously they pretended to respect our religion only in order to deny our national identity as Jews. We would not play their game; we would defend our right to eat bacon as part of our right to be equal—as a symbol, not as a commodity.

The strike lasted a couple of hours. The British did not understand what we wanted, but they realized that it would be difficult to explain why they had to jail a unit of Jewish volunteers because they insisted on eating bacon. The whole thing was absurd, but it could reach London and the House of Commons, where there was always someone ready to listen to the Zionists. Our commanding officer announced that beginning the next morning bacon would be served to the Jewish units as to everyone else in the camp who did not object to eating pork, and we celebrated this achievement in our bungalows as if we had won a political victory. The Welsh sergeant major became more acid and disparaging in his comments. He now accompanied his commands on the parade ground with phrases such as "Heads up, chins in, don't look at the ground: there are too many Jews and Scotsmen around for money to be lying about."

Resting on my barracks bed, I had tried to put some order into my ideas as I watched the movement of the flies on the unattached ceiling of the bungalow. By now only Ben-Yosef and I were left in the room. Throughout the discussion about the strike he had kept quiet, sitting next to his accordion case, and he was now playing on the instrument, improvising a new tune.

"What's the sense," I asked him, "of calling this strike?"

"None," he answered, "but it's the nature of the weak to show that they are stronger than they are. Gandhi, too, believing that the superiority of the British was linked to their carnivorous habits, ate meat, breaking the religious vegetarian traditions of his family. We, too, will mature in time and won't need to demonstrate our national identity by eating bacon, but our problems are much more complicated than those of India."

To win, he explained, Gandhi only had to wait; nobody can control half a billion men and women in their own country. Zionism, however, had to build up a free people and a land at the same time. The strike over the bacon was just an indication of how confused our ideas still were. The Zionist movement, Ben-Yosef continued, had two faces, one turned toward the outside and one to the inside; one looking at political independence, the other at social revolution. "Our trouble is that we don't want to be just like the others; we want to be similar and different at the same time. We are more interested in realizing a messianic dream than a political plan. The religious tradition against which we have just revolted may contain a lot of superstitions, but it also stands at the root of our legitimate rights in Palestine. Those who want to substitute this old Jewish legitimacy with a new, historically and morally debatable one, risk throwing out the baby with the bathwater, as the British say. We no longer have the patience to wait for the Messiah to come and get us out of trouble; Zionists have decided to do the job themselves." Had I ever heard, he asked me, of a writer called Agnon? He lived in Jerusalem and was telling people that the day we got a state we would lose the Messiah forever.

Ben-Yosef did not like to think too much about these problems; they were too big for him. If, as many people believed, the God of Israel was a God who liked to reveal himself in history, the history that the war was now in the process of writing would give him plenty of occasions to reveal himself to his people. We were living in momentous, bestial times; the soul is corrupted less by the evil of action than by the passivity of the individual within the collective action. "Is there anything more unreal," Ben-Yosef asked me, "than the silence of this military bungalow, surrounded by flower beds, in the middle of the military camp in which we play soldiers far from danger, conscious of, and at the same time untouched by, the hell in which the people whom we have the cheek to pretend we are going to liberate are roasting? Is there anything more absurd, more illusory? Is there any greater sin than our beer-drinking parties, our gobbling bacon, while in

Europe millions are dying of hunger, and our own people, the Jews, are literally burning at the stake that the Nazi inquisition has set up in honor of Aryan gods?" He, Ben-Yosef, had a personal antidote to all this—the music he made on his accordion. "A clown remains a clown," he said to me with his sad smile, "even when dressed in khaki."

One day, three or four months after I had joined the army, feeling that I was turning into a clown myself, I decided to go to Kibbutz Givat Brenner to have a talk with Enzo Sereni. I had not seen him for two years. I knew that he had volunteered for British intelligence, but I did not know that he had had trouble with the authorities in Cairo. He was now back in his kibbutz, brooding over his inactivity and planning other daring operations, which would eventually lead him to his death behind the German lines in Italy in 1944.

I found him in the small kibbutz library poring over old European newspapers. I told him at once that I was so fed up with my military service I was ready to desert if I could not get a transfer to a unit where I could do something more interesting and meaningful for the war effort. Sereni listened to me without interrupting but with obvious signs of impatience. At the end he was so irritated by my babbling that he almost shouted at me. There was nothing he could do for me, he said, but even if he could, he wouldn't lift a finger to help me. Who on earth was I to claim special consideration? What had I done in my life to expect more than the others? Who gave me the right to use this terrible war, in which the Jewish people and half of humanity were dying, for my personal satisfaction? What I was looking for, he said, and he was right, was not promotion of a cause but my own advancement. Unable to associate myself with any collective work, I was now trying to run away from the army life for which I had volunteered, in the same way as I had run away from the kibbutz and from my school. I was forgetting that nothing could be built without the patient humility that inspires common action. The cathedrals in Europe did not bear the names of their builders; none of the trees I could see growing around us could be linked to the labor of a particular person; Zionism could not succeed through bombastic speeches or parades, as the Jabotinsky Revisionists—the "orthodox" secular parties of the right—claimed, but only through the ant-like work of devoted people who understood that the Jewish homeland could only be built gradually. This was the meaning of Chaim Weizmann's call for "one dunam at a time; one cow at a time." Better than anybody else I should have known, he concluded, without realizing how deeply he wounded me by quoting Mussolini's famous slogan, that "it was possible to serve a cause even by mounting guard over a petrol can."

I left Givat Brenner full of resentment at Sereni, whom I was not to see again until the night in Bari when he left my unit to be parachuted behind the German lines on a mission without return. In my rage I did not realize what I came to understand years later, that the best way to obtain something is to stop asking for it. In fact, while mounting guard over an oil depot at the Tel Aviv power station, less than two months after my meeting with Sereni, I received a most unusual call from my company commander. He told me that an officer from the Special Intelligence Service had just arrived from Cairo and wanted to see me in private. He left me alone in his office, and after a short while I was faced by a major who spoke perfect Italian. He told me that he was in the process of organizing a propaganda service in Italian (paradoxically enough it was the same unit Sereni had been forced to leave) and was looking for speakers with good Italian pronunciation. He had gone through the list of Palestinian volunteers of Italian origin and wanted to meet me personally. He asked me about my studies and my family, and after half an hour's conversation—which already created a bit of a sensation in my unit—he asked me to go with him to the army broadcasting station in Jaffa for a voice test.

Many years have passed since that day. The officer, a Greek Jew by the name of Nakamuli, a rich paper merchant from Cairo, has long been dead. For me he remains the greatest friend I had in the six years I served in the British army. On more than one occasion after I had left his unit, he helped me without apparent reason. He was not ashamed to invite me to his splendid mansion on the Nile to dine with Egyptian notables and British officers, in spite of my being then a simple NCO. Nothing endears him to my memory more than the way he helped me to read and reread the text for my voice test, making it clear to me that he wanted me to succeed although he knew absolutely nothing about me. He had probably sensed my anguish and my desire to break away from garrison life. I do not know how well I read the article from *Il Popolo d'Italia,* which Nakamuli had brought with him, but I was recruited on the spot, and when I left the studio in Jaffa I knew that I had been touched by the wand of fortune.

However, all these were things to come in the future as I waited to be called in as a witness at the court-martial. Sitting on the veranda, I concentrated my thoughts on the answers I would give to the judges when asked if I recognized the padlock.

A padlock: a piece of iron upon which depended the freedom of a comrade-in-arms whom I hated, and my own dignity, which I knew I was on the point of losing. Not that I had never told a lie before, but to lie on the Bible was quite different from lying about a piece of chocolate cake eaten without permission. And that was exactly what I was on the point of doing, because of the padlock that closed the gate of depot number 6 at Wadi Sarar.

Wadi Sarar was a big ammunition depot. It was reached by the train which ran from Tel Aviv to Jerusalem along the old, winding Turkish line. Our unit had been sent there in the autumn of 1941 to replace some of de Gaulle's Senegalese troops. The guard posts, scattered over a large area alongside big huts full of military equipment, consisted of one tent and eight soldiers, headed by a corporal or lance corporal. Only the British had the right to enter the buildings. Day and night, we colonials were supposed to stop anybody approaching the site by shouting, "Stop! Who goes there?" and pointing our Enfield rifles with fixed bayonets at him. If the unknown person stopped and answered "Friend," we were supposed to shout back, "Advance to be recognized." What happened after that stage we had not been told. If the friend turned out to be an enemy, we would have had to scare him off by our ferocious appearance and our bayonets since we were forbidden to keep our rifles loaded. If, however, the enemy was kind enough to give us time to open the pouches hanging on our battledress, take out the clips and load the rifle, he would still have had a chance to survive because we had to fire the first round in the air. Only with the second round, said the regulations, were we authorized to "shoot to kill," a highly unlikely situation since there was no enemy in sight for miles around. The only really important thing in this game of war was the procedure with which one guard commander handed over the inventory of his post every eight days to his replacement.

During Corporal Attiah's period of guard duty, a few thousand cartridges had disappeared together with the original padlock from the door of depot number 6. Attiah told the British who discovered the theft that the new padlock on the depot gate was already there when he took over guard duty from me. Since nothing was missing from the depot while I guarded it, nobody could accuse me. But if I stated that the padlock in question was different from the one I had observed two weeks previously, the suspicions against Attiah would be much stronger. And since I remembered perfectly well the shape of the padlock that had been broken and replaced, my evidence could be decisive.

From the day Attiah was arrested I had known no peace and quiet. In Palestine at that time Jews formed a closely knit, state-like community, with their own independent institutions, schools, clandestine military organization, the whole consolidated by a loyalty based on a highly politicized feeling of historical experience, discrimination, and persecution. This cohesion was even stronger in our army units, consisting entirely of volunteers, in which the real authority was vested in the Jewish NCOs. In fact, back in 1941 the number of Jewish colonial officers was still very small. Those who completed the first officers' courses opened to them were sent to join service units such as transport, engineers, quartermasters, and so on, which the British needed more than infantry. The few "native" officers in our regiment came from the best local Arab and Jewish families—Ben-Gurion, Margolis, Nashashibi, Dajani—and nobody wanted to endanger their promotion in the military hierarchy by involving them in political problems. They had to be kept out of trouble as much as possible, while the NCOs, most of whom had joined the army on instructions from the various Zionist political parties of the clandestine military organizations, were charged with the political guidance of the soldiers. This unofficial but very real authority, distinct from that of the British, naturally did not manifest itself every day. The Jewish NCOs carried out their daily duties according to orders from their British officers, behaving toward us as NCOs behave toward enlisted men everywhere in the world. We all knew that in matters of "national importance" they enjoyed an authority far higher than their rank.

When Corporal Attiah was indicted for the disappearance of ammunition at depot number 6, I immediately found myself facing the categorical instructions of "the organization," brought to me by a "native" sergeant, who was shocked by the fact that I could raise "moral scruples and objections." As soon as it became known that my answer to the court-martial was not certain, a void was created around me. It was not yet a clear case of ostracism but a sudden unresponsiveness to any attempt on my part to establish contact with other soldiers.

The human setting around me ceased, so to speak, to exist. It was neither hostile nor provocative, just mute and expectant. Marginal as I was to the Zionist society in Palestine, devoid of Jewish culture, and ignorant of all ideologies, not to speak of being unable to share with others the romantic vision of national revival that I had brought with me from Italy, I was terrified by the idea of living until the end of the war totally isolated in the middle of a society that was itself rejected by the rest of the world. The dread of having to command a squad of soldiers who might refuse to obey my orders in front of the entire unit on parade tormented me no less than the fact that I was being asked to do violence to my conscience. I had nobody in my unit to talk to. I knew that the answer to my questions would be that it was a holy duty to trick the British who had betrayed all their promises to the Jews through the white paper limiting the sale of land to Jews and their immigration into Palestine. "The one who robs the robber is absolved," says an old Jewish adage, and I had nothing against that. What held me back from perjury was the feeling that by swearing falsely in the name of God I would be breaking the very "crystal of my soul," cracking the innermost core of my conscience. Two types of morality, the national and the religious, clashed confusedly in the solitude of my anguish, neither one succeeding in overcoming the other. When I finally received an order to present myself as a witness to the court-martial, and my sergeant asked me what I had decided to do, I was surprised to hear myself answering with feigned confidence, "to lie under oath, of course."

For about an hour the warm approval I thought I read in my comrades' faces made me happy; for the first time I was tasting the strange, sensual pleasure of sinning in full consciousness, the relief of a mind that had decided to leave all doubts behind and accept whatever the future might bring. But it was a short-lived relief. My conscience renewed its constant attacks on my decision, and I could not sleep that night. In the morning, after receiving my travel warrant, I boarded the first Arab bus going past the Wadi Sarar camp and went to see my botany teacher at the Mikveh Yisrael agricultural school. I had not met him since the day I joined the army. His name was Meshiach, and he had studied agriculture at the University of Naples. He wore a pince-nez, and a bow tie on Saturdays, which made him strangely elegant in the untidy surroundings of the school, and he had always received me with great kindness in his home during the months I spent at the school and attended his lessons.

He listened to me with rapt attention. When I had finished describing the morass into which I had fallen, he took off his pince-nez and began polishing the lenses for a long time with extraordinary precision, while I observed the deep indentations that the springs had left on either side of his nose. When he finally replaced the pince-nez, his eyes bore a look of ancient sadness.

"Our sages were asked," he began, "why it is written in the Bible that only the sons of Israel cried at the death of Moses, while both the sons *and* daughters of Israel cried at the death of Aaron. Can we say that Aaron was better or more important than Moses? Certainly not. But Moses had said 'Let justice—if necessary—break the mountain.' He could not accept compromises because only by following absolute justice could he remain at one and the same time the servant of God and the servant of his people. Aaron, on the other hand, accepted compromise for love of peace and for a truth that could not be divine because it was a human truth. Had he not lied to the people when he built the Golden Calf and told them, 'This is your God, O Israel?' He did so because he felt that the idol could serve as a banner, as a rallying point for unity in a herd of sheep left temporarily without a shepherd. Aaron was a great patriot, probably greater than Moses, who could not separate his love for the people from his love for absolute truth."

"You are faced at this moment," he continued, "by the dilemma of Aaron: it is the dilemma with which the devil (remember that for the Jews he is still a divine messenger) faces every one of us sooner or later. The entire Zionist movement, the very essence of our national revival, is a kind of Golden Calf, because the state we want to create is a human construction, with a human morality, not a divine one. We have chosen to come to terms with the devil, with material power, human passions and interests, because we simply no longer have the strength to do anything else. 'The dead praise not the Lord,' says the psalm, and we are on the point of being destroyed.

"If you could ask Moses' advice," he concluded, "he might tell you to break the mountain with your truth. I cannot tell you that, if for no other reason than because while God himself sent Moses to save and guide the people morally and politically lost in the Egyptian exile, he has not sent anyone to bring a message of hope to us and to the Jews whom the Nazi Pharaoh is in the process of destroying in Europe, and here too, with the help of British despots. We stand alone, without guidance, and we have the duty to defend our people. Perhaps we shall have to pay for our arrogance with our lives and those of our sons for generations to come. This, too, may be part of our destiny. I cannot tell you whether you must or must not lie tomorrow; all I can tell you is that the roads that will open before you, whatever you do, will be equally painful, although the covenant with the devil is less difficult to sign than the covenant with God. Free will is the weightiest gift God has made to mortal man in order that everyone may at the end be able to save himself."

Together we left his apartment. We passed in front of the silent synagogue and through the gardens and then started walking down the long sandy avenue leading to the road that links Jaffa with Ramle, between the colonnade of palm trees and amid the uninterrupted buzzing of insects.

When I heard my name called, the conversation with my botany teacher flashed through my mind. Like a marionette I marched into the room of the court-martial at the order of the duty sergeant major. Under my topee, as I stood stiffly at attention, I could not see who was standing to my right or my left. I only felt a score of eyes fixed on me. The colonel, sitting between two other officers, told me kindly to stand at ease. The secretary of the court, an NCO of the Royal Hussars, brought me a Hebrew Bible and made me repeat the formula of the oath. I could feel sweat running down my back and creating a damp feeling in my trousers. At a sign from the president, the military prosecutor walked up to me holding a padlock in his hand. "Corporal," he said, "do you recognize this padlock?" "Yes, sir," I answered, surprised at how simple it was to lie. "Are you absolutely sure of that?" asked the military prosecutor, looking straight into my eyes. "Let me remind you that you have sworn on the Bible to tell the truth, and that God is at this very moment present in this court." "Yes, sir," I repeated, without the slightest effort, with a deep sense of relief, "this padlock is the one that locked the gate when I took over my guard duty." "Very well," said the military prosecutor. I heard behind me the roar of the sergeant major shouting "Ten-shun! About face! Left-right, left-right, halt!" and then a voice tinged with anger, "Dismissed: go back to your camp, Corporal."

With a light step I went out, passing under the cascade of bougainvillea, barely touching the hot sand on the ground with my shining boots. My mind was perfectly clear, my heart totally confused. I felt a strange smile on my lips. I knew I had just signed a pact with the devil, and I was anxious to know what I would get in exchange for my eternal soul.

8.

Jerusalem

WHEN I rang the bell at the apartment in Ibn Ezra Street in Jerusalem, I did not realize this gesture would have so many important consequences for me.

It was a three-room apartment on the ground floor with two entrances: the door at the side opened onto a staircase leading to the floor above; the other, at the front, opened onto a veranda. This was separated from the street by a small garden, at that time full of flowers, today overgrown with weeds. Through the veranda a small sitting room could be seen, clean and tidy, with part of the furniture concealed by curtains. A notice in full view, in Hebrew and English, read: TO LET. I crossed the garden in a few steps, walked onto the veranda, and rang the bell to inquire about the rent.

It was six o'clock on one of those summer evenings when a discreet wind waves the cypresses of Jerusalem, wakes people from their siestas, takes them under their showers, and invites those who have the time to get ready to admire the sunset. In less than an hour, the sky would turn red, then violet, and finally enter into the bright obscurity of the night.

I was dressed in civilian clothes, happy to be allowed to shed, after twelve months, my army uniform. I was wearing gray flannel trousers falling inelegantly onto a pair of heavy black boots, a checked jacket, which I carried hanging from my thumb over my shoulder, and a white shirt without a tie —a set of clothing halfway between that of the poorer, untidy dress of the immigrant Jews and the better-cut but climatically unsuitable wear of the British civil servants. It was indeed a hybrid outfit, undefined, like my new status of Italian announcer in the military broadcasting service of the Middle East.

I did not feel in the least embarrassed by it. I had just been promoted to the rank of sergeant; I had ten pounds, which I considered a fortune, in my wallet. In my pay book I carried a card issued by Field Security asking "civil and military authorities" to extend me all possible help in case of necessity. I was nineteen years old and felt free to live like a bird in the middle of a war that raged far away and which would open up, at least to me, the road to fame and success I so much desired.

A middle-aged woman appeared on the threshold. She wore a blue scarf on her head, which disclosed a few faded blond curls. Her unmade-up face revealed a shade of hardness and arrogance behind her delicate features. She wore frayed overalls with a colored apron around her waist. In her right hand, gloved in tan chamois leather, she held a duster as if it were a riding crop. She was obviously the landlady, a typical example of that German-Jewish bourgeoisie impoverished by immigration to Palestine but determined to preserve at all costs the decorum of a past social position.

She looked at me with a hint of a questioning smile on her thin lips. I explained that I was interested in renting a room with half-board and that I was a serviceman authorized to wear civilian clothes because I was temporarily serving with the foreign languages department of the radio. I asked the price and accepted it without arguing since it was below my billeting allowance. She understood this and suggested taking care of my laundry for an additional ten shillings a month.

As we talked, standing face to face, she on the veranda, I on the grass of the garden, I felt her psychological resistance gradually weakening. When she eventually became convinced that I was a Palestinian Jew serving in the British army and not one of those exotic types brought to Jerusalem by the war in the wake of the Allied troops, her face relaxed into a wide smile of agreement and complicity. Months later, when we happened to talk about our reciprocal impressions during that first meeting, she told me that her first impulse had been to turn me down, suspecting me of being an agent of the British Secret Service or, worse, of the Palestine Police. But as I kept talking, I sounded to her so infantile and looked so amusing in my attempts to appear self-assured and important, that she felt the need to offer me "a nest where I could let my feathers grow." Before he met me, her husband had been quite suspicious, asking himself whether it was prudent to allow into the house someone obviously linked with the Intelligence Service. He was convinced that my job as announcer was a cover-up for some more secret operation. But after we were introduced me, he shared his wife's opinion that whoever I might be and whatever I might do, I was, above all, a confused youngster in search of family warmth. Thus, without knowing it, I was accepted from the first moment as a kind of stray dog by two gentle remnants of a destroyed world.

Frau Luise, my landlady, took great care to uphold the dignity of her husband, a doctor from Hamburg who, in 1942, had not yet received a permit to practice because of the great number of Jewish refugee doctors who had flooded into Palestine. Dr. Wilfrid lived by translations and small commercial transactions, the most rewarding of which was the search for British and Arab buyers for the silver, rare books, and miniatures he or his friends had brought from Germany. The rent

I paid for the room and half-board was an important income for him, especially since the whole family could live on the army rations I brought to the house.

Their parental attitude toward me had also been awakened by the fact that their son, an engineer not much older than I, had gone from Germany to England. Their daughter, however, had chosen the life of the pioneers in an extreme left-wing kibbutz in Galilee. Even before knowing her, I thought that she had been right to run away from the padded, conventional atmosphere of her home, to which I, however, found no difficulty in adapting. I was curious to meet this farming daughter who was probably milking cows in her remote kibbutz and whose silver-framed photograph standing on the grand piano attracted my attention by its long, thoughtful face, seemingly absorbed in remote visions. But during the first week I spent in my new dwelling I was too busy with my new work at the broadcasting station to become interested in the life and family problems of my hosts.

They had given me a room at the end of the corridor overlooking the courtyard. Silent and shady, this room offered me, after many months of no privacy, the luxury of a sofa bed with two real linen sheets, freshly washed and ironed, and a table and a chair that did not shake. The cupboard was too big for the one change of underwear I possessed, the two summer uniforms, the winter battledress, my only civilian jacket and trousers, the three striped shirts, and the woolen tie the radio administration had requested me to wear while on duty. The most important thing in the lodging was, however, the bathroom. When I opened the shower tap I was free to let out of the perforated iron rose over my head as much cold or hot water as I wanted. Only those who have slept for weeks in the desert, experienced the hardness of an army shirt disgustingly stiff with sweat under the armpits, and had to face the shame of open-air showers and latrines can value the privacy of a separate bathroom and the exhilaration produced by the myriad water drops on sweaty skin, the indescribable pleasure of the primordial meeting of flesh and water.

In that bathroom, which my landlords took care to leave at my disposal after six in the morning, I sang, dreamed, and enjoyed every instant of the good fortune that the war had brought me, heedless of my future and rarely mindful of my past. If at night I was assailed by melancholy, I usually succeeded in overcoming the pangs of my Italian memories with reveries of my new military career, a psychological process undisturbed by the austere, old-fashioned atmosphere prevailing in the other two rooms of my new residence.

My landlords lived in the dining room, a small space occupied for the most part by a square table and two divan beds. Under the window there was a lace-covered shelf with some porcelain statuettes on it and a vase full of fresh flowers. Under the other window was a cupboard with crockery and cutlery, with the family's Sabbath ritual objects well in view on top —two silver candlesticks, a kiddush goblet, the spice box for habdalah. Hanging from the wall was a Hanukkah oil lamp.

Dr. Wilfrid was an observant Jew, but more in a "conservative" manner than in strict orthodoxy. He prayed alone at home in the mornings, afternoons, and evenings, and went to synagogue only on Saturdays and festivals. He did not usually keep his head covered but presided at the Sabbath meal with style and a feeling of pride that bore witness to the long religious tradition of his family. His wife and daughter were not observant at all. Frau Luise, however, gave the same punctilious care to the laying of the Sabbath table as she did to the ironing of the slightly frayed clothes and the starched shirts of her husband. For me, who had never celebrated the Sabbath in Italy, and who was certainly not particularly impressed either by the sabbatical rites in the kibbutz or by those in the homes of local Italian friends, these intimate Friday evening dinners, always accompanied by excellent food, revealed an unexpected and captivating aspect of Judaism. I enjoyed and relaxed in the peaceful quiet of a dining room in which the golden gleam of the Sabbath candles set at the center of the embroidered tablecloth shone more brightly than the fully lit crystal candelabrum. I was grateful for a tidiness that reflected not only the civility of my hosts but also a larger, ancient order of things to which I felt I somehow belonged in spite of its strangeness. On these evenings Frau Luise always appeared dressed in an elegant, outmoded suit, always wore for the occasion an ancient family pendant round her neck, and before nodding to her husband to start reciting the blessings she threw a last authoritative look at all the objects lined up as though on military parade to "receive" the Sabbath: the gold-rimmed plates laid on the table, the silverware on either side of them, the breadbasket covered with an embroidered cloth, the silver goblet for the blessing, the saltcellar, and, standing in a larger circle around the table, all the other objects in the room.

During these Friday evenings, when the noises had died away in the streets of Jewish Jerusalem and the shadows from the oil lamps quivered in the empty synagogues, Dr. Wilfrid appeared transformed. Impeccably dressed, in summer in a white linen suit, which he exchanged in winter for one of dark English tweed, he sported a silk bow tie under a starched piqué collar, which made him look slightly ridiculous on any other occasion. Now, however, the air of uncertainty and shyness that accompanied him throughout the week was replaced by a proud demeanor, just as the sandals in which he plodded the city streets in search of buyers for his books and miniatures had been replaced by a pair of shiny black shoes. With his head covered by a silk-embroidered skullcap, he recited the Sabbath blessings with an assured voice and a benevolent smile on his lips. This smile must have belonged to the rich and famous Hamburg doctor he had once been, to the director of the great military hospitals in the Great War, to a man who had tasted the comfort of his father's villa in the Black Forest and who now wanted, at least on the Sabbath, to forget his refugee status and his middleman trade.

After dinner we used to move into the third room of the apartment, a sitting room in which nobody slept and which my landlords tried to preserve as an island of culture and affluence. The largest part of the room was occupied by a grand piano. Frau Luise played on it when she entertained friends or when engaged in a harmonious dialogue with her husband at the end of the Sabbath. On those occasions he listened to her, seated on a frayed, brocade-covered armchair, nodding his head in gestures of rhythmic approval and occasionally allowing unashamed tears to roll slowly from his closed eyelids.

Frau Luise, in a way, also talked to me while playing the piano. With her music she was describing to me places and landscapes in Germany, telling me stories of a people whom she had obviously not stopped loving but about whom it was no longer possible to speak except with expressions of hate. I felt the same toward Italy and shared her nostalgia for a country I doubted I would ever see again. Yet this common melancholy did little to melt the layer of indifference that I felt gradually building up in myself—an apathy toward everyone and everything, the result of a destiny that in Italy made of me a Jew in spite of myself, while here it was seemingly turning me into an alien in the midst of so many Palestinian Jews.

Dr. Wilfrid used to gather a few friends in his sitting room on Saturday afternoons. For several weeks I was not invited to join this symposium of good German-Jewish bourgeois. The excuse was that they spoke a language I did not understand. The truth was that they were suspicious of me, not knowing exactly who I was. I had told my landlord of the circumstances under which I had left Italy, how I had enrolled in the Mikveh Yisrael agricultural school, how I had joined, as everybody did in my class, the Hagana. I had described to him my swearing-in ceremony in the wooden hut at the edge of the school's botanical garden, the oath I took while keeping my right hand on a Mauser pistol, my eyes blinking because of the floodlamp that concealed the faces of those who administered the oath. I told Dr. Wilfrid how and why I had left the school at the beginning of 1941 and joined the British army after protracted discussions with my companions and teachers on the advantages and disadvantages, the political morality and the ideological principles involved in serving the king of England instead of the Palmach, the Jewish striking force, which was being organized in the kibbutzim in readiness for a German-Italian invasion. For my schoolmates the choice was simple: those who wanted to share in the Allied war effort but refused to become an integral part of a foreign army enrolled in the Palmach. Those, like me, who were looking for adventure, money, and career could and should serve in the British army.

In spite of my sincerity, my indifference toward ideology seemed suspicious to Dr. Wilfrid and some of his friends, who were emotionally involved in the war even if they did little to contribute to the war effort. They lived riveted to their wireless sets, listening to the news in every understandable language and making the war bulletins the principal subject of their conversations. Under its quiet surface, Jerusalem in 1942 teemed with mysteries, pacts, treason, and plots, imaginary or real. The Jews, the British, and the Arabs plotted against each other and within their own communities, each hating and double-dealing the others in their own particular style and logic.

The unity of the Jews had never been complete. Side by side with the orthodox Jews, clustered in their neighborhoods and hostile to the secular Zionists, there were the "orthodox" secular left-wing parties that hated the "orthodox" secular parties of the right—the Jabotinsky Revisionists. All three maligned the bourgeois, despised the Arabs, and aped the British. The British refusal to open the gates of the country to the refugees from Europe and the first horrendous news that seeped in about the fate of the Jews at the hands of the Nazis, had begun to dissolve the Zionist collective discipline and make it difficult for many Palestinian Jews to respect the Jewish Agency's promise not to fight Arab nationalism and British imperialism as long as the war against Hitler was being waged. There was a lot of talk about groups that had decided to take armed action against the mandatory government. It was even said, in great secret, that some were ready to come to an agreement with the enemy if the Germans would agree to stop the slaughter of the Jews.

The Jewish Communists, who for years had suffered because of the Soviet Union's hostility to Zionism, were now able to defend openly their idea of creating a binational Arab-Jewish state in which Marxism would triumph over the "tribal" Jewish nationalism. All over the country there were political visionaries, military prophets, and ideological parasites; human relics and bureaucratic caliphs; naive heroes and opportunists; charlatans and saints. To me, most of them seemed like hallucinatory figures and recalled to my mind the paintings of El Greco: human beings inhumanly stretched toward unlimited horizons of hope, hate, rancors, and revolts, and at the same time chained down in Jerusalem to the tiny space of a provincial city, aware that in fact they were already witnessing the fall of the greatest colonial empire in the world.

In this gossipy, exalted, mysterious, and parochial atmosphere, palpitating with history and faith, made up of shadows and sudden gleams of light, I could not avoid being an object of suspicion. I represented the "other," although biologically a member of the Zionist "family." At the same time, conditioned as I was by my British uniform, infatuated with my role of "clandestine" speaker, I invited mistrust with my unnatural condescending behavior to the "natives," satisfied with an artificial isolation that so well fitted my immature psychology. Quite often, however, and in spite of this complacency of mine, I felt the need to find someone in whom to confide and with whom to discuss what I was doing in the middle of all these explosive contradictions. Dr. Wilfrid, with whom I often talked, was the person least suited to help me clear my ideas. This good, liberal, German, religious, Zionist doctor dreamed of nothing better than to become a British citizen and to live in a mandated territory.

Sometimes after dinner when Frau Luise asked us to leave the dining room in order to turn the divans into beds for the night, we sat next to the silent piano, he smoking a carved clay pipe, I crouched on the round ottoman near the door. The sliding white muslin curtains at the windows of this quiet sitting room reminded me of the puppet theaters with which I used to play, with one difference; here we were the puppets, manipulated by invisible hands that pulled the strings of our existence, concealed by mountains of words to which, night after night, I added my vocal contribution, reading the war bulletins and the political commentaries of our clandestine radio station. In those few square meters of tidy space, full of fragments and reminiscences of a world destroyed for Dr. Wilfrid and new for me, it came naturally and easily to both of us to speak about the ill-concealed doubts that perturbed our consciences.

For him Zionism was an option, a choice for collective life made by Jews who had lost most of their religious identity and were clumsily trying to build a new one around the idea of a nation that they had picked up piecemeal in the countries of their enemies. In Palestine, Jews were trying to live—so thought Dr. Wilfrid—in a "national home" built according to foreign architecture on our ancestral land, the use of which we had handed over to others throughout centuries of forced absence and which we now wanted to recover in a couple of decades. Under such stress nobody could hope to revive a civilization, a culture of our own. Zionism was a utopia with no moral obligation when turned into a reality. Even if we ignored the Arabs, who after all were an external nuisance and paradoxically contributed to our unity, our problem was how to incarnate our lofty ideas and create a genuinely new Jewish style of life in which our faults would coexist with our follies. The assimilation we had embraced with such enthusiasm in Europe had hastened Hitler's disaster. If we continued to imitate the outside world, the national home we wanted to create for Jews in Palestine risked turning into a vehicle for a new collective assimilation. What new disaster would then befall us?

For him the problem was how to find a way to blend the heritage of Esau, to whom had been promised the world of matter, with that of Jacob, who was chosen to live in the world of the spirit. Zionism wanted to integrate both, not just conciliate them, as for centuries Judaism had tried to do in the ghetto. It was a dangerous exploit, which had never succeeded before and which, in addition, Jews had undertaken in the midst of the chaos in Europe.

Dr. Wilfrid was not particularly worried by the Arab hostility. In World War I he had served as a military surgeon in Turkey and that experience in the East had forever conditioned his mind toward the Orientals.

The Turks had taught him that the Arabs could never be citizens but only subjects. Such, he believed, they should remain within a Zionist state, provided that the Jews would be able to establish with them relations of economic interest stronger than those of political antagonism. The Arab revolt was a beautiful legend created by Colonel T. E. Lawrence, warmed up after the Great War by the romanticism of an English elite touched by moral and political decadence. The Zionists were certainly paying the price of this legend, but in the end the myth of Arabism would produce a flood of words and perhaps of blood, which would eventually extinguish itself in its own contradictions. Arabs, in any case, counted little because they did not know who they were and what they wanted. They possessed a collective political-religious identity as long as Islam had linked them with the other Muslims through the Ottoman Empire and, in a looser way, with the Muslims of other colonial territories. The bedouin of Arabia who created Islam were unable to keep it alive in modern times and inherit the strength of the Turks necessary to impose on all or most of the Arabs a political control based on the collective identity of the Muslims. Once the unity of Islam broke into pieces, the caliphate was abolished, the provinces of the Ottoman Empire were transformed into states without national character, common history, and social or religious equality, what could the strength of the Arabs be? Nothing, since the Arabs would continue to yearn for a dying Europe, clothed in the veils of the Lawrence myth, while incapable of absorbing Western values since these belonged to the Christian world. In the caricature of local imported nationalism, the Arabs would lose the little indigenous creativity they possessed. "You Europeans," a wounded Turkish colonel once told Dr. Wilfrid, "do not want to accept the fact that the Arabs are the fathers, not the sons of the desert, and incapable of creating a state. They are converted Christians who preserved only the shrewdness and the memory of the Byzantine oppression. We, the Turks, coming from the steppes of Asia, have prevented them for centuries from cutting each other's throats as defenders of the legitimizing role of Islam—a faith that befits the believers in it because it is equally accepted by the rulers and the ruled, even when applied in a different manner. The unity of Islam once destroyed, the community of believers will return to being what it had always been in the East—a mosaic of nomadic tribes and masses of peasants exploited by merchants or by robbers masquerading as rulers. The Ottoman Empire will be succeeded by another imported empire, or by chaos. In both cases the Arabs would be the losers."

The Jews, too, would be losers, Dr. Wilfrid believed. "We are not a tribe of robbers but a family of slaves. We have lost the sense of statehood like the Christians who converted to Islam. Our Islam is the European culture. It has drawn from its Greco-Christian roots the poison with which it revenges itself upon us for having given Jesus to Athens and Rome."

The Zionists' error consisted for him in thinking themselves capable of guaranteeing the material survival of the Jews through the creation of a pagan "house" outside Europe. Perhaps one day they might be able to create even an independent state of their own. But it would not last and would be counterproductive. A Jewish Westernized state would look for strength, not for justice; for compromise, not for uniqueness. These were Greek ambitions, not Jewish. Jews had always drawn their energy from the opposition existing between man and God, between the pure and the impure, the sacred and the profane, between pride and piety. Their system of life had developed through the centuries the art of living in balance between stars and dust, subconscious and superego. It worked for a sacred people confined to, but also protected by, the ghetto; it would not work in a modern state in which the "raison d'etat" would replace the "raison de Dieu," because ideology ends in self-destruction. Jews would never be able to put into practice the abstract ideas of human, rational perfection to which they aspired.

The national religion in which Zionism believed was not only alien to Jews, it was the worst of all political beliefs. It had neither limits nor brakes, the interests of the state being above everything. "My country, right or wrong" was a principle totally opposed to the spirit of the Ten Commandments, which were given to the Jews coming out of Egypt and which turned them from slaves into an elitist nation. "If we cannot find a way to turn ourselves from assimilated, pagan Jews into an elitist modern political society," he said, "we run the risk of dying before being born." Dr. Wilfrid was scared of a freedom founded on the principle of self-determination since it implied perpetual opposition to values and ambitions equally valid for others. He was prepared to exchange Jewish national rights for the rescue of as many Jews as possible and the time needed to educate them to statehood. This could be achieved only through the maintenance of the British imperial power over Palestine for the longest possible time. "It may turn out to be like living under a shed that will not protect us from cold or heat," he said, but at least it will allow us to prepare ourselves to face our true enemies: ourselves."

I listened to him, amused and irritated at the same time. I could not share his pessimism or agree with his praise of political immobilism, but I did not find myself in total disagreement with what he was saying about Britain. I did not perceive her foreign presence, as some of my schoolmates did, as fundamentally hostile, as a kind of octopus whose tentacles we had to hack off. For me, Britain represented the sporting field on which I had been invited to participate, the authority that in the sticky confusion of the Orient, projected an image of equity, of order, of fair play. It may all be due to imperial self-interest, but it was more than just exterior pretense. Anyway, Britain was now fighting the worst enemy of the Jews. She had the right to expect our loyalty, and in my case even more than that. After my choking experiences at school, in the kibbutz, in colonial garrisons, my present work in the field of psychological warfare made me dream of a future in which I might rebuild, in a "British" key, the class security I had enjoyed in Italy but without its "Latin" bourgeois straitjacket —a future in which I could take a confused, social, and personal revenge on the humiliations of my past.

To me at that time, Britain seemed the antithesis of provinciality, the opposite of Mussolini's buffoonery and of the cultural banality in which I had grown up. Still fed by heroic films seen in Italy, I abandoned myself to the attraction of the immense red-colored spaces submitted to British power in the geographic atlases; to the influence of a language I was now using more than my mother tongue; to the fascination of an

English style of life that in Palestine was, for the most part, a caricature of Victorianism. My admiration for the British was, as with Kipling, in direct relation to my colonial, psychological marginality, and I was unaware that I was in the process of becoming an "assimilated native" without the shrewdness of the Levantine.

In the years to come, this juvenile experience would help me to understand the mentality and the development problems of the peoples of the Third World. But at the time of the battles of El Alamein and Stalingrad, I did not feel that I was becoming what the French call an *évolué*, parroting what I believed to be signs of English culture and way of life: a moustache, which I found difficult to grow; a sauntering walk copied from some officers; an affected detachment from other people's troubles; a haughty indifference toward the dramatic war events I discussed with the arrogant ignorance of a football expert; and the ill-conceived superiority with which I treated the local "natives," Jews or Arabs, in the streets or in the market. This behavior was not peculiar to me. Jews, Moslems, and Christians competed with each other in those days in aping the British, each in his own way. At the Palestine Broadcasting Station they even had a booklet that explained the secrets of the new language, Pinglish. This mixture of local and Anglo-Saxon words—and especially the adaptation of English syntax to the local mentality—was one of the signs of the cultural disintegration of at least some of those groups of Palestinians, Arabs and Jews, who came in close contact with a foreign society totally convinced of its natural superiority.

Listening to the arguments of my landlord with the foolish righteousness derived from my temporary status as a British soldier and the curiosity of my ignorant exoticism toward a Judaism totally unknown to me, I could not understand the dangers of the pagan rationalism that obsessed him. Zionism was not a ghost that disturbed my sleep. On the contrary, fed as I was by romantic dreams and Fascist ideology, the thought that the state could be an idol, the nation a cruel chimera of which one should beware, never crossed my mind. For me the state was as natural a thing as the air or my mountain vacation. It was the organization that made people go to school, cleaned streets, minted money, distributed medals, gave a meaning to symbols, decorum to churches and uniforms, made trains arrive on time, and protected the legitimate interests of good families like mine in Italy. The state was an institution that had to be defended. Without internal order and protection from external enemies, one could not enjoy the normal pleasures of life, consisting for me mainly in fox hunting, skiing, watching Westerns, and conquering the only thing that at that time was to me of inestimable value—a woman.

And yet my conversations with Dr. Wilfrid made me aware of an aspect of my character that I tried to conceal even from myself. I perceived at the bottom of my consciousness something like an icy spot: I could suffer, hate, enjoy myself with every fiber of my body; I could listen in ecstasy to a piece of music; I could embrace with enthusiasm any cause; I was faithful to friends, sensitive to honor. To lie (as I frequently did) made my stomach ache for days. In sum, I knew that emotionally I was hypersensitive. But I could not help maintaining a selfish reserve even toward those I trusted most and toward the ideas that seemed to me most reasonable and noble. I developed an inability to give myself up totally, as if at the root of my conscious mind there existed a layer of indifference, a core of psychological ice that made it impossible for me to identify myself completely with anything or anybody.

I have never freed myself from this visceral indifference to which I probably owe my capacity to overcome both physical and moral pain. Only with advancing age have I given up the need, slightly sadistic, to have the roots of my teeth treated without an anesthetic. On those few occasions when I broke one of my limbs, I noticed a strange mechanism developing in my brain, a kind of levitation of my consciousness which, without reducing the pain of the flesh, transferred it outside my body.

To this splitting of my senses, I owe my psychological and moral survival in circumstances in which others would probably have gone mad. A word, a gesture of contempt, can still wound me more deeply—as the Arab proverb puts it—than a knife. But even the most terrible burning in the soul quickly cools at the contact with that icy layer. Only the anguish produced by fear of physical danger remains for me a permanent nightmare. To free myself from this I have often committed irrational acts of apparent courage just to overcome, through the fear of fear, the terror I always feel when faced by danger. In these circumstances, just as when confronted by strong physical pain, I feel a splitting of my senses that sometimes lasts for days. I then see myself trembling with fear and shame, pleading for a chance to run away. And opposed to this, another self, who stares from imaginary, empty eye sockets, indifferent and mocking.

A lady friend, endowed with parapsychological powers, told me once that I carried the mark of Cain on my forehead. I was born, she said, with a natural vocation for crime from which I have been saved by my innate animal fear. When I tried to explain to Dr. Wilfrid my occasional splitting into my two selves, he teasingly commented: "It is possible that in you Cain and Abel have not yet separated. You need a woman capable of choosing for you between life and death."

The idea that that was the choice of Faust came to me suddenly a few days later when, returning home late at night, I found Dr. Wilfrid's daughter waiting for me with a book of Goethe in German open on the table. She had arrived in Jerusalem from her kibbutz that afternoon, and her parents, who had gone out for the evening, had asked her to prepare my supper.

Without getting up, she held out to me her long-fingered, warm hand. I felt the two thoughtful eyes, which had been looking at me from the silver-framed photograph on the piano for the past two weeks, scrutinizing me as if I were a laboratory specimen.

"I am Berenika," she said softly. As would often happen to me when with her, I did not know what to answer.

9.

Broadcasting Intermezzo

THE "CLANDESTINE" Italian radio of the British headquarters in the Middle East operated from the studios of the PBS (Palestine Broadcasting Station). Our office was located in two rooms of the requisitioned monastery of Saint Peter in Gallicantu on the slopes of Mount Zion, a long, rectangular stone building, six floors high, with a queer cement balustrade of a floral design around its flat roof. From it one could see the entire valley of the Final Judgment (the Valley of Jehoshaphat), and at the foot of the Mount of Olives, the village of Silwan, engulfed in the wadi, which ran down through the Judean Desert toward the Dead Sea.

Beneath the monastery, on the left-hand side and looking eastward, one could see, partially concealed by two lines of cypresses, the square stones of an ancient Roman street. After celebrating the Last Supper on Mount Zion, Jesus had walked on it to reach the Garden of Gethsemane, where he was arrested—a distance of less than two miles magnified by history and faith, which the eyes had difficulty in equating with the images created by legend and religion in the mind.

Mount Zion, at that time, was a silent hill, oppressed by the enormous Teutonic church that Kaiser Wilhelm II of Germany had built at the end of the last century in honor of the Virgin Mary and to please his Catholic subjects, jealous of the favors that German Protestants enjoyed in the Holy Land. The basilica, with its tower-like, copper-plated cupola, would soon become a battered, Jewish advance military position facing the Arabs in divided Jerusalem. In 1942 it was just another religious building whose shape broke the gentle line of the hill during the day and became, like everything else in Jerusalem, just another mysterious shadow in the evening.

From the roof of my office, where I used to go to enjoy the sunset, this tower looked to me like a kind of Tyrolean hat planted on the head of the mountain, a fanciful stone decoration imported into the Orient from the north, a symbol of that metamorphosis of Jewish beliefs which, transplanted from here into the Greco-Roman world, had turned the competition between old and new Israel into a suicide story for Western civilization.

From the monastery one had the impression in the evening of being almost able to reach, with one's outstretched hand, the massive Zion Gate. Through the dark opening of the donjon, orthodox Jews crossed furtively into the street. Bearded and lanky, wrapped in their caftans, their large felt hats bordered by fur, earlocks swinging on both sides of their faces in unison with the nervous movements of their bodies, they moved like shadows to and from the Old City quarters, quickly swallowed up by the stone alleys leading to the Tomb of David. I admired their courage in moving about alone at night in places where we British soldiers were advised not to go for fear of getting knifed. I knew nothing about them, although I was aware we belonged to the same people. They lived in their closed world surrounded by Arabs, keeping apart from the modern Jews whom they considered more impure than the Moslems or the Christians because of their heretical Hebrew nationalism. Only near the Wailing Wall, which at that time consisted of a narrow cobbled corridor, could I perceive the link between me and people so different. Here, swaying and moaning, Jews of all types, orthodox and liberal, native and visitor, young and old, Oriental and Western, felt the weight of the past that united them, often in spite of themselves.

This feeling of unity was strengthened in me by the revulsion I felt for the two British policemen who, at the entry to the passage, watched over our behavior. Their task was to see to it that nobody should blow a shofar—the Jewish ritual ram's horn—to remind the Lord of the promises made to His people. Like the Arabs, the mandatory government did not believe that a Jewish Messiah, let alone the Zionist Jews, would eventually build a Jewish state. But the howl of the shofar was considered political provocation, contrary to the delicate religious status quo. Those two unarmed policemen, looking impassively at the Jews crowding along the wall, seemed to me full of contempt for our native, rebellious superstitions. They stood like mannequins, carefully dressed in their colonial uniforms, probably bored and unaware in their northern, barbarian ignorance of the passions condensed by history in this miniaturized scene of suffering and prayers. To me they were a reminder both of the irritating difference of political status separating us in spite of our common uniform and of the comic marionettes I watched as a child in the theater in Turin, with their angular, wooden gestures moved by invisible strings. Who was the puppeteer activating all these people near the Wailing Wall, each devoted to his own cause and God? I could not find a satisfactory answer. And it was probably this lack of a satisfactory response to a primordial question that would one day push all of us, men and women in search of new roots, to join the fanatics. One day, without really knowing the reason, but moved by a visceral need for action, we would rise up and break all religious laws, demystify all political incantation. We would kill the British whom we admired because they stood guarding us against the Arabs, because they watched us mockingly near the wall; and then we would give vent to our perverse desire to cut off all the beards of the Jews, strip our impossible brothers of their stinking caftans, which weighed so heavily on our Zionist conscience, and start everything anew.

And yet the Wailing Wall was the only place where I felt that our secular national movement, even in its most extreme socialist forms, had a historical meaning; the only place where one could dream of a miracle—without imagining how close we stood to its coming.

In that warm summer Rommel menaced Egypt and Palestine, and people spoke of the inevitable retreat of the British army toward the mountains of Lebanon. These black forecasts did not disturb the sensation of peace and eternity that at nightfall surrounded the monastery where I worked, canceling all traces of the events that troubled the world. In the deep silence, broken by the howls of the jackals, I could let my imagination run wild, as had probably been done before me in these same premises by prophets and thieves, scribes and slaves, Pharisees and Crusaders, Roman legionnaires and merchants, without feeling part of the history that made Jerusalem the crossroad of the world. I was interested in living, in tasting and enjoying the strange adventure that Jewish persecution in Italy and the war in the Middle East had opened up for me. I was anxious to exploit whatever occasion fate offered me and desperate at not being able to explain to anyone why I felt such a need to climb up to the roof of the monastery at night to call my mother softly; to cry without shame over the dog my father had given, without my permission, to my uncle, over the mare on which I had galloped in Italy, and over the tin soldiers I had buried, together with my Fascist Youth dagger, under the cedar in my mother's garden—now probably all waiting, like the dead in the Valley of Jehoshaphat stretched out at my feet, for me to blow the trumpet of their resurrection.

I used to let myself go into these infantile reveries while, under the roof where I was standing, a legion of strange human beings, more unreal than those who inhabited my imagination, were busy, each one with earphones on his head in order not to disturb his neighbor, following the broadcasts of the enemy stations. Their task was to gather the material with which the army's psychological warfare service supplied the many clandestine broadcasting stations, like the Italian one in which I was working.

In those few hundred square meters under my feet there were Bulgarians and White Russians, Frenchmen and Germans; there were Croats who hated the Serbians and Macedonians who hated the Greeks; Moslems hostile to the Jews and Armenians who dreamed of avenging themselves on the Turks. They were tied to powerful receivers for two-hour spells. With one hand on the radio knobs and the other furiously scribbling on paper headed "On His Majesty's Service," these men and women fought against a faraway enemy and at the same time engaged in continuous battles to defend their own linguistic territory, as if it were a piece of the country they served or betrayed according to their own political faith. It was a mosaic of human relics kept together by a war that allowed each one to pursue the illusion of influencing the fate of distant peoples who were probably unaware of their existence and indifferent to their broadcasts. With most of them I had no contact. They were all older than I and belonged to that class of people I considered inferior because of their being "enemy aliens." They seemed to ignore my existence, and I did not realize that for them I was an unexplainable being: the only non-British soldier employed as a civilian speaker, who at the age of nineteen dealt with political questions reserved elsewhere only for senior officers.

With my military superiors I had no special problems. Some of them had come to Jerusalem from Cairo in the wake of the German advance in the Western Desert. Enzo Sereni, who had run the Italian section in Egypt, had clashed with the British HQ and left the Psychological Warfare Department. Of the original group created by Sereni, only one member remained —an officer of the Italian Alpine Corps, captured in Greece by the British and who switched to their side. He called himself de Robillant, drank a lot, pretended to be consumed by TB, and dreamt of—and indeed later succeeded in—becoming a writer. Neither with him nor with the other Italian expatriates, Jews and non-Jews, who had created in Jerusalem an anti-Fascist group affiliated with the movement "Giustizia e Libertà," did I develop close relations. On the contrary, I developed a friendship with the director of the Italian broadcasting section, Renato Mieli, and with his wife, Isa, who worked as secretary of our office.

Their personalities were so different from those of other Fascist refugees or Zionist immigrants in Palestine. Among so many excitable characters, Mieli appeared like an incarnation of common sense, modesty, and courtesy. He spoke softly, accepted philosophically the arrogance of the military administration, and enjoyed making fun of our British controller without his ever realizing it. This controller was an RAF officer who had never been in the cockpit of a plane or near a front line. He belonged to a Hungarian family that emigrated to England and stressed on every possible occasion the aristocratic particle preceding his name. He was also particular about the "y" that ended it (we sometimes substituted a simple "i" in our internal service notes), as if this consonant acted as a phonetic watershed between his Balkan origin and the new status acquired in England.

Renato Mieli had to write a daily political commentary to be broadcast to Italy after the news bulletin. He tried to avoid making use of the slogans with which our British controller wanted to embellish our broadcasts. It was no easy job. "We are a clandestine radio," Mieli used to say. "Theoretically we are operating somewhere on an Italian coastline. To make our clandestinity credible we must give the impression of being constantly in contact with the local population, we must interpret its mentality, be aware of its problems, interest our Italian listeners who have the patience and the courage to tune in. We must therefore supply them with plausible news and only from time to time plant unverifiable items of propaganda and denounce personalities in the Fascist regime. Calumny is useful only if measured, and tendentious interpretation of facts credible only if based on verifiable events." It was counterproductive to conceal the successes of Rommel, or minimize the importance of British military reverses, such as the fall of Tobruk. On the contrary, they should be mentioned whenever possible, to explain the consequences of a war in which Italy, beaten by the Allies or made a satellite of Germany, would in any case become a loser. Mieli looked for every possible item of news on current life in Italy, news picked up from Fascist, Vatican, or Swiss stations, on which to base his political commentary, rather than speculating on major events.

Although monitoring was not my responsibility, I liked to spend hours listening to broadcasts in Italian from wherever they came. I was fascinated by the voices that reached me from Italy, and even more by the little pep talks that the famous "Colonel Steven" gave, in Italian, from London over the BBC. He was a British diplomat who had served for many years in Italy and had an intimate knowledge of the Italian mentality. At a distance of years I perceive how, in the absence of a proper school education, I learned from him, and in general through my work in the monastery of Saint Peter in Gallicantu, the trade of journalism. But it was to Fausto Nitti, the nephew of the former Italian prime minister, whom I owe the reading of my first serious books—Croce's *History of Europe* and *Estetica* —which so greatly influenced my way of thinking.

How this elegant and refined gentleman had ended up in Jerusalem reading daily news bulletins with me for a faked clandestine broadcasting station run by the British, I do not know. I admired him for the way in which he always dressed perfectly, for the free and easy manner in which he carried his Indian walking stick, for the dignity with which he combined an exceptional family past with his present precarious status. Nitti hated speaking about himself; he preferred to listen in silence to others. When we had to present a two-voice program, he reading the news and I the announcements, or vice versa, he took special care in hitting the gong that opened and closed our broadcasts. That subdued rumble of percussed metal, which the microphone was supposed to propagate on the air until it reached the ears of some Italian listener thousands of miles away, seemed to have for him a value greater than any political commentary. I watched him standing near me in the studio, his eyes riveted on the technician through the sound-proof window who had to give us the signal to start the broadcast. In his left hand Nitti held the gong, dangling from a cord tied to two holes on its rim. Bent slightly forward, he raised the hammer with his right hand, waiting like a hunting dog pointing its prey. When the technician gave the sign, with a finger aimed like a pistol, Nitti struck two chimes on the gong, one stronger, one weaker. Then he stretched himself forward, as if he wanted to follow with his entire body the sound he had just produced, as if a tiny part of himself could fly through skies and reach a secure place that none of us knew, where perhaps somebody was waiting for him. Perhaps it was a woman, perhaps an accomplice, perhaps a faithful dog, like mine, now lonely in its kennel, like me, like Nitti, like all those whom the war had uprooted, separated, dismembered. Perhaps it was just the echo of our thoughts thrown toward a faraway, unreal Italy, which we were pretending to help and prepare for its political future, returning deprived of sense to its source in a provincial corner of Britain's cosmopolitan empire.

Isa was the opposite of Nitti. Minute, blond, loquacious, quivering with communist passion, she kept full control of herself in her working relationships but went wild in the style of the bulletins she typed on small sheets of paper. She was indeed quite a strange "comrade": too intelligent and too much conditioned by the Levantine atmosphere of Egypt to insert quotations from Marx and Lenin into her daily conversation, she never let an occasion pass to mention the Red Army without adding the word "heroic." For her every Fascist was a plutocrat, every worker in the vanguard of the people. Cosmopolitanism was doomed, the USSR was saving Europe from the Nazis, and true democracy could exist only in a socialist world. Many of these expressions got lost between the old Underwood on which Isa hammered them out and the broadcast sheets we used in the studio. It was not the British censor who corrected the style of this ardent Alexandrine; it was her husband and sometimes Nitti who expurgated from the text as many of her ideological superlatives as the arrogant banalities of our British controller—one with his modest smile, the other with his impenetrable silences.

In August 1942, when the appointment of Montgomery as head of the Eighth Army had strengthened everyone's courage and faith, the reinforcements the Intelligence Service had requested from its American counterpart arrived in our section. They consisted of two Italo-Americans who, I was told in strict confidence, had been sent by the gangster "Lucky" Luciano to prepare the Allied landing in Sicily. They were supposed to supply us with coded messages to broadcast to Sicilian patriots belonging to political movements that wanted to separate the island from Italy. Our British controller, that RAF officer with the "y" at the end of his name, explained to me that these messages were of two types. There were coded sentences addressed to the Sicilian members of the Mafia, so secret that nobody had the right to know their meaning; apparently they were explosive material that could change the course of the war, if not in the entire Mediterranean, certainly between the towns of Gela and Caltanissetta. Then there were the messages that the captain called "musical accompaniments." These were to be written in a hermetic style supposed to give credibility to our broadcasts in certain Sicilian milieus that theoretically listened to them. These regional-separatist lucubrations would, according to him, prepare the ground for the forthcoming landing and make the inhabitants of Sicily more sensitive and conscious of the history of their island. My captain sincerely believed himself involved in an ideological effort to promote the political consciousness of a pro-British, independent Sicily, even if more controlled than ever by the Mafia.

Ignorant as I was of the history of Sicily, which I had never visited, I could make no sense of the arguments the captain expounded to me, especially in the absence of the head of our station. I was, however, surprised by the fact that the two mafiosi whom we had received from America—one fat and the other thin, lugubrious and comical like Laurel and Hardy —lived an existence totally detached from our section. I do not remember ever having read a message, coded or uncoded, prepared by them. What I immediately noticed was that the two "advisers" spoke a strange, Anglicized Italian that nobody in our section was able to understand. It sounded more like the language spoken by the Bulgarians and Albanians who worked on the top floor of the monastery than the dialect of any Italian province I knew. I also discovered that at least one of these two strange figures (the other soon disappeared from sight) could not write. When I accompanied him—he was the fat one—to the quartermaster's office to sign some administrative forms, I saw him inscribing the paper with scribbling similar to that which my father's illiterate peasants made on the documents he prepared for their signature.

Fortunately for everyone, the two representatives of "Lucky" Luciano knew how to keep their mouths shut. They had been quartered at the American Colony Hotel, one of the most elegant residences in Jerusalem, and there they spent their days, drinking lemonade and beer. Throughout the period of my work at the radio, I do not remember anybody ever making use of their services, partly because—as I said—nobody could understand their language. The British controller of our section had tried to overcome this linguistic difficulty by using sign language which, according to him, expressed fundamental concepts of the ancient Sicilian culture. To me they looked like the gestures children make at monkeys in zoological gardens, but it was probably because I had not been let into this type of state secret. Later, however, it came to my knowledge that, perhaps due to an error of interpretation of languge or of judgment by overly zealous police, the two mafiosi, who were supposed to advance the Allied cause in Italy, had been advancing that of hashish dealers in Palestine. It seems they had no difficulty in making themselves understood in the local Jerusalem markets.

During my time at the radio I never asked to what political or religious creed Mieli and his wife belonged. Only many years later in Rome when I met Mieli (then the editor of an important communist weekly) in the home of a mutual friend —a noble landowner who tortured himself about whether to divide his land among his tenant farmers—did I learn that both of them were Jewish. It was not surprising, since the Communist party in Egypt in the thirties had been to a large extent supported by Jewish intellectuals, the sons of some of the richest families in Cairo and Alexandria. I met one of them during a recent trip to Egypt. He was one of the survivors of the age of Nasser and Sadat, reduced by age, prison, and political failure to a pathetic political relic, rather like one of the characters in Durrell's *Alexandria Quartet*. In retrospect I tend to believe that in Renato Mieli the Jewish strain remained alive even at the time of his active participation in the Communist party. He was, in any case, the only one among the

strange figures working at the monastery of Saint Peter in
Gallicantu who did not share the general disbelief in the
Zionist movement. All the others forecast that Jewish nationalism would die out with the end of the war and provoke a
massive return of Palestinian Jews to Europe. Nor did Mieli
believe that the British would be able to uphold their White
Paper and make Zionists agree to remain forever a minority
protected by Britain in an Arab land.

In spite of my work at the Psychological Warfare Department, I was naturally interested in the future of the Jewish
National Home far more than in that of Fascism in Italy or
in that British-imposed democracy, which I could not even
conceive through the lenses of Allied propaganda. My experience with Zionism in Palestine, even if diluted by my Anglo-
philia, did not help my political and social contacts with the
cosmopolitan world in which I worked nor with the larger
world outside. If, in "town," I was suspect to the Jews because
of my connection with the Intelligence Service, within our
"monastery" my status of Jewish Palestinian military personnel
among foreign civilians was the object of not particularly
friendly comment, usually made in an anti-Zionist key. It was
strange how these cosmopolitan refugees, each one strongly
supporting the sovereignty of his own native land even when
this clashed, as in the case of the Balkans, with that of their
neighbor, were unwilling to admit that Jews, too, possessed a
nationality of their own and a right to political independence.
This debate around the legitimacy of Zionism as a national
movement did not cease with the creation of the State of Israel,
and it has become more acute since the 1970s with the development of a parallel and opposite Palestinian Arab "Zionism."
Going back in my mind to the political discussions of that
time, it seems to me that the major difference between then and
now does not reside in the topics of the discussions but in their
intensity. In whatever language people spoke there was an
emotional passion and, I believe, a level of intellect, which in

Israel today remains the patrimony of very limited groups.

I have no clear recollection of how I used my time in the mornings—probably sleeping and making up for the long night hours spent in the studios. I have, however, the impression that from the setting of the sun until dawn, the entire Yishuv did nothing but argue. One of the reasons was certainly the nonexistence of other types of entertainment. Sports were not popular in Palestine; television did not exist; the cinemas screened old films; food was rationed; social life was rigidly divided between those who frequented the British and those (the majority) who shut themselves up in the ethnical, religious, ideological sectarianism of their respective communities: Jews, Christians, Moslems, Greeks, Armenians, socialists, orthodox, etcetera. In the cafés of the new Jewish quarters of Jerusalem, where orange juice, locally produced beer, chicory coffee, and apple strudel were the only edible items, or in the dining rooms, which invariably served as bedrooms, people argued, dreamed, plotted, listened to endless poetry readings, to the music of gramophones, or to foreign broadcasts, without ever looking at their watches. They, or at least those Jewish friends with whom I used to meet, loved, hated, hoped frenetically, splitting hairs over every argument, with impassioned speeches. Fear, hunger, and pain were concealed by a generalized tendency to laugh at the worst situations. We all shared the apocalyptic, messianic, albeit provincial atmosphere of Jerusalem with the ravenous irresponsibility of youth never sufficiently satisfied by action.

The topics of our discussions varied from homemade strategy to the planning of impossible trips; from religious duties to ideological heresies; from the functioning of weapons to free love; from the compilation of subversive posters against the British to the denunciation of some real or imaginary betrayal; from the critiques of books we had learned to the exegesis of the writings of Marx—which most of us had never read. The most stimulating arguments were those between kibbutzniks and city dwellers, between those who rebelled in words against the presence of the British and those who rebelled in thought against the discipline imposed by the Zionist movement. Few acted on their own initiative. Of these I hardly remember the words, but only a troubling succession of faces: faces of young people bronzed by the sun, faces of old people dessicated by sorrow; eyes of women lightened by passion and lust, faces of philosophers and of priests; faces looking at you with slit-like eyes, inhaling their cigarette smoke together with the recondite meaning of their words; faces of youngsters searching for exploits, faces of cowards and faces of saints; faces marred by sentiments toward which one felt attracted as though by an animal force; faces whose expressions said the contrary of their voices, whose eyes turned in the emptiness of anguish; faces of princes and faces of slaves, all of them exposed to the challenges of this land's passionate beliefs.

Among so many different faces, two belonged to the only non-Italian colleagues in my office, with whom I had established a complex relationship. One was Anna, a German Jewess converted to Christianity, living in a convent in the Old City of Jerusalem. The other was Robert, a Christian Arab who had returned from London at the outbreak of war. They had in common a singular hatred for the Zionists and an impelling need to give expression to these sentiments in my presence.

Robert was not gifted with brilliance or culture, but he possessed a sufficient smattering of both to upset me with his political arguments. According to him and—he always added —without the least possibility of error, the Zionist cause was doomed and fundamentally immoral. He proclaimed his certainty with aplomb, choosing in the composition of his sentences as many Anglo-Saxon words as he could, avoiding with care words rooted in Latin, which sounded to him too vulgarly Mediterranean. Impeccably dressed, with jacket and tie even in the most torrid heat, he did not affect an Oxford accent, nor did he try, as so many Arabs and Jews were doing, to imitate the manner of speech and the behavior of the higher British officials. There was, however, in his manner, something as unctuous as his brilliantined hair and as arrogant as the movements of his hands, with which he used to wave away my answers as if they were bothersome flies. My rancor against him was mainly due to the fact that he flirted with Anna with an insistence that seemed to me improper and at times even insulting. I suffered seeing him leaving the office in her company, disappearing in the evenings into the winding alleys of the market leading toward her lodgings, which were impenetrable for me. I imagined them walking in the labyrinth of the native market toward secret, perfumed divans, first arm in arm like two good colleagues, later entwined in amorous struggles in alcoves lighted by candles, filled with oriental carpets and damask cushions, she a ravishing blond, he like the sheikh of Araby, possessing this Jewess, freed by her religious conversion from her tribal loyalties and clutching like an octopus the body of this Arab with all her tentacular complexes.

Anna attracted me enormously. She was older than I by at least ten years, and her feminine charm was blended, for me, with a feeling of motherhood. I looked for every opportunity to meet her inside the office but had not the courage to approach her outside. I felt for her a childish passion and embarrassment, a fear mixed with some familiarity that made me sit next to her in the canteen, wait for her when she left the monitoring hall, accompany her to the NAAFI shop, where one could buy cheaper beer and locally made chocolate. Robert joined us, always elegant and sure of himself, looking for every opportunity to develop his anti-Zionist theories in front of Anna, convinced by my confused reactions that he had succeeded in demolishing my political faith.

Anna preferred to divert the conversation toward religious questions. She seemed to feel the constant need to explain to me why she had converted. She attacked Judaism but never the

Jews, as if she wanted to defend that secular Zionism that had broken with the Jewish tradition and proclaimed the right of the Jews to free themselves from the yoke of the Law. To her this meant a process of collective assimilation, inevitably fated to turn the first Jewish community in history into candidates for Christian conversion. It was a thesis that infuriated her friend Robert, even if he tried to conceal his irritation behind the understatements he formulated in the language of Shakespeare. The Zionists, he believed, even if they converted to Christianity or Islam, would remain somehow Jewish if allowed to exist autonomously. In Palestine their political beliefs would forever remain for him nothing but a new, cowardly form of European colonialism. He turned livid when Anna retorted that the Arabs, too, even when Christians, remained Moslem at heart; that they were men from the desert but incapable of achieving the level of morality that ancient Judaism had developed in the desert. If the Jews had accepted the message of Christ they would have been the true light unto the people. The Christianization of Zionism could herald the final salvation.

Robert and Anna disagreed on everything except the wrongness of the faiths in which they had respectively been born. They both loathed their parents' religions with the passion of a neophyte: she as a convert to Christianity, he as a convert to the British style of life. They took special pleasure in explaining to each other and, indirectly to me, the superstitions of the ancestral religions they had given up.

When Anna denounced her version of Judaism she did it with a detached professorial voice, as if she were describing a fossilized exhibit in a museum—a civilization dead and buried in the depths of time, without any ties with the Jewish life that throbbed so intensely around her, without any connection to the barbarous deeds perpetuated by the most Christianized societies of Europe. She spoke against Judaism with her eyes following a faraway vision, while the hollow of her throat, uncovered by the open collar of her blouse, palpitated more rapidly. At these moments I was struck by her extraordinary beauty, and I was scared by the coldness of her looks, the lack of feeling. There was a frost in her soul, like in mine, which made her sound deeply inhuman.

One afternoon when we stood alone on the roof of the monastery to watch the sunset, I found the courage to ask her what had made her convert to Christianity. I was interested to know, I told her, because my mother had gone the same way. She did not answer me. The sky was already red, the air translucent, a few restless birds flew among the trees. The walls of the Old City reflected on their stones the violet color of the dying day. The tolling of a bell, pulled by invisible hands, reached us from a distant church. I asked her if she saw her conversion as a way to escape from the yoke of her family's Judaism or as a way to be different. Anna remained silent, her thin lips barely open, one hand clasping the railing round the roof, the thumb and forefinger of the other fiddling with a button on her blouse. The very fact that she was listening seemed to me proof that I had at last succeeded in establishing real contact with her, perhaps in warming the ice in her soul. When she finally answered me, she did so with her eyes still fixed on the distance but with a new expression on her face, which reminded me of the portraits of saints on Annetta's bedside table. "I became a Christian because I believe in the purity of platonic thought," she said briskly, before moving away. Years after, reading a page written by Hanna Arendt, I remembered this answer I had not then understood. At the time I had only the impression of having collided head-on with a statue, at the feet of which, like those of an idol, lay my broken feelings.

From that day on, Anna avoided discussing with me questions of religion, directing her arrows against Robert. He was a convert, she kept telling him with the hint of a sneer in her voice, not to a divine faith but to the mundane faith, the cultural values of Europe in which he had been educated. Everything in him, from the way he dressed to the ideas he expressed, was imported from or influenced by the West. He was ashamed of his origins, of his ancient Assyrian Christian family and did not want to be reminded that he belonged to a community that the Moslems had exterminated in Iraq at the beginning of the thirties and the British partially saved by recruiting the surviving men into the auxiliary imperial troops. This was the true reason for his hatred of everything Islamic and his unlimited admiration for everything British. But since he could not be either English or Moslem, he deluded himself with the romantic vision of Arabism he had brought back from England. This allowed him to share in the indigenous nationalism without shedding his hostility toward Islam, while his aversion to Zionism was in inverse proportion to the attraction that British culture exercised on him.

Anna was right, and Robert could hardly bear the truth she was telling him, especially in my presence. I had difficulty understanding how so many complexes could coexist in a single person. But Robert was the Arab counterpart of many Jews I knew: fanatically nationalist and at the same time hostile to their religious traditions, obsessed by the need to express their hate for British colonialism and at the same time fascinated by everything British. His Arabism was a form of exoticism in which he hoped there might sooner or later be a coexistence of the Arab and the English. He could not admit to what Anna kept telling him, that Christian Arab nationalists like him would be the first to suffer from the disappearance of British imperialism from the Middle East. The Moslems would then monopolize all the power and aggress against all the minorities in the lands of Islam. In Palestine common sense and common interests should have united Christians and Jews in upholding the British presence. Instead they were both fighting, for opposing reasons, against their natural ally, Great Britain. Robert laughingly discounted this kind of talk, just as many Fascist Jews I had known in Italy had refused to listen to unpleasant truths.

His relations with Anna, a converted Jewess who tried to fulfill her visions of purity and intellectual clarity in a world of confused, burning passions, probably meant for this Arab-Christian in search of his roots an attempt to patch his broken identity, which later pushed him into joining one of the armed Arab bands during the war against the Jews in 1947–1948. Anna, too, remained on the Arab side, refusing to leave the Christian Quarter of Old Jerusalem. She was found raped and with her stomach slit open on the very day when the Jews surrendered to the British-officered Arab Legion of King Abdullah of Transjordan.

IO.

Berenika

Berenika was not beautiful, certainly less so in life than in her photograph. Her eyes were wide, her hair cut too short. Her white cotton shirt, which the women of the kibbutz wore on Saturdays, reminded me of the uniform of the Fascist girls youth movement. Her shoulders were slightly bent forward, adding a sinuous curve to her body in contrast to the controlled passion that she expressed in every movement. This slightly concave line of her physique fitted her character: introverted but turned toward action, ready to receive but also to conceal and exclude. The image I immediately formed of her in my mind when I saw her for the first time was that of a cradle in which one could rock but from which one could also fall out at the slightest push of an invisible hand—an image still present in my memory although smoothed by time, passions, and wounds, like one of those silhouettes cut out of black paper by hungry artists on the steps of the Louvre.

I was certainly confused to find her, suddenly, in front of me, waiting to give me my dinner, with the book of Goethe open on the table. I was also overcome by the violence with which her perfume awakened in me the need for a woman. She must have perceived it, and from that very first moment a double dialogue established itself between us made up of banalities and deep, unexpressed feelings, of mechanical gestures and furtive glances. It was, as so often happens between young people, a sentimental ballet of two beings equally attracted but unable to give expression to their sentiments.

Berenika had arrived from her kibbutz, recently established in Galilee, because she thought she was pregnant. Aged twenty, she had thought it her "duty" to accept into her body a "comrade" in need of affection, although she had had no intention of starting a family. She told me this with the detachment of a nurse prescribing the proper use of a medicine to a patient. Her kibbutz in any case was too poor to allow itself the luxury of new children, especially from unmarried couples. Her case had been discussed by the kibbutz secretariat, with tact but without false prudishness. It had been decided that the best thing would be for her to have an abortion. She had agreed. She would not have known what to do with a baby—even if raised communally in a kibbutz. The war was transforming the country and, more important, would certainly change the whole world. In such circumstances men and women did not have any more right to dispose freely of their bodies, of their lives, than millions of soldiers locked in battle, or the myriad human beings, reduced to an animal existence, who were enduring the war. The body of a healthy young woman like hers should serve some more useful purpose than turning out babies, many of whom would probably be killed before being weaned. The idea of having an abortion seemed logical to her because of its very brutality: it was part of the general atmosphere of violence in which we had to learn sooner or later to live.

The doctor who had visited her was not, however, fully convinced of her pregnancy and had advised her to wait. Out of this involuntary pause emerged her unexpected vacation, a brief period of life she was spending in a kind of moral and biological limbo. But this state of uncertainty had persuaded her to break off relations with her boyfriend and come to stay with her parents in town. She was not particularly suffering from the break. She had rather the impression of having abandoned a patient in the middle of treatment. She felt toward the human wreck with whom she had copulated a strange maternal feeling, an instinct of protection stronger than toward the being who perhaps was already growing in her womb. Both appeared to her weak, naked, skinned alive. She imagined them as shapeless masses of blood, sinews, and ganglia, exposed to the indifference of the world, easy prey to predators, in need of delicate care, of bandages, of baths, but differently related to her. Her comrade was something physically detached but ever present in her mind; the other—she did not know what to call it—was ever present in her body and in her deepest, irrational consciousness but intellectually alien to her and in possession of a selfish vitality over which she had already lost all control.

I listened to this talk with a shameful, confused, and at the same time tense and excited mind. From the very first moment we met—I do not remember whether it was the same evening when I found her waiting for me in her parents' apartment or the following day when we went out together for the first time to walk along the crenellated walls of old Jerusalem— she had explained to me the reasons for her coming to town with such a simplicity and frankness that I felt my own feelings for her were becoming wrapped in aseptic thoughts. When, in the quiet of my office, I thought about her, I tended to compare her with certain booklets of military instruction that I carried in my knapsack. These manuals aimed to prepare soldiers to face the most violent events. And yet they described them in the same tone Berenika had used to narrate her personal story: front lines where people were dying were translated into colored graphs; battlegrounds into maps dotted with arrows; mortal weapons into mechanical toys. Everything was made one-dimensional; existence was a simple matter of causes and effects, of variable solutions, of schemes. Everything was clear and simple, "like a printed book," my uncle's cook—who was illiterate—would have said, and yet everything was so obscure, mysterious, convulsive.

Behind Berenika's cool logic stood passions and humors clothed in a nurse's apron, and I was unable to link them with the man from whom she had just separated and the creature who might be growing in her womb. I was disconcerted in front of this girl, only one year older than I but who seemed so experienced, who had drunk to the dregs the poison of the senses and uninhibitedly answered the animal call that often kept me awake at night. Walking at my side along the walls built by Suleiman the Magnificent, she unveiled to me the secrets of a body equally attracting and repelling. From her eyes and from the curves of her shoulders I received both inviting messages and signals of icy detachment. I was divided by the desire to throw myself into her, forgetting myself, the war, and the past, and the anxiety and fear of losing myself in the obscure meanders of her dangerous character. But all the time, in spite of my confusion, I felt that something secret, unspeakable, and strange existed in this woman, concealed behind a cool shamelessness of logic. I imagined, for lack of a better idea, that her strange manners were dictated by her political ideas or that she might be involved in some clandestine affairs that imposed on her this complex behavior.

Imprisoned by my doubts and fantasies, I believed her to be involved in sordid affairs with Arab beys or British officials from whom she probably stole secrets. Or that she ensnared some local effendis ready to sell to the Jews land in the areas forbidden by the British White Paper. Everyone at that time, in any case, was plotting, counterplotting, and had some private or public secret to conceal. Only I was living in the grotesque clandestinity of a radio station broadcasting in Italian from Jerusalem, trying to make probably nonexistent listeners believe that we were located somewhere in Italy. There was nothing really to brag about. With shame and sadness I kept telling Berenika what I was doing, why I had joined the British army, about my boredom at performing guard duties in the middle of nowhere, dreaming of the battles in which I never took part. Now at least I had become, by mere chance, an announcer in a camouflaged broadcasting station. But I still felt alien in my new country, estranged from the queer cosmopolitan people who populated my office, unable to rebut Robert's arguments on Zionism and Anna's ideas on Judaism, while looking for fame and adventure through the cracks that the British administration, the war, and my knowledge of Italian had suddenly opened before me.

Berenika listened to me with her ironic smile and her absorbed eyes. She let me talk for hours without interrupting me, without asking questions, curious only to know some details of my mother's personality, of our village home, or of my dog, Bizir. She never asked me what I did in the office, and I carefully avoided asking her about her political activities. I knew that as a member of a collective settlement she must have belonged to some clandestine military organization. But I could not imagine what task could have been given to a woman of her age, free from family ties, attractive, educated, and fanatic.

There was another aspect of her behavior that intrigued me. Like her mother, Berenika was not observant. But even more than Frau Luise, she showed great respect toward her father's religious beliefs. I wondered where she had found the courage to tell Dr. Wilfrid, so prudish and strict in his moral principles, the reason she had come to town. Yet it looked as if her troubles had brought her closer to her father. She, a member of the Hashomer Hatzair, the leftist pioneer movement, which never lost an occasion to attack rabbinical Judaism, took greater care than her mother to make the apartment ready for the Sabbath: she spent hours polishing the silver; she arranged the flowers; she made sure the tablecloth was smooth and the table settings were perfectly aligned. With great concentration she lit the Sabbath candles, and when in the kitchen, she—who outside her home ate every kind of forbidden food—was more particular than her mother in separating the pans used for cooking meat from those used for milk. This, I thought, must have been her way of thanking her father in silence for his understanding. But beyond her feeling of gratitude, I sensed something deeper, an intellectual and moral engagement, devoid of religious conviction, but meant to make of every gesture an act of devotion, a family, daughterly prayer.

When I caught her making my bed I laughed at her for the precision with which she made hospital corners. Once she allowed me to help her. She made me turn the woolen blanket three times in order to make sure that the factory label was underneath and in the top left-hand corner. That was its place and there it must stay. For those who could understand it there was an order in everything, she told me, just as there was a language for everything created: flowers, stones, furniture. The dignity of things should never be violated. When I asked if this were not a kind of ritual of her personal religion, she avoided answering. She insisted that her passion for reading the Book of Psalms was purely literary and wanted me to listen to the rhythm of the Hebrew language. When she read them for me, her harmonious voice became metallic, stressing ancient words as if they were square stone. But in order not to mislead me about the spirit in which she read the psalms, she never failed to add: "Goethe and Schiller, too, have written verses as beautiful as those by David. Pity you don't understand German."

Quite different, however, was her behavior in political matters. She vehemently discussed the progress of the war with her father. She exalted Russia and had doubts about the sincerity of the British military effort now that the fear of a Nazi victory had receded. She did not have clear ideas about the war aims of the United States. Italy did not interest her, or perhaps she avoided talking about it in my presence after what I had told her about my Fascist past and that of my family. However, neither with her father nor with me did she ever express any opinion on the Zionist movement and its ideological trends. As to her experiences in the kibbutz, she spoke like somebody telling stories to innocent children: the work in the chicken house, her adventures in the kitchen, her problems in keeping milk fresh. Simple facts of life that any Italian farmer's wife could have told a visitor without ever touching on the ideas, the psychological and moral problems that united or divided the inhabitants of these egalitarian communities, usually made up of uprooted people of bourgeois origin, trying to reconstruct their lives in the framework of an idealistic, collective family, free from biological constrictions.

When I sometimes questioned her about the policy followed by her party toward the Arabs and the British and its postwar program, she looked at me with a strange smile without answering, as if to say, "You can't understand these things." Only once, when I told her that in my view the kibbutz, in spite of its pretensions to equality, was a collective aristocratic institution, whose members would sooner or later behave like "feudal collective knights," did she throw me a look full of anger and answer me almost in a hiss: "Only someone who grew up in a Fascist milieu could reason like that." But her face soon softened, and her smile became coquettish and inviting.

As the days went by, I found my situation more and more ridiculous and unbearable. I was full of desire for this woman, so attractive and physically so near me, and at the same time I behaved like an elderly friend of the family, spending hours listening to her personal situation. I wanted to make her share my life, my thoughts, my anguish, and, instead, I spent most of my time with her discussing literature and philosophic subjects totally unknown to me and which, on top of that, did not interest me at all.

One day Berenika mentioned to me the financial difficulties she might have if she were forced to have an abortion. I immediately offered her fifty pounds sterling, a fabulous sum at that time, which represented all my savings. She accepted the offer without a word of thanks. I felt so deeply offended that I spent an entire night fantasizing how I could revenge myself, furious at having given away my money in a fit of generosity dictated solely by my need to appear what I was not, namely rich and generous. In the morning, with heavy eyes and my head more than usually confused, I got up with the stern intention of informing her that our relationship could no longer continue, at least not in the way it had developed up to that moment. I had had enough of playing the "squire of dames" to her and of being treated like a schoolboy. Sitting at the breakfast table, where toast waited to be spread with the margarine of my military rations, I searched in my mind for the most offensive phrase with which to wound her.

Berenika entered the room with a mug of steaming milk in her hand, put it on the table, sat down next to me, and in silence took my hand, accompanying the gesture with a look full of sweetness. I felt a sudden void in my stomach and was overtaken by an uncontrollable fit of coughing, which sent me running to the kitchen for a drink of water. When I returned, my eyes were still watering and I had difficulty talking. Berenika was still seated at the table, stirring the sugar in my coffee cup. She did not give me time to open my mouth. She took a slice of toast, started to spread it with margarine, and staring at it as if it were the most important object in the world, she said, almost talking to herself: "Something happened to me last night. I don't need to go and see a doctor."

I could not find a more intelligent reply than to say—"You see? In the end everything turns out all right," and I was happy that my coughing gave me a pretext to conceal the emotion that now really made my eyes water. Berenika must have noticed it, although I kept rubbing my eyes with my knuckles. This was the first time I realized that the eyes are sunk into the hollows of the skull, and by running my fingers over my cheekbones I could feel the shape of my face and perceive the reality of my "impersonal" skeleton concealed under the skin. Thus, my first, vibrant impulse of love came accompanied by an equally violent sensation of death and the taste of a slice of toast covered with Australian margarine.

Now that she was no longer preoccupied with her biological problem, Berenika decided to return that morning to her kibbutz in Galilee; she wanted to get involved in activities that would take her out of the chicken run and make her forget the anxieties of the last few weeks. Probably, she said to me, she would ask her comrades to authorize her to volunteer for the British army. Whatever the case, she would return to Jerusalem as soon as possible since there were a lot of things we now had to talk seriously about with each other. A short break was necessary for both of us. She needed a few days to look inside herself; I should do the same. I agreed and told her that I would wait for her return with great impatience. At that moment Dr. Wilfrid entered the room. Berenika told him that she had decided to leave Jerusalem. "Does your mother know?" he asked. "Not yet," Berenika said, smiling softly. "Then it's better that you go and tell her about it." And there was that air of naive complicity between the two.

By the time Berenika returned I must have been well on the way to my office. At one corner of the street I bumped into an old lady who was taking her dog for a stroll. Both looked at me with a stupefied air as I bowed to them and went on my way whistling, euphoric.

From the morning she left Jerusalem until her return ten days later, I did nothing but think of her, of her body, and of what I would tell her about us and our future. There were moments when I was so deeply immersed in my erotic thoughts that I must have given the impression of a sleep-walker. One evening, when dressed in uniform, I was followed by a patrol of military police while on my way to the radio station. They stopped me, believing I was drunk since they had heard me talking to myself. I told them I was reciting a piece of poetry I had learned by heart for a party we had organized in the mess. They checked my pay book, made no comments, and let me go, happier than ever.

In the office, too, people realized that something had happened to me. I showed little interest in the news bulletins they prepared and I read every day; I did not discuss the progress of the war. I spent most of my time looking out the window of our monastic office, looking at the flight of birds and at the changing colors of the Mountains of Edom beyond the Dead Sea.

Those were days of great tensions and hopes. The British were dashing toward Tripoli, the Americans had landed in North Africa. The end of the war seemed suddenly near and the defeat of the Axis powers inevitable. In our section there was a lot of talk about the political system that would replace the Fascist regime in Italy. Names of persons unknown to me were continually bandied about. Our commentaries mentioned political groups such as the Partito Popolare, the Communist party, Giustizia e Libertà, names that sounded to me as unreal as those of the Longobards or the Bourbons, who ruled Italy centuries before and about whom we had learned at school. Only Isa Mieli, who looked more excited by these political events and speculations than anyone else in the office, took an interest in my emotional state.

One afternoon, while walking along the path from the Church of the Last Supper to the Zion Gate, she suddenly asked me: "Does your girlfriend bother you a lot?" I blushed to my ears, but I was grateful to have at last an opportunity to talk about Berenika and confide my pains to somebody. I felt a growing need to share my anxieties, my fears, the passion of this first love and at the same time to explain my anger toward her. As I started to answer I realized how difficult it was for me to describe her: not because I knew so little about Berenika's life but because of those strange, enigmatic aspects of her personality and the mystery that I felt surrounded her. I had the impression that Berenika had gone through experiences that had split her character, clouded her soul, and made it impossible for her to live at the pace of the rest of humanity. All I could say to Isa was that indeed I was involved with a girl who was making my head spin as never before.

We had just gone through the Zion Gate and ascended the high steps leading to the top of the bastion to admire the sunset. Sitting in the niche between two massive battlements, the fragile figure of Isa, already undermined by the illness that would soon lead her to her death, faded into the shadows of the advancing night. Without questioning me, she urged me by her silence to talk. I told her how I had met Berenika, what I knew about her kibbutz, and the problem she had had with her "fiancé." I tried to explain why she seemed to me so different from other girls, especially from Annemarie, of whom I suddenly realized that I had not thought since the day I first set foot in Palestine.

Annemarie was a student I had first known in 1937 at the tennis club in Alassio, owned by an Englishman—Bennett, I think was his name—who had not been persuaded, either by the sanctions imposed by the League of Nations against Italy for the invasion of Ethiopia nor by Fascist propaganda against *perfide Albion,* to leave Italy. I did not like tennis particularly; I preferred fencing and riding. But it was considered quite fashionable in Fascist times to play tennis, and in that particular club two things attracted me—buttered toast and Annemarie, who had initiated me into many secrets of that sport: how to hold the racket at the proper angle; how to pronounce correctly certain English words that sounded ridiculous to me, such as "play" and "ready," without which the game was not supposed to begin.

Annemarie was easy to be with. She laughed at everything I told her about my schoolteachers, the horses I rode during my vacation in the Alps, Annetta's pretended fright when I suddenly jumped out at her from behind a door in the hope of making her drop the plate or glass she was carrying. With Annemarie, sitting on the green benches of the club in the shade of the hedge, caressed by the Mediterranean breeze, I could talk about everything without feeling embarrassed or bored.

A year later, in 1938, after the racial laws against the Jews had been published, I went back for a week to Alassio as the guest of an aunt of mine who lived nearby. Quite naturally I ran to the tennis club to look for Annemarie and to play in a place where Jews were still admitted, since it was private ground.

Annemarie had arrived in Alassio a fortnight before. She looked quite happy to meet me and her company became, for me, quite indispensable. I waited for her in the mornings when she returned from her swim and in the afternoons when she came to play tennis. She herself seemed indifferent to my changed status. I did not discuss the matter with her, but I thought it impossible that she could not be aware of it, and the fact that she continued to deal with me in such a straightforward manner made her friendliness to me more dear. When I told her, for instance, that my family had moved from Friuli to Piedmont and that I would stay with my grandmother in Turin in order to continue my studies, she looked truly happy and suggested we should continue to play tennis at the Fascist headquarters, which had the best grounds in Turin. I did not react, telling myself that either she was not aware of the anti-Jewish laws or did not realize that I was a Jew. I was too afraid to upset our relationship by explaining to her the situation to which the Fascist laws had relegated me in Italian society. So I went on behaving until the end of my vacation as though nothing had changed, hoping that her ignorance would continue forever. The day before I left, we were resting on a bench after a fierce match, panting and sucking a lemonade with a straw.

"Do you think people like Mr. Bennett would have been able to defend the British Empire against an attack by the Italian Army?" I asked.

"Why do you ask me such a question?" she replied, surprised.

"Because," I said with perfect nonsensical logic, "I may leave next year for Palestine, and Palestine is part of the British Empire."

"And what on earth are you going to do in Palestine?"

I told her that I was a Jew, that I no longer had the right to study in an Italian school, that my father had lost his job, and that I was forced to emigrate. I thought, therefore, that the best place to go would be where nobody could reproach me for the crime of having been born a Jew.

Annemarie had heard about the racial laws in her home, but she did not link them with me or with any other person she knew. She could not understand what "those people in Rome" wanted from me. Nobody in Italy was able to distinguish between Jews and non-Jews. Her father had explained to her that it was a problem that had never existed in Italy and that Mussolini had been obliged to invent it to please Hitler. In any case, she could not see how the laws could influence our relationship. We had nothing to do with politics, we were both members of the Fascist Youth, and it seemed absurd to her, in fact impossible, that I should not be allowed to go and practice at the Fascist headquarters in Turin. If this was indeed so, we could find some private tennis court to continue playing. She said these things, a bit angry, with her legs drawn up to her chin and her heels on the bench, the empty lemonade bottle held between her knees, into which she blew bubbles of air through the straw. We promised to meet each other in Turin. She lived at the side of the station; I, in my grandmother's apartment just a few hundred yards from there.

Not long after, a few days after the beginning of the school term, I decided to phone her. I was attending the Jewish Secondary School established in a great hurry by the Turin Jewish community to accommodate the scores of young Jews suddenly expelled from public institutions. She answered, seemed quite embarrassed, and told me that she was very busy. I insisted, and she finally agreed to meet me under the portico of her house early the same evening.

I had forced her hand and was sorry and a bit ashamed about it. But all I wanted was to tell her that this should be our last meeting because I realized the difficulties it would cause her to maintain relations with a Jew. I wanted to part as good friends, to let her know that I had decided to go abroad. I wished to take with me the memory of our nice friendship and the image of an Italy that, at least among young people of my age, made no distinction between Jews and non-Jews and did not share the view of "those in Rome." I wanted our friendship, which was obviously beginning to turn for me into a romantic love, to be an expression of secret, common revolt against the injustice that separated us: a token of hope I could carry with me in order to remain linked with my past wherever I went.

It was a rainy, melancholy evening that forecast disaster. I was walking into it, pushed by the desire to see her again as much as by the need to face a Jewish destiny that up to that date I had been able to avoid.

I saw Annemarie come out of the doorway of her house, hesitate a moment, look around, and then proceed straight toward me. She was accompanied by a man. I noticed that he wore a black overcoat, a felt beret, and a pair of yellow shoes on which fell the cuffs of a pair of badly pressed trousers. He held Annemarie closely with his right arm as though he were pushing her forward against her will—a reluctance that probably existed only in my imagination. When they got close to me I noticed that he had a small moustache.

"My father," Annemarie said. "Pleased to meet you," I replied shyly, stretching out my hand to him. He kept his own under his daughter's arm.

I felt my throat become dry and my face pale. I thought of the day when a schoolmate of mine had hit me on the chin and knocked me backward onto the ground. I had not felt any pain but only the sensation of leaving my body and entering into a kind of black cave full of fluttering birds. This time, if I had fallen on the ground, nobody would have come to my help. I was alone, standing under the portico, my brain emptied of ideas and blood, unable to react, while another part shouted at me to disappear from there, to be swallowed up by the earth.

Annemarie was switching her alarmed, sad gaze from her father to me. I caught in her eyes more embarrassment than compassion. Suddenly her father started to talk. He had a slightly raucous voice marked by a strong Piedmontese accent. "You are a Jew," he said, without resentment or any particular spite. "I and Annemarie are Italian. I understand that you are on the point of emigrating. You are right to do so, but it would not be good either for you or for my daughter if you two continued to see each other. I preferred to tell you this personally, as man to man. Do you understand me?" "I understand perfectly," I answered. Later I hated myself for not having been able to find a more offensive reply. Perhaps it was the trembling I spotted on Annemarie's lips that prevented me from doing so. Perhaps it was the fear that had overcome me together with blind rage. I should have turned my back haughtily on them; instead I stood there immobile, under the portico, until father and daughter had gone back into the house, then pushed my hands into the pockets of my overcoat with such force that the lining tore.

I caught myself doing the same thing with the pockets of my battledress trousers while I was telling Isa the story of Anne-marie. She noticed it and said: "A girl of that type is not worth tearing your trousers for. Time, you will see, will soothe the pain. There is an Egyptian story that says that when God created the world he made everything small so that it could grow up with time: the grain into the wheat, the baby into the man, the bud into the flower. Only sorrow was created fully grown, so that it might decrease with time and man be able to live with it."

We climbed down from the wall, and I accompanied her through the narrow alleys of the market up to the Damascus Gate, along the old Roman street that crosses the entire walled city of Jerusalem. We passed Arabs pushing donkeys laden with sacks of flour in front of them; Jews going to the Wailing Wall, their eyes riveted to the ground, their bodies shrouded in black. On the corner of the Road of the Cross, a Franciscan friar passed us with a great billowing of his brown habit. On both sides of the street merchants were closing their shutters; in the cafés young Arabs played *shesh-besh* while older ones, wearing red fezzes, inhaled, dignified and absorbed, the taste of their water pipes. At the Damascus Gate a police patrol—the British constable with his elegant blue peaked cap, the Jewish and the Arab auxiliary constables with their imitation astrakhan cossack hats—eyed with indifference the passersby. It was a world full of life, in which everyone went about his affairs absorbed in his own thoughts, indifferent to my feelings as they were indifferent to the slabs of paving stone worn smooth by feet and history.

Berenika returned from her kibbutz on a Sunday afternoon. She told me that the community secretariat had agreed to her request to join the British army. She was now waiting for the announcement by the British military authorities of the formation of a new company of volunteer women drivers in order to report to the enlistment office. Then, after two months of training at Sarafand, the same camp where I spent my time as a recruit, she would be posted to Transport Command in Egypt. The war, she said, had at last reached a decisive turn: after El Alamein and Stalingrad the destiny of the Axis powers was sealed, whatever their capacity to carry on fighting. It was the destiny of the Jews that remained unknown. No one could forecast how many of them would still be alive in Europe at the end of the hostilities. All the survivors would be in need of help, and the British would be the last to extend it to them. The Jewish Agency hoped that London might allow the creation of a "Jewish Legion" to take part in the fighting and eventually be allowed to rush to rescue the remnants from the ghettos. These were pious illusions, Berenika said. A large Jewish fighting unit would acquire political rights on the battlefield that the British had no interest to grant. So, she continued, the men had to be patient and prepare themselves for the struggle that would certainly take place in Palestine against the British and the Arabs once the war was over. The women in uniform, especially if they were in charge of transport, would, on the contrary, be more free to move around within the liberated territories and probably be able, without arousing suspicion or opposition, to bring concrete help to the Jewish survivors. This was the reason the Jewish authorities in Palestine had decided to speed up the recruitment of Jewish women. Berenika felt herself more available than her "women comrades" after all that had recently happened to her. In any case, if she did not join the army she would certainly have felt obliged to leave the kibbutz, and most of her friends were against her doing that. So she had returned to Jerusalem to wait for her call-up, but she did not want to stay in her parents' apartment. There was not enough space, she told me with an understanding smile, for both of us. She would rent a room in the neighborhood by the end of the week. Meanwhile she would go to Tel Aviv to prepare her "military accoutrement."

In the few days that followed I did nothing but think about how and when we would meet. Even when reading the news bulletin I could not take my thoughts away from her face, her body, and stop asking myself how I would tell her that I wanted to make love to her. I could not, obviously, go straight to the point. I had to create an appropriate "ambience"—for instance, to go and see a boring film in order to have an excuse to leave the cinema in the middle of the screening. Or to invite her to a cozy restaurant for dinner, or for a trip to the Dead Sea, or better, to go horseback-riding, this last scenario looked more romantic but certainly less comfortable. The only scheme I did not conceive was the quite unpredictable one that eventually took place.

Berenika returned, happy and suntanned, from Tel Aviv. We dined with her parents and then went out for a walk along the old battlements of Jerusalem.

It was a warm autumn evening, when the stars of the East shine so brightly that they look like iridescent butterflies, palpitating in their efforts to break away from the sky. Along the path from Jaffa Gate toward the Zion Gate we did not meet a soul. I walked next to her, carefully avoiding touching her, clutching in my left hand the handle of my pistol, my right hand sweating in my trouser pocket. She walked absorbed in her own thoughts, turning her face toward me from time to time with an oddly sad smile.

I suggested we climb to the top of the Zion Gate and look at the darkness of the Jehoshaphat Valley, spotted by the trembling lamps in the Arab houses. She agreed without demur, and I understood that it was quite unnecessary for me to look for a pretext to tell her what she obviously already knew: that I desired her, that I had not had the courage to say it before for fear of a refusal, that I was not quite sure of really loving her since I had never loved anyone before, that I had nothing to offer her but was even prepared to join a collective settlement to be near her.

She listened to my confused talk in silence, and when at last I found the courage to put my hand on her shoulder, she bent her head toward it, inviting me through that gesture to kiss her. Then she asked softly whether I had ever been with a woman. I told her, blushing, that I had not and she, with her detached, sweet, and cruel way of speaking, explained to me that people could be caught in the nets of sex more easily than by the nets of religion. The only way not to fall prey to sexual instincts was to treat them with indifference like any other bodily need, without trivial fantasies. The bourgeois world in which I had grown up had replaced godly religions with the religion of money but had preserved many taboos of the past. Among them sex was still predominant. She had freed herself from them for quite a while. There was nothing wrong in my desire for her; she also felt a strong attraction for me. She would not let my hunger for a woman go unfed, but I had to be rational in my passions because our physical link could not expect ever to enjoy the space and the time necessary to transform itself into a permanent link. Consequently, there was no need for me to engage in a romantic walk or other types of reveries in order to satisfy my biological aims. She had a room, we could go there straight away, if, of course, I wanted it and was not afraid to face the experience with her.

I was not just afraid, I was trembling, and I continued to tremble for the whole way back, which seemed to me much longer than the way we had come. I do not remember what I said to her, walking next to her, and I think I did not even embrace her. But I still clearly remember most of the details of the apartment, of which Berenika gave me the key so that I would be the one to open the door.

It was a wooden door with a slit in the middle for letters. Behind it there was a step from which one entered a small hall.

Fixed to one side of it there was a bronze rack, and on the other side a shelf. The kitchen opened to the right of a small corridor, the bathroom to the left. The corridor led to a large room with two bay windows, protected on the outside by iron bars. There were no curtains, and cases full of books stood everywhere. In the middle of the room on the square table covered by a sheet of glass, there was a large basket full of fruit—oranges, dates, nuts, and raisins. A big box served as a cupboard without a door, and under the windows an iron bed was covered by a crude, floral bedspread. On the floor, on the old gray tiles, was a mat. All was still.

Berenika looked at me in silence. I, more embarrassed than before, did the same. "I'll go into the bathroom," she finally said. When she came out she was completely undressed. "Naked as a worm," I thought to myself, quite disenchanted. But that was not quite an appropriate moment for aesthetic speculation. When we parted, she said: "You see, the whole thing is not very important." I answered that it was not true, that it had been a sublime moment for me, but I knew, as much as she knew, that I was lying. What, in fact, I could not get out of my mind was an advertisement for padded brassieres I had seen in a local newspaper that read: "In any case, when they fall, it's too late." What she did not realize was that once more I felt that I had killed something in me.

The emotional anticlimax provoked by this meeting, so long awaited and then revealed as so disappointingly aseptic, created a break between us that deepened with the passing of time. It sharpened the contrast between the trepidation of my senses and the icy core of my soul. I probably exaggerate in attributing to that single event a state of mind that was obviously part of my nature. Be that as it may, after that night my relations with Berenika became increasingly atrocious. I sought her body with fury, and she tore my soul to shreds. I told her I loved her, and she replied that love, as physical enjoyment, was a delinquency at a time when our people and the Western civilization were dying. I told her that once the war was over I would take her to Italy to introduce her to Annetta who used to hold my hand until I fell asleep. She insisted I should read Freud and Marx to understand to what extent human sentiments are the product of the economy. I talked to her about my village in Piedmont, about my father's horses killed in the Great War, about the streams along which we played cowboys and Indians. She urged me to abandon these infantile dreams and remember that true nobility is the fulfillment of collective obligations. I meekly suggested that Marxism was a populist aristocracy that often forgot the individual. She held that the state of Jews to be created in Palestine should be unique in its nature—planned by men and women who looked for a perfect model society in a promised land, not born out of chaos as in the case of other nations. I retorted that she was deceiving herself in believing that an uprooted people would turn into a nation of saints by virtue of socialism. As soon as the British relinquished Palestine to the Arabs, they would engage in an all-around, cutthroat battle among themselves and with the Arabs.

We kept on arguing even when we went out riding. It was possible to hire good horses for a shilling an hour at stables near the Jaffa Gate and in less than ten minutes to be out in the fields, leaving behind us the city, which at the time was much less extensive than today. I liked to gallop, to make the sheep and goats I occasionally met on my path scatter amid the barking of dogs and the swearing of shepherds. She, on these occasions, walked her horse and kept me waiting for her in the sun, full of reproaches for my "arrogant" style. There was no way of convincing her that if the Arab shepherds had been mounted and I on foot, they would have acted in exactly the same way as I did, for the pleasure of showing off; or that the galloping of a well-ridden horse, even if it scattered a flock, possessed a beauty of its own, which an Arab in particular would appreciate. This kind of argument made no impression on her. As long as social distinctions were not abolished, she would patiently explain to me, linguistic expressions and styles of life would continue to reveal the inequalities of men. I was a typical production of class relations, unaware of acting according to the superstitions created by economic relations. If we, the Jews of Palestine, did not become conscious of this in the country we wanted to build, we would become worse than other people. It had always been the fate of the Jews either to rise up to the stars or to eat the dust—never to lead a life of mediocrity.

For me, these talks—apart from being boring and inappropriate for a ride—made little sense. I listened to her while making my horse prance at her side, looking with desire at her open shirt. When she became aware of my inattention she used to shake her head with the mocking expression of a schoolteacher who had lost all hope of educating a stubborn boy. I would then dismount, take her horse by the bridle, lead it under the nearest tree that offered some shade, help her dismount, and make her sit down on a stone or an old olive root protruding from the ground. I asked her whether the Crusaders, who perhaps had tied their horses to our same tree, entered into her economic system; if the knights of France and Germany who had come to die in the stony valleys of Judea had been moved only by economic motives; if the women who for years had waited for them, had done so out of economic superstructures. I asked her where she put the adventurer who had searched for the sources of the Nile, the desert hermits who had searched for the message of God, the Zionist youth who left Russian universities to drain swamps. Who forced the orthodox Jews to live in their ghettos in Jerusalem? Were they not obeying an "economic" determinism quite different from the one the Marxists wanted to sell to the world? If it were true, as she kept explaining to me, that the class that controls the means of economic production also controls the means of spiritual production, how did it happen that in Rome, slaves and freemen educated their masters, and in Europe the priestly commoners educated the noblemen?

Irritably throwing pebbles at the horses' hooves, I sometimes found myself almost shouting my questions, asking her whether it was so difficult for her to understand that a person could abandon home, treasure, and power for the sake of a woman; whether it had never passed through her mind that it might be easier for someone to fight for a lady than for a party. As for myself, I would have no difficulty in joining her kibbutz, but for her sake, not for Marx or Freud. In any case, I was not alone in the world in needing a woman to overcome the fear of the dark, the shame of poverty, the fear of war, the dread of facing people stronger than I. After all, a perfumed handkerchief could be more encouraging than a party card.

Berenika listened to me patiently. Sometimes she would make a brief comment, such as "How stupid your Crusader knights must have been"; or "What good does a hermit bring to the world?" On other occasions she would explain to me, kindly, why I was dreaming and gently scold me for being unable to realize that I was living in the twentieth century. Once she almost shouted at me that it was high time I remembered that I was a Jew whose duty it was to demand justice and vengeance from the world, not a squire in a feudal court searching for occasions to impale a Moor on his lance. If we wanted to continue our relationship I must learn to remember that she belonged to her kibbutz, to her party, to her people, before she belonged to herself. The war was not the same war our fathers had fought. It was truly the war to end all wars because it would end only when the tree of Nazism and Fascism, both fruits of capitalism, had been uprooted. The sacrifice that humanity was now making would be useless if an entirely new society did not emerge from all the horrors of the war.

Our state would also be different from the others. The true strength of the Zionist movement consisted of the fact that most of its members were uprooted people who searched for a land in which to strike new roots. In this sense the fight against the British and the Arabs was a secondary aspect of the Zionist revolution, which had broken the centuries-old traditions of Judaism and in so doing had released an energy choked by millennia of prayers and submission. Our transition from a situation of passive objects of history to active factors in history was something unique. We were indeed our own ancestors, building from the very beginning the life of an entire people, creating a new race of Jews, free from the cultural chromosomes of secular suffering. The spirit of the people could—and indeed should—become stronger through the macerations of the flesh of its members.

In pronouncing these phrases, Berenika's voice became sharp and metallic. I perceived in it a dry hatred of material things, including the body that encased, or rather kept, her spirit in shackles, and a desire for vengeance against her own senses, whirling in a black hole of passions. She always startled me with her suppressed, inexplicable anger, and at times she scared me. Our conversations then turned into monologues that made me feel I was standing alone in the peace of the olive trees, the beauty of which Berenika seemed unable to taste, just as she seemed oblivious to the buzzing flies that made the horses paw the ground.

Meanwhile, day followed day rapidly, and we both knew that the time of our separation would soon arrive. The newspapers announced the formation of a new ATS (Women's Transport Service Unit) company. Berenika volunteered for it, and I was posted to Cairo, no longer to a clandestine radio outfit but to an intelligence unit preparing the Allied landing in Sicily. We both felt sorry and relieved at these developments. Our relationship had become too complicated, artificial, and unreal, our physical relations shrieking and painful. I proposed to her that we should say goodbye with a last horseback ride.

At half past seven in the morning, the two horses I had ordered the day before from Abu Selim at the Jaffa Gate stables were waiting for us, fed and saddled. They were two white mares, spotted with black, unable to walk quietly, already profusely sweating after a few minutes of cantering. Rain had fallen during the night; every clod of earth, thirsty from the long drought, glistened. The unshod hooves of the horses caressed the wet paths, crushing here and there the weeds and the stalks of dry wild oats.

We were trotting in line, enjoying the fresh air, the early sun, the flight of birds, casting around handfuls of thoughts in the silence of a morning as young as our bodies. At the entrance to a wadi I let Berenika ride ahead of me, so that she should not have trouble in controlling a horse anxious to run. She put her mare at a gallop and I looked with passion and sadness at her mass of brown hair flying in the wind.

Suddenly I saw her mare swerve and Berenika, jerked out of her saddle, clinging to the neck of the animal, which fortunately stopped immediately. Not far from her an Arab shepherd stood, arms upraised, waving a stick menacingly in his hand. In a second I caught up with him and, without thinking, raised my riding crop over his head and hit him violently, I believe on his back. Only then did I realize what had happened: Berenika was about to ride into a flock of goats, which she had been unable to see because of a rise in the land, and the Arab shepherd had moved forward to warn her and try to stop the horse. He had had no evil intentions, and I had hit him without reason. I could not even apologize because he had run away in fear.

Berenika, meanwhile, had got up from the ground, fuming with rage and indignation, her horse, unaware of her tumultuous feelings, already grazing peacefully nearby.

"I'm sorry for what happened," I told her, trying to help her to remount, "but I thought he was going to hurt you." She looked at me with a tense face, her eyes almost closed with rage, screaming two words that still burn me: "Nazi! Nazi!" Turning her horse, she trotted back to Jerusalem without looking at me.

When we returned the horses to the stables we were like two strangers. Abu Selim sensed it and did not insist on our drinking the usual cup of coffee he had prepared for us. He followed us with a curious gaze as we walked into town.

A shower is a wonderful remedy, I thought to myself as I stood under the hot water and sponged away the perspiration of that disastrous ride. I was quite decided not to request an explanation from Berenika for an insult I felt I had not deserved. The incident, I told myself, would make our break easier, if not less painful. The convoy I had been attached to was leaving for Cairo in the late afternoon. I would return to the apartment at three o'clock, an hour I was sure Berenika would not be there, take leave of the doctor and his wife, settle my account, and drink the cup of tea that they would certainly offer me. I felt full of energy, and I thought of my schoolteacher in Italy who had once explained to our history class that the Romans had conquered the world because they practiced water therapy. From alternate hot and cold baths, he said, the Romans drew the energy that modern Italians had lost because they did not bathe themselves enough. In fact, especially in summer, there was always a smell of young bodies insufficiently washed in our classroom.

Thinking back to that good old man as I vigorously toweled myself, I burst out laughing. I felt a sudden urge to sing and started to hum the march of the Alpine troops, as I did when returning from the lake where I had been fishing for the trout still wriggling in my creel.

How far away that lake was now, with its pine-tree forest; Luza, the big old mare I was allowed to ride; my father's mountain cottage where he used to read the Book of Jonah on the Day of Atonement; the sleigh rides over the snow; the Indian tepee; the old gramophone that I wound up while my sister and her friends danced with the army officers during the summer maneuvers. Almost without my being aware of it, the tune of the Alpine soldiers froze the smile on my lips, and two big tears started rolling down my cheeks. How shameful if anybody had surprised me crying in such a shameless way. It was a good thing I was leaving that same day without having time to see Berenika again.

But she was there, waiting for me outside the bathroom, leaning on the jamb of my bedroom door, thoughtfully nibbling at her thumbnail. Her hair was still untidy, her unbuttoned shirt showing two wet patches under her armpits. "Come," she said, "we must not leave each other like this."

The room was fresh, shady, and silent. The bed was too narrow for us both, but we lay enlaced as though we would never part. Her body was cold, and her voice sounded altered —raucous, not out of passion but out of pain mingled with fear. She was talking softly, with her face half buried in my shoulder, and spoke as though I was not present.

It had all happened, she said, on a summer afternoon, the last she had spent in the Black Forest. The house was big. One entered it through a glass door that opened into a hall, from which a wooden staircase led to the bedrooms upstairs. Three men came in; she did not recollect their faces. They looked like three carnival masks, their cheeks red with perspiration, and their mouths smelling of beer. They wore brown shirts and boots against which one of them continuously snapped his whip. Frau Luise had faced them first, with considerable courage. Her father, on the contrary, had immediately lost his head and his countenance. He started to shout that he had fought in the war, that he had received the Iron Cross, First Class, that they had no right to enter his house. They just laughed at him, spat in his face, shouted all sorts of insults at him, and then knocked him to the ground. This was too much for her mother; she started to scream and call for help. Berenika rushed down the stairs. In her agitation she forgot that she was only half dressed. It was probably this that gave them the idea. Two of the men dragged her father into his study and locked him in. The third grabbed Berenika in front of her mother. Now Frau Luise had stopped shouting; she watched the whole performance like a statue, her eyes and mouth wide open. She did not even move when she saw that they were throwing her daughter to the ground.

"It was very painful," Berenika sobbed, "very painful, especially at my back when they pressed me against the first step of the stairs. From that moment I have no longer been in possession of my body. These arms, this stomach, these legs are strangers to me. For this I am unable to love, only to render some service. But at least I am no longer the prisoner of my flesh. I am free. No one can ever do me more harm. No one can affect my spirit. Only memories wound me; and the whips that hit human beings. They are all Nazi whips. Even if handled by someone like you, like you."

It was the first and last time I saw her crying without shame.

II.

Bitter Fortune

THE E-BOATS of the Royal Navy dashed along at full speed on the glassy waters of the Adriatic. In the fresh April morning I tasted a deep, satisfied peace. The sun's rays, the wind, the smell of the sea became part of me together with my new fantasies about the future.

The war was nearing its end. With this operation I would gloriously complete my military service, canceling out the disillusions of the past. Once more the gates of chance were being opened to me. With childish satisfaction I touched the two brand-new pips of a second lieutenant on my shoulders. It was a temporary rank, given me for the duration of this operation. They did not change my status as warrant officer, and with the imminent surrender of the German troops in Italy, there would be no time to turn them into a permanent rank through that Royal Commission about which I had dreamt for so long. Between going to an officers' course in England and a quick demobilization, my choice, after four years of war, was irrevocably made. But on the ship taking me to Yugoslavia, I was what I appeared to be from my army papers. The way the first mate had offered me a double ration of rum from the ship's earthenware jar left no doubt about it —like the pass I still have in my files, tattered by time, delivered to me by the HQ of Tito's Fifth Army. It explicitly states that on 9 November 1945 I was authorized to circulate freely in every zone held by the Partisans. It bore the signature of a political commissar, a certain Major Branko Mamula, clearly written under the only sentence in Serbo-Croatian that I knew by heart: *Smaart Fascismu-Sloboda Narodu* (Death to Fascism—Freedom to People). If the major had been aware of the true purpose of my mission he would certainly not have granted me this permit. My orders were to report to the HQ of a unit of British rangers stationed in Zadar and continue with them into Istria. Officially our task was to harass the retreat of the troops of General Vlassov, the Russian officer who had linked his destiny with that of the Germans. But in fact we were asked to contact the X MAS, an elite unit of the Fascist Republican army, commanded by Prince Valerio Borghese. According to certain reports, the prince was ready to surrender south of Trieste if the Allies could reach him before Tito's Partisans. Even today I still do not know how reliable our information was. We never made contact with the X MAS because the Partisans, who wanted to reach Trieste ahead of the Allies, stopped the rangers north of the town of Pola. Here we got the news of the surrender of the Germans in Italy and went back to Zadar.

Anyway, what counted for me on that morning when I was rushing toward a new horizon of my life, was not the surrender of Borghese, but the fact that the task I had received and the temporary promotion that went with it soothed the feeling of shame I had been carrying with me since the day I refused to parachute behind the German lines.

How that refusal burned in my soul! And how easily I could have avoided getting into trouble. It would have been enough to explain to the medical officer what I felt after my harrowing jump from a plane at Gioia del Colle. Instead, out of pride and out of fear of admitting being afraid, I had kept quiet, like the beadle of the Jewish school in Turin, whom I had gone to take leave of before my departure for Palestine. "I will kill myself," he told me, "because I am too afraid to die." I had laughed in his face, without thinking then that one day I would find myself in the same situation.

At the field hospital near Bari, where I had been lying in bed for two weeks after the night jump that had broken my ribs, the nightmares had become more violent and more frequent than ever. I had tried to overcome them by persuading myself that statistically it was less dangerous to jump from a plane than to travel overland in a military convoy. I tried to raise my morale by repeating to myself the stories I would be able to brag about once my mission was over. I imagined the face of my father seeing me suddenly appear in his study, hundreds of miles behind the enemy lines. I imagined myself hiding behind one of the big, black-and-white pillars in the church of my village in Piedmont, ready to scare Annetta as she came in to pray early in the morning. I shut my mind to the dangers waiting for me on the ground, convinced as I was that the war would remain for me a beautiful adventure. Yet I could find no remedy for my nightmares.

I kept seeing myself sitting on the edge of the hole in the bottom of the plane, flying in the night toward unknown destinations. I felt my legs dangling in the void, frozen inside my padded overalls less from the cold than from fear of the jump. I could not take my eyes off the green light, which by changing to red would signal me to throw myself into emptiness. Then there was the fall: a long, interminable descent, in darkness, with a parachute that refused to open and the blood that rushed ever more violently to my head. All around me was the silence of the grave, as if the entire universe, while watching my fall, was holding its breath. In my dreams, the violent jerk, just above the ground of the airfield, which had made me yell with pain and relief, never came. In them, no one asked me whether I was all right, no one carried me like a bundle to a jeep and rushed me half-fainting to the hospital. In my dreams there was only the thud of my body hitting the ground. It woke me up each time I tried in vain to extricate myself from the black embrace of the mud.

Why didn't I go and talk to the doctor of my unit? Nobody, after all, forced me to parachute behind the enemy lines; it was only my desire to play the hero. But the fear of seeming afraid had been stronger than common sense. I had kept quiet until the very last days before my mission—after I had drawn the operational equipment, the belt with two hundred gold sovereigns in it, discussed the code and the area of landing with the intelligence officer, and waited with growing anxiety to be called by the CO to learn the date and hour of my jump.

When I entered his office I was convinced that one way or another I would leave it unscathed because I would certainly lack the courage to tell him that I was afraid. Instead, the confession came out by itself, in short, broken sentences. I was dismissed with a dry "Very well," which still feels like a knife in my stomach. I gave back the belt with the sovereigns, the equipment, the code, and went to my room on the roof of the villa where we were stationed to collect my personal effects before returning to my intelligence unit. From the military kit bag I took out an Italian revolver, which I had stolen from a captured enemy depot. I laid it on the edge of the bed. The weapon, falling on the ground, fired a shot. The bullet grazed my forehead, burned a lock of my hair. I looked at myself in the mirror, my ears still deafened by the explosion, which no one else in the building had apparently heard. At that moment I told myself that it had been a fortunate accident.

Here, on the deck of the boat that sped toward my beautiful future, I knew that it was not true, that on that evening in Bari I had seriously wanted to die. An invisible hand had diverted the bullet, as when my father, cleaning a pistol in his study, had fired a shot at my head by mistake. Obviously I was not yet destined to die. In this war, which had swallowed millions of men and women and children, it was written that I had to pursue my military masquerade, going on drinking barrels of beer in the messes while my people were dying. That evening in Bari there was only one thing for me to do: disappear, throw my uniform away, take back my original name, which I had changed when I joined the army, and thus close twenty-two years of existence and try to start one totally different. I had to change my looks and my soul, do away with what I was, become a different person.

With these black, determined thoughts, I walked out of the villa, convinced of having passed the point of no return. But I had walked less than five minutes in the direction of the fields when I bumped into Francesca.

How different was Berenika from Francesca. Not in her general appearance, although there was some resemblance between the two women in spite of the fact that Francesca was more than thirty, but in her face, as I remembered it on the top of the stairs of Kasr el-Nil barracks in Cairo.

After my transfer from Jerusalem to Egypt, Berenika had followed me as an ATS driver in a transport company. For weeks I had hunted for her without success, as I was not aware that she had changed her name. When I finally saw her again it didn't occur to me to ask her why she had done so. It was quite common for Palestinian Jewish volunteers born in Germany or Italy to change their names when enlisting in the army, in order to ensure their safety if captured. I had done it myself. Only when I found myself standing in front of her with a bouquet of flowers in my hand and told her of my firm intention to marry her, did I understand from her embarrassed answer that her new name was that of her husband.

It was a rude shock, but at the age of twenty, and in wartime, nobody ever died of love. Still, I continued to feel

rancorous and could not cancel from my memory the enigmatic expression on her face. There was in it something tragic
and dark, like an appeal to death, an incurable sadness. It was
a kind of inexplicable anxiety I noticed also in the eyes of some
of the Jewish soldiers who had arrived in Italy from Palestine.
They somehow lived, like Berenika, in the world of the Holocaust. I, on the contrary, in spite of the fact that all my relatives
were in places occupied by the Germans, had never connected
their lot with the news that was reaching us with increasing
frequency about the systematic extermination of the Jews by
the Nazis. This was probably due to the fact that I could not
imagine them dead, and that the few Italian Jews I had met
in Bari had told me about the dangers they had run in crossing
the lines, but also of the help they had received everywhere
from the local population. The tales of their escape sounded
like adventure stories, often punctuated by humorous anec-
dotes. The idea that my father or mother could have been
deported thus never crossed my mind. And in fact, as I have
already related, they saved themselves, my father by playing
the itinerant peddler for eighteen months along the streets of
Piedmont, and my mother by taking refuge in a convent with
my sister.

Francesca, unlike them and unlike Berenika, was neither
Jewish nor Italian, but Yugoslav from Dalmatia, and did not
carry on her face any trace of her tragedy. I had met her several
times on the tramway passing in front of our HQ. I had noticed
her less for her refined features framed in a mass of Titian hair
than for the contrast between her elegant bearing and the
vulgar atmosphere prevailing in the town.

Every corner of Bari at that time exuded humiliation and
sadness. The war had spared the center of the city but the
harbor had been torn up by the explosion of an Allied ship full
of ammunition. The old palaces, run down by time and ne-
glect, looked much the same as the houses of the poor in the
ancient parts of the town. Everywhere mud turned into dust

when the sun dried the street, and dust turned into slippery mud when the rain mingled with the sewage from the broken drains. Tangles of telephone wires underlined on the longest walls of the town the historical pronouncements taken from Mussolini's speeches, which now sounded grotesque, fading away under the effect of the elements.

The Italian civilians, with whom we Allied soldiers had not yet received permission to fraternize, looked like ghosts. On the Teatro Petruzelli Square long lines of horse-driven carriages waited for customers. The skinny horses slept on their feet with their ears protruding from holes cut into straw hats. They looked as miserable as the drivers. Only in the open country, where the Allies concealed their guns and lorries under camouflage nets among the olive trees, did the ancient people of Puglia, who had passed within a few months from the Fascist regime to a foreign occupation, seem capable of retaining some dignity. With these silent and surly people, whose dialect I did not understand, we soldiers had no contact. The cooks who prepared our food; the women who cleaned our offices; the few clerks who knew enough English to run the gasworks, the slaughterhouse, the telephone exchange, and the harbor were all refugees. They came from all over: Italians from the north; Yugoslav monarchists fleeing from the communist soldiers of Tito; Yugoslav Partisans who came to collect their rations and cure their sick and wounded in Bari; Greeks and Albanians who crossed the Adriatic, transporting in their boats men, animals, spies, and explosives.

Each group had its own internal and external hierarchy, created by the changing fortunes of war, by misery, and hate. The Jews stood one step above the Italians; the Partisans one step above the soldiers of the disintegrating Royal armies of Italy, Greece, and Yugoslavia; the British officers felt superior to any minister of the new, provisional Italian government. And then there were the black marketeers with their wobbly carts, their shaky tricycles, with some old, gas-operated vehicles, who traded in everything—from women to currency, from soap to weapons. With or without permits, one would find them in the middle of military camps, inside political offices, offering real or faked influence. Despised by all but compromising everyone, these black marketeers represented new channels for the energy of a people who had lost the structures of their traditional authority. Finally, everything and everyone was submerged by the masses of soldiers coming from overseas, whose conquest of an ancient European land seemed to have gone to their heads.

There was neither hatred nor violence toward the local population among the Australians, the Scots, the South Africans, the Indians, the British, the Palestinian Jews, the Cypriots, and the Canadians, who walked aimlessly in the streets of Bari. Few of them were able to appreciate the artistic treasures of the city; none had clear ideas about Fascism, especially since the signing of armistice with Italy the war was being fought only against the Germans. But to this flood of uniformed men and women coming from the deserts of Africa, accustomed to dividing the world into white men and colored, the Italians who shined their shoes and sold them whatever they possessed gave a feeling of vulgar pride, of petty domination, and of certainty in a victory that the humiliation of a defeated people made at last palpable after years of war.

In this atmosphere of arrogance and misery, the healthy, modest beauty of Francesca shone with particular vividness. She was sitting on the wooden seat opposite me in the tram, her legs clamped together and her knees showing under her short, clean skirt. She wore a simple but elegant black-and-white striped blouse, tied at the neck with a velvet ribbon, and her posture roused in me feelings of admiration and respect. I would not have dared to approach her if, on a particular afternoon, I had not noticed two large tears rolling slowly down her cheeks from behind her dark sunglasses.

When she got up and moved toward the exit, it came

naturally to me to ask her whether I could help her in any way. A question of this kind, put by an unknown Allied soldier to a woman on her own, could at that time be easily misunderstood. She looked surprised, but either because I spoke to her in Italian or because she could not bear alone the trouble that oppressed her, she did not hesitate to answer me. Her daughter, aged four, had been struck by meningitis. The doctor had told her that the Allies possessed a new drug that might save her. Penicillin was the name, or something like that. She had spent the whole morning looking for somebody who might find it for her. She was now on her way to the doctor to tell him that she had had no success.

Without any certainty of being able to help her, I told her that I could probably solve her problem. I was ashamed at my showing off but happy to have established contact with such an attractive woman. Not knowing what to do, however, I went to the Jewish Soldiers' Club, she following me closely with the uncertain trustfulness of a lost dog that has suddenly found a protector.

The major attraction of the Jewish Soldiers' Club, theoretically open to military personnel of all religions, but in practice frequented mostly by Palestinian volunteers, was the cheese sandwiches. A number of Jewish refugee women, more hungry than ourselves, prepared these cheese sandwiches in enormous quantities from ten o'clock in the morning to ten in the evening. There were a couple of local Italian youngsters who did nothing but clear the tables of coffee cups and empty bottles and refill the urns with water for tea and coffee. These drinks were considerably more tasty than those offered by other military canteens since nobody in the Jewish Soldiers' Club poured into the urns packages of soda bicarbonate, which was supposed to dampen the sexual urges of the soldiers. Unlike other canteens, beer was consumed in relatively small quantities and was replaced by soda water, the most popular drink of the Jews in Palestine. A current joke claimed, in fact, that it was also the best way to locate wounded Palestinians on the battlefield. The Italians, the British, and the Germans could be identified by their asking for "acqua," "water," and "wasser," respectively, and Palestinian Jews by their call for "soda."

The Jewish Soldiers' Club was poorly furnished. There was a silent radio by the side of one window, an out-of-tune piano that came to life under the hands of transient musicians usually playing the songs of the Jewish pioneers who had dried the swamps of Zion and other nostalgic Eastern European tunes. On those occasions the Palestinians clustered around the piano singing arias that Jewish soldiers from other countries tried to follow with affectionate humming. But this happened rarely. The great sport in the smoke-filled rooms was to discuss politics, to revive, in Bari, the ideological quarrels of the Zionist movement, to embroider on the gossip from the Tel Aviv cafés and from the kibbutz general meetings, which reached Bari after weeks of delay. The discussion always ended on the question of what would happen in Palestine after the war, a subject on which everybody held a different opinion.

At the far side of the club's larger room was a brown door, always half open although nobody dared go through without some very specific reason. It led into a room even more sparsely furnished than the others, which served as an office for "the committee."

Nobody knew how many members made up "the committee." They were NCOs belonging to the various Jewish units stationed in the area, occasionally joined by mysterious civilians coming from far away. They represented the various political currents of the Yishuv and the different clandestine military organizations—the Hagana, the Irgun, and the LEHI. At home they could fight and betray each other; in Bari they worked together in an atmosphere of suspicious concord, dictated by the need to act in unison for the benefit of the Jews who had escaped from the Nazis. In that room people sat up late every night. Decisions were made that caused military vehicles full of food and blankets to run up and down the roads of southern Italy, and plots were made to trick the British, on the principle that the Zionists had to fight the Germans as if the white paper did not exist, and fight the white paper as if the Germans did not exist.

I did not belong to any of these groups. The badge of the Intelligence Corps that I wore on my beret and the parachutist wings that I had recently added to my uniform made me, if not suspect, at least unclassifiable to the club habitués. But on two or three occasions I had brought to the "committee" sums of money I had confiscated from German or Fascist agents. This now authorized me to ask for help, or at least for advice. To my surprise, help was given on the spot by an elderly member of the committee in the form of a scribbled note addressed to a nurse at the field hospital located outside Bari on the road to Barletta. "Her name is Sara, Sara Bauman," he told me with a wink, and then added: "Best wishes for the health of the daughter and for your success with the mother." I blushed to the roots of my hair.

It was not possible to ask for a lift for Francesca on a military vehicle. I hired a carriage pulled by a horse more sleepy than his driver, who must certainly have been surprised by our destination and by the strange silence of the couple behind his back. We arrived at the hospital after half an hour of slow trotting and embarrassed conversation, made more difficult by the onset of a cold, rainy evening. Francesca had married a Yugoslav engineer in 1938 and had had a daughter just before the German invasion in 1941. One year later they had gone underground. The husband, surprised while hunting for food by a band of Ustachi (the Croat nationalists who collaborated with the Italians and the Germans), had been tortured and then shot. Francesca and her daughter were transferred by the Partisans first to Tito's headquarters on the island of Lissa and then to the mainland. Knowing Italian and English well, she worked as a secretary at the Allied office running the harbor. Hers was a war story like many others, full of the usual violence and sorrow.

The field hospital on the road to Barletta consisted of a big house surrounded by Nissen huts used as wards. Somebody pointed out to me the hut where I would find Sister Bauman. I had no difficulty in recognizing her: small, with her hair pulled into a bun under the starched cap, obviously a non-Anglo-Saxon, with her nose slightly squashed. Nobody would describe her as a beauty queen, I thought to myself, and quickly classified her: spinster, thirty years old, Russian origin, formerly employed in a kibbutz kitchen, ideologically involved.

As if she had read my thoughts, Sister Bauman answered my Hebrew greeting icily. She threw a suspicious glance at the chit I held out to her, and with eyes that pierced like a gimlet, asked me what I wanted the medicine for. I told her the truth. With a raised eyebrow she asked: "Yehudia?" (Jewish?). "No," I answered, and felt at once that I had ruined my chances.

Without saying a word, Sister Bauman turned her back on me and disappeared into the ward. I was left standing next to her table, miserable and furious, waiting for her reappearance. I did not dare to leave before speaking to her again because I wanted to have something to tell the woman who was waiting outside in the carriage. I had kept her away from her sick daughter for hours, had raised her hopes, and now had to find an excuse to explain why I could not help her. But what enraged me even more was the idea of having to stand there like a pillar, exposed to the spiteful judgment of a nurse who, from her point of view, had every right to treat me like a black marketeer. She was certainly thinking that the medicine was going to be used in some dirty business that had nothing to do with Jewish or Zionist solidarity. Ashamed and impatient, I stood at the end of the ward, cursing the moment I had offered my aid to an unknown woman, asked the help of the "committee," and now exposed myself to the contempt of this insensitive and ugly woman who clearly enjoyed punishing me by letting me stew in my own confusion.

After an eternity of time, Sister Bauman reappeared. She held in her hand a tray full of gauze and thermometers and a round, metal box, similar to the mess tins in use in the American army. She laid the tray down on the table, took her navy blue cape off the hanger, threw it over her shoulders, covering the round box in the process, and signaled me to follow her. "I've taken four vials," she whispered to me. "I put them in a thermos—they are double-size—distilled water and powder—you will have to mix them—they must be kept in cold storage. I'll give them to you outside the hospital; here there is a danger that some doctor might stop you. They are worth more than gold."

Only then did I realize how unjust my thoughts about her had been. I prayed silently that the driver would have moved the carriage away from the hospital entrance so that I would not have to show her that I had a woman with me. Instead, he was standing, with his horse asleep, in the same place where I had left him, some twenty yards away from the gate, with Francesca barely visible in the depths of the carriage, crouched in a heap, her arms crossed around her shoulders to keep out the cold.

As if she had understood my embarrassment and the careful behavior of the nurse, Francesca did not move, looking at us with eyes full of uncertain hope. When we came closer to her, Sister Bauman asked me in Hebrew, "Does she understand English?" I nodded my head, and she started babbling to Francesca, still seated in the carriage, in a tone completely different from the one she had used with me. She asked what the illness was, the age of the child, her general condition. Shaking her head in a movement of sympathy, she repeated, stressing every word, the instructions she had already given me. "Now go straight home," she finished, "and look for a doctor or for a nurse to give the injection. You will see, everything will turn out all right." Francesca stretched out her hand to take the thermos. There was an instant of uncertainty between them. Then, to my astonishment, they embraced each other. After a moment she smiled at Francesca, turned her back to me, and with a brisk "Shalom," returned to the hospital.

I went back to Bari with Francesca in the carriage. She refused to let me pay the driver because, she said, she wanted to go straight on to the doctor. We parted like that at the entrance to the city—she, moved but in a great hurry; I, happy to have been able to help her but full of desire to see her again. We had not disclosed our family names to each other, nor our addresses, only our first names. We had both felt the need not to ruin the beauty of a disinterested happening, which had given hope to her and had helped me for a moment to forget my nightmares. Now, after more than two weeks, and at the very moment when I was grieving for myself and on the point of doing something rash, I found her in front of me, as if she had been sent by destiny.

Francesca greeted me with a big smile. She had been looking for me for quite some time to thank me. The medicine had saved her daughter's life, and she was now convalescing in a Yugoslav Red Cross home for children. She had noticed at which tram stop I used to get on and off and decided to try and find me. She wanted to know the name of the nurse, to send her at least a bunch of flowers. We had not only saved the life of a child but also given her back faith in a world in which human beings had changed into beasts. But here she stopped abruptly. She looked into my face and asked, "Don't you feel well?" Since I only answered by shaking my head, she said in a kind but firm tone, "I don't live far from here. Come with me. I'll make you a good cup of tea or coffee. It will do you good."

Rocked by the movement of the ship, I was smiling to myself, thinking back to the room in which Francesca had received me on the day when, unable to kill myself, I had decided to disappear from this world. Without her I would certainly have got myself into great trouble. Also I would not have been transferred from Bari to Rome; I would not have seen my uncle again; I would not have reestablished contact with Italian society; I would not. . . . Once more I felt protected by my little star, asking myself why things happened to me so differently from others; why an angel or a devil kept rushing to my help every time I got myself into trouble. For others, life was a drama; for me, just a game. Was it still the result of the Faustian pact I had signed by perjuring myself on the Bible at the court-martial to save a fellow soldier whom I hated? Would there never be a final price to pay?

The Dalmatian coast began to emerge on the horizon out of the quiet sea. The first mate, his face framed by a black beard straight out of a packet of Players cigarettes, kept explaining to me the route we were following. Neither from him, nor from the sea, nor from the land far away did I get an answer to my questions. I decided to give myself up to the pleasure of living without thinking of the morrow, without trying to understand why there are those in the world who suffer and those who are happy.

That decision, however, came straight from the room of Francesca. Located on the first floor of a house inhabited by refugees, the room was connected to others by an external passageway on which a common latrine let out a feeble smell of urine. While she was looking in her purse for her key, I noticed the eyes of two children, of an old woman, and of a man peering at me curiously and enviously from doorways in which glass panels had been replaced by cardboard. An Allied soldier meant tinned milk, cigarettes, laundry to wash, and some other minute chances of making money. I paid no attention to them; that evening I felt only a great need to hide, to sleep, to forget, and to confide my pain to someone. With great relief I heard Francesca closing the door behind us.

The room was big, poorly furnished and lighted, with a red brick floor and a ceiling held up by crude wooden beams, badly whitewashed. Opposite the entrance, on a bed covered by a red bedspread, the whiteness of two pillows stood out. At the foot of the bed was a chest with a swinging mirror on top, a few toilet articles, and a candlestick. Between the chest and the chairs, a rough table covered by a red-and-white-checked piece of oilcloth. Next to the bed there was a big peasant cradle, a bowl, and a small, enameled baby's bath. In a niche was a grate for a wood fire with some pans on it. Behind a curtain one could discern a washbasin and a tap. There was a deep silence, a sense of peace, of order—a smell of woman and home.

Francesca drew two chairs up to the table and made me sit down. She took out of the cupboard a tray, a tin with biscuits, and from behind the curtain, two cups. Then she started lighting the fire to boil water. She moved with controlled gestures, without making any noise. Her actions, both intimate and unembarrassed, filled me with infinite melancholy. Rocking myself backwards and forwards on the chair, I ended by leaning against the wall, closing my eyes, and falling asleep. When I opened them again, Francesca was standing in front of me with a steaming cup of coffee in her hand and a worried expression on her face. "It seems to me that something serious has happened to you. If you want to tell me, you can speak to me without fear, just as I did to you that day on the tram. We live in a cruel world, but human beings can still help each other sometimes." She looked at me with great kindness while I slowly drank my coffee, slightly bitter and not of the best quality. But it was hot, like the atmosphere in the room. My first words were: "I have committed a shameful act." She, thinking in wartime terms, replied with a mischievous smile: "I find it difficult to believe. Anyway, certainly not with me." Her sentence made me laugh and freed me a bit from the oppression that had been tormenting me since the morning. It was not easy to open my mouth, but once I started speaking —I do not know whether for half an hour or an hour—I was no longer able to stop.

I spoke in disconnected sentences; memories sometimes preceded the words and sometimes followed them. I spoke of my village in Piedmont, of my school years at Udine, of my dog, of the chickens in the kibbutz, of the court-martial in Ramle, of the Jews whom I had had no courage to go and save behind the lines, of my joining the army, of my night parachute jump. I spoke about my dreams, my solitude, my fears, about the red flowers my mother wore on her evening dress. I explained to her why I had wanted to kill myself; why I had decided to desert, disappear, to go around in the world with the mark of Cain on my forehead, which marked twenty-two years of wasted life; no, only sixteen, because those of my childhood did not count; indeed, only nine, because we Jews become responsible people only at the age of thirteen. I spoke, I spoke, without really knowing what I was saying, and she listened to me almost without blinking, without moving a muscle of her face, her chin supported on her clasped hands, her elbows on the oilcloth of the table, intent, very beautiful, clean, maternal, with only her nostrils quivering.

We sat like this, facing each other in the quiet of the room, even after the disconnected flood of my words had exhausted itself. When her turn came to speak, she did so with a voice that sounded detached, as though she were talking of a third person.

"If I had married at the age of eight, which happens to some Moslem girls in Yugoslavia, I could now, at more than thirty, pretend to be your mother. But with the millions of minutes that I have lived through, full of fear, shame, tears, broken hopes, I really feel at this moment like your grandmother. Not just tired . . . decrepit. And I have gone through so much that I don't feel I can judge anyone anymore—certainly not you. I have known you for too short a time to be able to do so, even if I wanted. But I will tell you something that still gives me, too, a lot of nightmares.

"You know that the Ustachi captured my husband. They tortured him and killed him, together with some peasants who had nothing to do with the Partisans, out of sheer cruelty, vengeance, out of their need to show their own authority through the suffering of other human beings. Before I left for Lissa, the Partisans attacked a German convoy. They took some prisoners among whom was a Ustachi leader and his woman —wife or mistress, whatever she was. They ordered me and other people of the area to go and witness their execution because, they said, these were two human beasts and had to be executed in an exemplary way.

"They kept the two locked in a house at the edge of a wood. There were flowers under the windows, a small river running limpid between the trees, grass, and moss. A place where death looked unreal. The Ustacha and the woman waited with resignation, their faces swollen by beatings, he with a torn uniform, she ridiculous in a dress that once upon a time must have been quite elegant.

"The woodcutters arrived. They carried their axes on their shoulders. One of them told me that the Ustacha had killed two sons of the old man who was leading them. In Indian file, with the other local inhabitants the Partisans had rounded up, we went into the wood. It was a wonderful day, with the sun penetrating through the pine trees in bundles of golden rays and with birds singing. When we arrived at the sawmill, the old man who led the march activated the circular saw. The blade turned, gleaming in the air, emitting a sound of strident metal that tortured the eardrums. When they grabbed the Ustacha by the shoulders and tied him onto the sliding bench in place of a log, the man, who up to that moment had maintained a dignified countenance, started screaming like a wild beast. They quieted him with blows on his head. Then it was the turn of the woman to be tied up, about a yard away from him. She kept quiet. She did not open her mouth even when the old man, lowering a handle, started the sliding platform moving toward the blade.

"The two bodies tied astride the platform looked like rolled up carpets on the railing of a balcony. People around me held their breath; I had the sensation of having turned into a block of stone. When the blood of the Ustacha spurted onto the sawdust there was a shriek of wounded flesh that almost immediately stopped. Now it was the woman who was moving toward the blade. She continued to keep silent. Half a meter from the blade, she succeeded in twisting herself to one side and turned her head toward us. Her mouth was wide open, her eyes fixed, and her body agitated by a kind of repulsive orgasm. A Partisan went up to the old man and raised the handle to stop the movement of the bench. Two men, walking on the sawdust soaked in blood, untied the woman. On the other side of the blade, two pieces of the man's body looked like marionettes whose strings had been dropped.

"The woman, raising herself, leaned first on the bench, then bent her knees and started vomiting. With a kick, they made her stand up. She staggered away into the meadow. Among the trees, the sun continued to throw its rays in a cascade over the grass, the birds went on singing. When the saw stopped turning, there was utter silence, full of the scent of pine trees and moss. The woman staggered and fell face forward onto the ground. They left her there. They told me afterwards that she had gone mad."

Francesca had placed her arms on the table. She convulsively contracted her hands while continuing to talk with her detached manner, as if she were relating an event of no importance. "I told you this story," she said, "because even around the most horrible things, life goes on. God has given to every being the gift of fear, and the animals have learned to use it better than men. If my husband had been afraid, he might still be with me. If that Ustacha had been afraid, he would not have committed the crimes that made him tremble at the moment of death. How can you know how the adventure you wanted to embark on, in order to show other people that you were not afraid, would have ended? Perhaps the fear you are so ashamed of today will one day appear to you like a virtue. But that is not the main thing I wanted to tell you: the essential thing is that this rotten war is coming to an end. Those who have come through it, like us, alive, have the duty to live as long as possible to repair the disasters that men without fear, small and great, have caused, believing themselves in the right to change the face of the world. If we have sinned, our punishment will be to atone for our sins by living, not by looking for death. Otherwise there would have been no reason or sense for you and the nurse to steal penicillin for a child you did not know."

She spoke softly, with warmth, and with a light in her eyes. I sensed her perfume and followed with my eyes the rising and sinking of her blouse, tightly buttoned at the neck. I had a great desire to touch her, but I could not find the courage to do so. "It's late," I said, "and it's time for me to go. It did me a lot of good to speak with you."

She looked at me and murmured: "If you want, you can stay." The sudden change from the formal *lei* to the informal *tu* in the Italian had the effect of a punch in the stomach. My head was empty and my face, I believe, very pale, when I put my hands on her shoulders. We remained for a long moment immobile, standing at arms' length. Later, when, lying next to her, I measured the passing of time by the beats of her heart, I heard her whispering into my ear: "Don't be afraid, little soldier; life is stronger than evil."

ABOUT THE MAKING OF THIS BOOK

The text of *Memoirs of a Fortunate Jew* was set in Bembo by ComCom, a division of The Haddon Craftsmen of Allentown, Pennsylvania. The book was printed and bound by Fairfield Graphics of Fairfield, Pennsylvania. The typography and binding were designed by Tom Suzuki of Falls Church, Virginia.